Peoples of the Inland Sea

NEW APPROACHES TO MIDWESTERN STUDIES

Series editors: Paul Finkelman and L. Diane Barnes

Peoples of the Inland Sea

Native Americans and Newcomers in the
Great Lakes Region, 1600–1870

DAVID ANDREW NICHOLS

OHIO UNIVERSITY PRESS

ATHENS

Ohio University Press, Athens, Ohio 45701
ohioswallow.com
© 2018 by Ohio University Press
All rights reserved

Printed in the United States of America
Ohio University Press books are printed on acid-free paper ⊗ ™

28 27 26 25 24 23 22 21 20 19 18   5 4 3 2 1

Library of Congress Cataloging-in-Publication Data
Names: Nichols, David Andrew, 1970- author.
Title: Peoples of the Inland Sea : Native Americans and Newcomers in the
  Great Lakes Region, 1600-1870 / David Andrew Nichols.
Description: Athens, Ohio : Ohio University Press, 2018. | Series: New
  Approaches to Midwestern History | Includes bibliographical references and
  index.
Identifiers: LCCN 2018000074| ISBN 9780821423196 (hardback) | ISBN
  9780821423202 (pb) | ISBN 9780821446331 (pdf)
Subjects: LCSH: Indians of North America--Great Lakes Region (North
  America)--History. | Great Lakes Region (North America)--History. | BISAC:
  HISTORY / United States / General. | HISTORY / Native American.
Classification: LCC E78.G7 N53 2018 | DDC 977--dc23
LC record available at https://lccn.loc.gov/2018000074

For Patrick

Frater et philosophus

Contents

Illustrations

Series Editors' Preface

For much of American history the term "Midwest" evoked images of endless fields of grain, flat, treeless landscapes, and homogenized populations in small towns. Most Americans hear "Midwest" and think of corn, wheat, soybeans, massive feedlots, huge pig farms, and countless dairy herds. The cinematic Midwest was River City, Iowa, in *The Music Man*; Dorothy trying to escape Oz and get back to Kansas; the iconic power of small-town basketball portrayed in *Hoosiers*; or a mythical baseball diamond in rural Iowa in *Field of Dreams*. In the late twentieth century, images of deindustrialization and decay linked the region to a new identity as the nation's Rust Belt. For too many Americans, the Midwest has been "flyover country."

This book series explores regional identity in the nation's past through the lens of the American Midwest. Stereotypical images of the region ignore the complexity and vibrancy of the region, as well as the vital role it has played—and continues to play—in the nation's economy, politics, and social history. In the antebellum and Civil War periods the Midwest was home to virulent racist opponents of black rights and black migration but also to a vibrant antislavery movement, the vigorous and often successful Underground Railroad, and the political and military leadership that brought an end to slavery and reframed the Constitution to provide at least formal racial equality. A midwestern president issued the Emancipation Proclamation, and midwestern generals led the armies that defeated the southern slaveocracy. Midwestern politicians authored the Thirteenth Amendment ending slavery and the Fourteenth Amendment mandating legal equality for all Americans. The political impact of the region is exemplified by the fact that from 1860 to 1932 only two elected presidents (Grover Cleveland and

Woodrow Wilson) were not from the Midwest. Significantly, from 1864 until the 1930s every Chief Justice but one was also a midwesterner.

While many Americans imagine the region as one of small towns and farms, the Midwest was the home to major urban centers. In 1920 three of the five largest cities in the nation were in the Midwest, and even today, despite massive migration to the sunbelt, there are four midwestern cities in the top fifteen. The great urban centers of the Midwest include Chicago, Detroit, Cincinnati, Cleveland, Columbus, Indianapolis, Milwaukee, Minneapolis, St. Louis, and Kansas City. For a century—from the late nineteenth century to the late twentieth century—the region was not only an agricultural heartland but also the nation's industrial heartland. Many of the key industries of the twentieth century began in the Midwest and developed there. Many midwestern cities were known by the industries they dominated, such as Detroit (automobiles), Toledo (glass), Akron (rubber), flour and milling (Minneapolis), and even breakfast cereals (Battle Creek). While most Americans associate the oil industry with Texas and Oklahoma, it began with John D. Rockefeller's Standard Oil Company in Cleveland. The airplane industry began with the Wright Brothers in Ohio and with the manufacturing of planes in Wichita. While Pittsburgh (which was almost a midwestern city) called itself the "steel city," more steel was manufactured in Youngstown, Gary, Chicago, Cleveland, and other midwestern cities, usually from ore that came from Minnesota's Iron Range. The Midwest was always America's agricultural heartland, producing grains, pork, beef, and dairy products. But this food production led to midwestern industries beyond the farms. Beef and pork raised in the Midwest were processed and packaged in Cincinnati in the antebellum period, and later in Chicago and other cities. Midwestern farmers and food processors fed the nation at lunch and dinner, while General Mills, Kellogg, and Quaker Oats, complemented by bacon from Swift, Armor, and Hormel, provided breakfast for the nation. The cows and hogs that fed the nation were themselves fed by midwestern feed companies, while the crops were cultivated and harvested using machines built by International Harvester, John Deere, Massey-Ferguson, and similar companies.

All of these products were grown, processed, and manufactured by migrants from the East and the South, and immigrants mostly from Central, Eastern, and Southern Europe and the Ottoman Empire. The

Midwest of the popular imagination was homogeneous and almost boring; in reality the Midwest that emerged in the early twentieth century was as culturally, ethnically, racially, and religiously diverse as it was economically diverse.

The books in this series capture the complexity of the Midwest and its historical and continuing role in the development of modern America.

David Nichols's *Peoples of the Inland Sea* provides a solidly researched exploration of American Indians in the region that we now call the Midwest. Its unique analysis begins in the seventeenth century, when Europeans and Native Americans first came into contact in the region, and traces events and important individuals through the late early republic, which by 1830 witnessed the almost total loss of Indian lands to American settlement. The removal of some 50,000 Indians from the Great Lakes region did not erase their history or their significant accomplishments, triumphs, and tragedies. Nichols captures those experiences, giving voice to the 170,000 Lakes Indians who lived near the Great Lakes basin by 1600. A diverse people, Lakes Indians represented more than a dozen different nations, lived in settled towns and villages, and traded over long distances. Their strong numbers began to recede as soon as Europeans found value in the trade and landholding opportunities surrounding the Great Lakes. Lakes Indian domination proved to be no match for the thousands of French and then British who flooded into the Great Lakes region. In the late seventeenth century their alliance with the French set the Lakes Indians on a path of cooperation and conflict that ended in the British triumph in the French and Indian War (Seven Years' War). Relations with the British soon soured and the stand Lakes Indians waged in Pontiac's War foretold generations of conflict between Europeans and Native Americans in the Midwest. Nichols masterfully captures this narrative, detailing the history of individual tribes and their interactions with other Lakes Indians and the Europeans. His study fills an important gap in the early history of the American Midwest.

L. Diane Barnes
Paul Finkelman

Introduction

VIEWING A PHYSICAL MAP OF NORTH AMERICA, ONE IS STRUCK, AS one's eyes move southward from the Arctic, by the countless thousands of large lakes gouged into the landscape. Products of glacial scouring during the last Ice Age, these immense freshwater reservoirs have long furnished human beings in Canada and the northern United States with a superabundance of resources: fish, timber, wild game, and transport, allowing lakeside peoples more easily to trade over long distances. The northern part of the continent contains six of the ten largest lakes (by surface area) in the world. Four of these, plus Lake Ontario, form part of an interlinked inland sea at the southern edge of the former Laurentide Ice Sheet, a sea commonly known as the Great Lakes.[1]

In the late nineteenth and twentieth centuries, the Great Lakes and their shorelands became the industrial heart of the United States, a vast marshaling zone for raw materials and the locale of some of the most productive commercial and industrial cities in the hemisphere. By then, however, the Great Lakes already had a very long history of human habitation, production, and trade, dating to the end of the Ice Ages. For all but a century or so of that history, most of the people who lived, worked, fought, and prayed in the Lakes region, who grew their crops in its fertile lowlands and valleys, who fished in its mighty freshwater seas and plied the waters of the Lakes and their tributary rivers with their birch-and-cedar canoes, who traded goods both exotic and mundane and built monumental mounds and smaller but still impressive longhouses and lodges, and who married and bore children and buried their dead there, were Native Americans.[2]

The Great Lakes Indians left (and continue to produce) a substantial record of their lives and achievements: archaeological sites, stories and myths, visual images and pictograms, recorded interviews and speeches, documents written by European observers, and writing generated by literate Indians. This grew particularly intricate and detailed after 1600, when Native Americans in the region began their sustained encounter with Europeans and European-Americans, who introduced them to alphabetic script and routine record keeping. Like material artifacts, oral traditions, and other forms of nonwritten evidence, textual documents require interpretation for modern readers to account for the biases of record keepers and to provide historical and cultural context. Since the 1950s, scholars have employed the interpretive tools of anthropologists, sociologists, and linguists to interpret European records and develop a more Native-centered history of American Indians. These scholars generally call themselves ethnohistorians.[3]

Ethnohistorians began applying their tools to the history of the Great Lakes Indians from the inception of their field, and by the 1970s and '80s they had produced a number of sensitive, thoughtful, book-length analyses of the changes occurring within particular Lakes nations. In 1991 the historian Richard White published a synthetic overview of Indian-white relations in the entire region, which had a powerful impact not only on ethnohistorians but on all American historians. White argued that Europeans and Indians enjoyed a rough balance of power on the Great Lakes frontier, and that this compelled them to create a "middle ground," a complex of diplomatic protocols, trading customs, and other "creative misunderstandings" that governed their relationships with one another until the nineteenth century. White's study provided an influential metaphor to all students of frontiers and borderlands, not just the Great Lakes region, and it was not for several years that scholars began to challenge it, arguing that the Lakes Indians enjoyed even greater cultural independence and political power than White already ascribed to them. Indians generally held the upper hand in their dealings with a French empire that claimed but could not enforce sovereignty over the Lakes region and Mississippi valley. Other historians argued that both the British Empire and the early United States labored under such restraints on their resources that Native Americans remained an independent political force in the region until 1815—even later in the north. The Lakes country now appears to have been not a middle ground but (borrowing Kathleen DuVal's term) a "native ground."[4]

Contact and conflict with the French, British, and American empires became one of the central dynamics of Lakes Indian history from the seventeenth to the early nineteenth century. Empires wanted Native Americans' resources and loyalty, and Native Americans desired European alliance and trade goods. The other factor dominating the lives of Lakes Indians was their struggle to survive and to preserve their customs and stories and agency, a practice Gerald Vizenor calls "survivance," in a changing physical and social milieu. The primary goal of this book is to explore these two struggles: one for political independence within a world of foreign empires, and one for cultural survival in an environment vastly altered by European goods, diseases, animals, and people. Like DuVal, Michael McDonnell, Cary Miller, and Michael Witgen, I will argue that in their dealings with Euro-American empires, the Lakes Indians often had the upper hand, for the Great Lakes was a region where France, Britain, and the early United States reached their logistical limits. The French and British had to make numerous accommodations to Lakes Indians' norms and expectations in order to maintain even a tenuous claim on their loyalty. While the early American republic proved less willing to accommodate Native Americans, it learned that it had to do so. In its dealings with the southern Lakes Indians, the new United States relied as much on diplomacy and trade as on force, and it drew the sword only when not one but two Indian confederacies directly challenged it, during the 1790s and 1810s.[5]

More disruptive than imperial conflict were the other effects of European contact, like exposure to new diseases or to new technologies they could not easily replicate. Epidemic disease and warfare slowly bled out the Lakes Indians' population, reducing it from approximately 170,000 in 1600 to a little more than 50,000 by the 1830s, while the fur trade led to intensified conflict between neighboring nations. Some compensated for land or population loss by intermarrying with Europeans, and epidemic diseases lost some of their edge as survivors became immune or as depleted nations (like the Iroquois) adopted war captives. Most avoided replacing all of their indigenous manufactures with European imports, continuing to wear skin and hide clothing, use bows and arrows, and manufacture canoes well into the eighteenth century. Some sought better prices for goods by trading with competing empires' merchants, and men and women avoided relying on animal pelts as their sole saleable good, instead developing more diverse commercial economies: marketing food and clothing to white traders and miners, mining lead, working as boatmen, and raising livestock.

By the 1830s, the American "empire" had acquired a sufficiently large population, army, and treasury to undertake the kind of conquest that neither the French nor the British dreamed of: effacing Native Americans from the landscape of the Lakes country. Even during the removal era, though, when fifty thousand Lakes Indians faced off against a nation of thirty million Americans, Native peoples found ways to resist and even thwart American power. Some managed to delay emigration for a decade or more, some hid out in Wisconsin or Michigan or took refuge in British Canada, and between one-third and one-half of the Lakes Indians, with the help of sympathetic white settlers and officials, managed to avoid removal altogether. Those who did move faced sickness, death, and the trauma produced by loss of homelands and loved ones, but the survivors built new homes north of the Lakes and west of the Mississippi River. Most modern Americans should take little pride in their ancestors' behavior toward Native Americans, but one can certainly appreciate the Lakes Indians' demonstration of human toughness, resilience, and cultural durability.

◆ ◆ ◆

Of the ten main chapters of *Peoples of the Inland Sea,* chapter 1 summarizes the long pre-Columbian history of the Great Lakes region, whose first human inhabitants arrived over ten thousand years ago. The early Lakes Indians began developing complex societies, with fixed settlements, ceremonial centers, and extensive trading networks, about three thousand years ago. One of these societies, the Mississippian culture, built settlements so large that the biggest of them, Cahokia, would have been a fair-sized city in medieval Europe.

Europeans surveying the mounds and earthworks that these pre-Columbian cultures built assumed that the post-Columbian inhabitants of the Lakes region had degenerated from more civilized predecessors. Actually, as chapter 2 observes, seventeenth-century Lakes Indians shared much in common with their "mound-builder" ancestors, as well as with each other. Though the 170,000 Native Americans living near the Great Lakes in 1600 belonged to more than a dozen different nations, most of them farmed, lived in towns, engaged in long-distance trade—the ethnic name of one nation, the Odawas, meant "traders"— and had complex social and political organization. Moreover, the early-modern Lakes Indians shared a common history of cultural disruption, if not trauma, in the wake of their first encounters (direct or indirect) with Europeans. Many succumbed to epidemic disease, or to Iroquois raiders whom the Dutch and English had armed, or had to abandon their homes and become refugees. Most succumbed to the lure of French merchandise, which improved their standard of living but also accustomed them to using goods they could not themselves manufacture.

By the end of the seventeenth century, where the narrative of chapter 3 begins, most of the Lakes nations shared another common trait: they had become military allies of the French empire. French officials viewed the Lakes Indians as future subjects and addressed them as the king's "children," but in practice France was the dependent partner in the relationship. Native American warriors defended, directly or indirectly, France's scattered outposts in the "upper country," and they effectively backed the kingdom's claim to the interior of North America. Hence the repeated concessions that Indians were able to procure from French officials: millions of livres' worth of gifts,[6] tacit permission to trade with the British, and the use of Native legal customs when prosecuting interethnic crimes. French officials certainly understood this imbalance in their relationship with the Lakes Indians, and their insecurity eventually propelled them into the military buildup that precipitated the Seven Years' (or "French and Indian") War. Chapter 4 explains how that war strained and broke French power in North America, but it also

observes that the same conflict demonstrated the power of France's Indian allies. Lakes Indian raiding parties took hundreds of captives and
essentially paralyzed two large British colonies, while several thousand
other warriors took part in early French offensives and came to Montreal to offer their services as late as 1760. Only an ill-timed smallpox
epidemic, skillful diplomacy, and a huge injection of military resources
allowed Britain to neutralize the Lakes Indians and defeat the French
army defending Canada.

Few British officials either tried or wanted to understand how much
the French-American empire had depended on Native Americans, and
how militarily powerful those Indians remained. And until they received a clear demonstration in Pontiac's War, fewer still appreciated
how readily the Great Lakes Indians could organize an autonomous
military alliance. Chapter 5 explains how the Lakes nations undertook that extensive and coordinated attack on the British posts in their
homeland. The motives driving Pontiac's allies included "nativism,"
the belief that whites and their material goods would poison Native
Americans,[7] but they also included opposition to British policies and
nostalgic allegiance to the French. France's political withdrawal from
North America and Britain's shift to a more accommodating Indian
policy helped prevent another anti-British alliance from forming
after the insurgency ended in 1764–65. Peace proved short-lived, however, thanks to the land hunger of colonial governments and Britain's
inability—and its unwillingness—to restrain colonial settlers.[8]

When those same settlers and colonies rebelled against the British Empire in the 1770s, the balance of power in the Great Lakes region finally began to tip against Native Americans. Chapter 6 observes
that many of the southeastern Lakes nations entered the Revolutionary War on Britain's side because colonial governments had injured
them in ways analogous to Britain's injury of the colonists, taking the
Delawares' and Shawnees' principal source of autonomy and wealth—
namely, their lands. Other Indians from the region fought for Britain
to ensure access to trade goods or win martial glory; still others managed to sit out the war. As in earlier imperial conflicts, Lakes Indian
warriors raided colonial settlements but could not permanently dislodge white settlers. Rebel militias then counterattacked and severely

damaged Native American towns in Ohio—indeed, as chapter 7 notes, their raids in the 1770s and 1780s swept most of the future state of Ohio clear of human habitation. Neither side, however, could deal the other a knockout blow during the War for American Independence, or indeed until the 1790s.

By that time, the American rebels had created a powerful national government that could project substantial military power into the southern Lakes region. Chapter 7 reveals that this political revolution in the United States coincided with a similar Lakes Indian movement toward political confederation, on a more ambitious scale than the pan-Indian alliance of the 1760s. By 1786 the confederates had created the United Indian nations, a military alliance with its own foreign relations and capital towns. While the United Indians remained open to a diplomatic settlement with the United States, their warriors continued to harry American settlements in Kentucky and in the new Northwest Territory, and they decisively defeated two federal armies sent against them in 1790–91. Gradually, however, the confederacy began to reveal signs of weakness: its constituent nations disagreed with and occasionally even fought one another, and its British allies and trading partners declined to risk a war with the Americans on the United Indians' behalf. The Americans, for their part, had begun building a stronger national government in the 1790s, one with sufficient resources to build forts, maneuver large armies, and win battles far from their Ohio valley bases. One of these battles, at Fallen Timbers in 1794, proved so successful that it compelled the United Indians to sign the Treaty of Greenville and break up their confederacy.

After 1795 the Americans became the dominant population in the southeastern Lakes region. Within a few years they began pressuring the southern Lakes Indians for land cessions that would enlarge the American empire's settlements and solidify its political power. Yet, as chapter 8 points out, the Lakes Indians still retained a lot of control over their own fates. Many, particularly in the northern Lakes country, continued to maintain their political autonomy and practice commercial hunting as they had done for over a century. Some, chiefly in the southern Lakes country, continued a shift to commercial agriculture that they had begun in the early 1700s. A third political and cultural strategy, proposed by the Shawnee prophet Tenskwatawa and his brother Tecumseh, emphasized a revival of nativism and the creation of a new, self-sufficient Indian nation-state. This last strategy, however, demonstrated the limits on Lakes Indian political autonomy, insofar as American officials like William Henry Harrison viewed it as a threat to the American regime's sovereignty and its steady transfer of land from Indians to white Americans. Ultimately, the Americans responded to Tenskwatawa and Tecumseh's movement with violence, and they crushed their confederacy on the battlefield within a couple of years during the War of 1812.

In many respects, the United States performed badly in that war, failing to obtain most of its military and political objectives. Chapter 9 notes, however, that the Americans did manage to win a major political and diplomatic victory: Britain largely withdrew its traders and officials from the Lakes country after 1815, giving the Americans a much freer hand with the Lakes Indians. During the next fifteen years, American expansion into the region proceeded in earnest, as soldiers garrisoned strategic points in the upper and western Lakes, treaty commissioners bought up most of the remaining Indian lands in Michigan and the southern Lakes states, American traders drew Lakes Indians ever more deeply into debt, Protestant missionaries tried to remake Native Americans in their own image, and American settlers engulfed southern Lakes Indian towns and turned them into enclaves in a white man's country.[9]

The Lakes nations could survive this invasion, and they even turned some of the invaders to their own advantage, but by the late 1820s the American national government had decided that it would not tolerate remnant Indian communities in the eastern United States. A combination of racism, fear of racial violence, desire for Native American resources, and a belief that Indians impeded economic progress propelled the Indian Removal Act of 1830, which authorized the relocation of the entire eastern Indian population to reservations west of the Missouri River. Over the following two decades, federal commissioners used a combination of economic pressure, veiled threats, and fraud to relocate nearly all of the southern Lakes Indians to modern Kansas and either removed or confined to small reservations the larger Indian nations of the northern Lakes region.

Chapter 10 demonstrates that removal occurred in the face of widespread resistance by Native Americans, and that the Lakes Indians fought hard against forced emigration and against political dissolution after removal. The Ojibwas, most of the Odawas, and the Menominees managed to remain in the Great Lakes region, and individual families and communities of Ho-Chunks, Miamis, and Potawatomis either illicitly returned to their homelands or moved to Upper Canada. Those Lakes Indian nations compelled to move west continued to exercise autonomous control over their collective fates, to manage their own economic affairs, and to organize new tribal governments and institutions. It was not until the 1860s that rapacious white settlers and another shattering continent-wide war forced many of them to migrate to new homes in Oklahoma or the Dakotas.

◆ ◆ ◆

Such are the chronological boundaries of this book. Its geographic focus deserves some explanation here, as does the author's particular definitions of "Lakes region" and "Lakes Indians." *Peoples of the Inland Sea* studies the Native American peoples of the six American states (Illinois, Indiana, Michigan, Minnesota, Ohio, and Wisconsin) located south and west of Lakes Erie, Huron, Michigan, and Superior, and of those parts of Ontario situated north and east of Lakes Huron, Ontario, and Superior. The Six Nations Iroquois, who historically lived in the geographic borderland between the Lakes and the Atlantic seaboard, have a similarly liminal presence here. The book does not provide a detailed overview of their history, but it does discuss Iroquois relationships with the other Lakes Indians, their alliances and struggles with the French and British empires (and the United States), and the migration of many into Canada and Wisconsin.

While defining my terms, I should note that Native American nomenclature is often a thorny subject, since Indians' self-labels (or eponyms) often differ from the national names that their indigenous neighbors or European explorers gave them. Generally, I have employed the ethnic names most commonly found in anglophone records, as a courtesy to readers wishing to conduct more research in specific Indian peoples' histories. Naturally, there are exceptions and qualifications to this rule. I employ the term "Ohio Iroquois" in referring to the so-called Mingoes, who received their derisive common name from the Six Nations Iroquois. The Ho-Chunks would not have appreciated the defamatory moniker that Anglo-Americans gave them, "Winnebago," so I do not use it here. When referring to more than one of the Three Fires peoples, I use the name "Anishinaabe" (plural "Anishinaabeg") and employ the modern spelling "Odawa" for the nation that Anglo-Americans spelled "Ottawa." For the Indians of the Illinois confederacy, I generally use the plural form "Illiniwek" and the singular adjective "Illini." American treaties generally use "Sac" and "Fox" to refer to the two interrelated nations that I spell "Sauk" and either "Fox" or "Mesquakie."[10]

"Native American" and "American Indian" are not names that Indians used for themselves before the nineteenth century, although because one of the first pan-Indian movements on the continent originated in the Lakes country, I found it appropriate to use both labels here. In accordance with modern usage, I have reserved the unmodified term "American" for the citizens, generally white, of the republican empire that fought, traded with, and ultimately displaced so many Native Americans. As part of their larger nation-building project, Revolutionary and Jacksonian-era Americans took for themselves a national label that properly belonged to Indians, thereby engaging in a kind of discursive removal of indigenous Americans. This book cannot easily offer redress for this expropriation, but I hope that my readers will not take it for granted.[11]

1

Once and Future Civilizations

BEFORE EUROPEANS BEGAN KEEPING WRITTEN ACCOUNTS OF THE region's history, the millennia of human experience in the Great Lakes country resided in the stories told by early modern Native Americans and the monuments their predecessors left behind. British and American travelers refused to integrate Indians' stories into their own Judeo-Christian chronology, and they drew entirely misleading conclusions from the thousands of mounds, fortifications, and earthworks that dotted the landscape. A sophisticated civilization, they believed, had once controlled the heart of North America, but barbarian peoples, the ancestors of the early modern Lakes Indians, had wiped it out. Civilization had given way to primitivism, and it remained to the European colonists to rebuild an advanced society.

Modern anthropologists have determined that this self-serving interpretation of precontact history is almost entirely inaccurate. The "civilization" that existed in mid-America was actually several different societies, which flourished at different times in different places.

These societies "declined" not when outside invaders overthrew them, but when large-scale settlements like Cahokia exhausted local resources, or when population growth became locally unsustainable, or when political elites lost legitimacy in the eyes of their subjects. Finally, the societies that built the great mounds and earthworks of the past were Indians, whom one could in some cases link to Native peoples (like the Ho-Chunks and Shawnees) who still lived in the region when the first French explorers arrived. The post-Columbian Lakes Indians all retained, moreover, the means if not the inclination to rebuild the monuments and cities of their past: they still practiced high-yield agriculture, built large and durable towns, and conducted long-distance trade for exotic goods. That they did not create a new mound-builder culture after 1600 one may blame on the actual foreign barbarians who entered and disrupted the region: the Europeans.

Lakes Indian history before 1600 was longer and more complicated than European invaders understood. Monumental societies like the Hopewell culture and the Mississippian settlements rose and fell, but beneath this highly visible superstructure of cyclical change, pre-Columbian Indians had children, built trading networks, adopted new forms of production like maize agriculture, and told stories that made sense of their people's place in the world. Seventeenth and eighteenth-century Europeans did not understand this underlying history, but fortunately modern scholars and Native peoples have been able to explain much of it.

＋ ＋ ＋

The Indians of the Great Lakes region traditionally did not assign a specific date to their peoples' arrival in America. Instead, their storytellers asserted that their ancestors had come to their contact-era homelands sometime in the distant past, usually from an otherworldly place of origin, often just as those homelands were coming into physical existence. The Hurons and Iroquois traced their descent from the Sky Woman (known to the Hurons as Aataentsic), who after falling from heaven birthed the first members of the human race on an island supported by a totemic Turtle. The Anishinaabeg told a similar story: angry manitous (spirits) destroyed their ancestors in a great flood, and the sole human survivor built an island refuge on the back of a great turtle. The Odawas identified the manitous in this tale as panther-like water spirits from an aqueous underworld who had flooded the world while chasing the trickster-hero Nanabush (who had killed their chief). The Ho-Chunks, a Siouan-speaking people from Wisconsin, focused their creation account on persistent links between the celestial and terrestrial: after creating the "island earth," Earth Maker fashioned four humans, named Hagaga, Henuga, Kunuga, and Nangiga, from dust and "a part of himself." He sent the four brothers to live on the world below but gifted them with fire and tobacco, which served as "mediator[s] between you and us" in the spirit realm. All of these stories conveyed similar lessons: human beings had both divine and earthly natures, and they lived in a world crowded with spiritual beings, some helpful and some dangerous.[1]

Modern archaeologists cannot affirm an otherworldly origin for Native Americans, but they do think that the first human beings arrived in the Western Hemisphere a very long time ago—approximately fifteen thousand years before the present day. These ancestors of the modern Lakes Indians reached their homelands just as the region was becoming inhabitable. The first people to migrate to America, the Paleo-Indians, probably crossed the Bering Strait during the last Ice Age. At the time, much of the world's water was locked up in the greatly expanded polar ice caps, and sea levels were lower, so low that the Bering Strait was not open water but a marshy, one-thousand-mile-wide land corridor connecting Siberia with Alaska. The Paleo-Indian migrants crossed this isthmus on foot or used small boats to follow the coastline. Whichever route they followed, they and their descendants gradually made their way down the Pacific coast, past the frozen, ice-covered lands of present-day Canada and the northern United States, and then spread east and south to people the hemisphere.[2]

During the time of this migration, the Laurentide Ice Sheet, a glacial mass larger than the present-day Antarctic ice sheet, covered the lands around the Great Lakes, as far south as central Illinois. As this ice melted in the late Pleistocene, the runoff flooded the region's rivers. Some rivers, like the older Mississippi and Ohio, carved deeper valleys that gradually filled with fertile silt. Others, like the Wabash and Wisconsin, took their modern courses when glacial lakes ruptured, discharging millions of cubic feet of water to the southwest. In the warming and now well-watered lands around the Great Lakes, many varieties of trees took root, first willow and birch, then conifers like spruce and pine, and (by 6000 BCE) maple, oak, beech, and other nut-bearing deciduous species. Browsing animals soon followed, living on the rich plant resources that the postglacial forests provided.[3]

Human beings began exploiting this new environment before the glaciers fully retreated. Archaeologists have located an eleven-thousand-year-old site in Calhoun County, Michigan, where hunters may have cached mastodon meat in a pond, whose cold water would have preserved their kill. Around the same time, caribou hunters left behind a campsite near present-day Holcombe, Michigan, and another Paleo-Indian party left fluted spear points near future Madison, Wisconsin. Paleo-Indian bands probably hunted large mammals, or megafauna, throughout the region during the late Pleistocene epoch.[4]

At the end of the last Ice Age, however, the human population of the Americas rose above the level where it could sustain itself through big-game hunting, while many of North America's large mammals (such as mammoths) went extinct from overhunting and climate change. Faced with a subsistence crisis, the Paleo-Indians began to develop new survival strategies and more sophisticated toolkits. They initiated what archaeologists now call the Archaic era of North American Indian history.

Native Americans of the Archaic period (8000–1000 BCE) learned to subsist on a smaller territory than did the hunters of the Paleo-Indian era. They made fishing hooks and gaffs, which allowed them to harvest the rich fish populations of North America's rivers and lakes: pike, bass, and catfish in the Mississippi River; sturgeon, perch, and mussels in the Great Lakes. They hunted smaller and faster animals, like birds and deer, using longer-range projectile weapons like the atlatl, a spear-thrower that increased the effective length of the hunter's throwing arm and thus his effective range. They learned to make wild plant foods (like acorns) edible by leaching out tannin and other bitter or toxic compounds. They domesticated dogs to serve as hunting assistants (and occasionally as food), a process that began early in the Archaic era—in fact, some of the oldest domestic canine remains in North

America, dated to 6500 BCE, were found near the Illinois River. They learned to make pottery, which provided them with rigid, leak-proof storage containers. Pottery making also indicated that the Archaic Indians had become less nomadic, since ceramics are heavy and easy to drop and break, and it probably also elevated the economic status of women, since women usually produced ceramics.[5]

Some Indians learned to mine copper from ore-bearing rocks, which the glaciers had deposited close to the surface in the upper Great Lakes region, and to anneal (strengthen) the metal by heating it and plunging it into cold water. Archaic Indians in Wisconsin were mining copper and turning it into spear points, fishhooks, and awls by 4,000 BCE. They apparently halted production sometime after 500 BCE, though Indians continued to mine and work copper north of the Great Lakes for many centuries thereafter.[6]

In the late Archaic era, around 1500 BCE, Indians in the Ohio valley began cultivating squash and several other North American plants that produced oil-rich seeds, such as sunflowers and sump weed. During the same period (ca. 2450–1000 BCE), they and their northern neighbors engaged in silviculture, promoting the growth of desirable trees by girdling rival tree species and burning undergrowth. The arboreal species that Archaic Indians favored, like oak and hickory, produced acorns, hickory nuts, and other "mast" that game animals could eat, attracting large populations of deer and turning some forests into de facto hunting parks.[7] All of these Archaic-era innovations in food production took several thousand years to unfold, but they allowed Native Americans to continue increasing their numbers after their old nomadic hunting economy became unsustainable. By 1000 BCE there were probably around one million people living in North America north of the Rio Grande. If the human population in the Great Lakes region maintained its proportion to the overall Native North American population, then it reached approximately fifty thousand people by the end of the Archaic era.[8]

The Archaic era ended with the rise of several sophisticated cultures in the upper Ohio River valley: the Adena culture (1000–100 BCE), the Hopewell cultural system (200 BCE–500 CE), the Mississippians (900–1500 CE), and the Fort Ancient culture (1000–1500 CE). The Adena people, named for the "type site" in Ohio where archaeologists first discovered their artifacts, had a social or religious elite whom they interred in wooden tombs covered by conical earthen mounds. With their former leaders they buried ceremonial goods like carved stone pipes and figurines of people or animals. The culture occupied a region extending from southern Indiana to West Virginia and from central Ohio to central Kentucky. Most of its people lived near the Ohio River and its tributaries, where large populations of fish, game, and wild plants provided enough food to support dense human populations—more than ten times as many people per square mile than in the uplands.[9]

The Adena people's successors, the Hopewellians, covered a much larger geographical area; they were a network of societies bound together by trade and some common cultural forms. The main Hopewell peoples resided in central Ohio and northern Kentucky, while their cultural relations and trading partners dwelt in Michigan, Indiana, Illinois, and Wisconsin. The Hopewell people lived in widely separated homesteads in river valleys and, like their Adena predecessors, spent part of their labor building large burial mounds for their elite. Hopewell mounds usually formed geometric shapes, and their builders sited them near other earthen buildings in ceremonial complexes, some of which covered several square miles. At the edge of these complexes, the Hopewellians built temporary dwellings where commoners lived part of the year, while they were constructing earthworks or attending religious ceremonies, before they returned home to hunt and plant.[10]

In their mounds, the Hopewellians interred not only their leaders but also hundreds of grave goods, many of which they fashioned from exotic materials: obsidian blades, copper jewelry, mica cutouts of human hands, and artifacts made of marine shells and grizzly-bear teeth. The trade network that provided these materials extended south to the Gulf of Mexico and west to the Rockies. The goods themselves were most likely "prestige goods," indicators of status that circulated in a different economic sphere from ordinary goods like food or animal skins.[11]

It is not easy to draw conclusions about the nonmaterial lives of Hopewell peoples from the remains they left, but the anthropologist Matthew Coon has made some thought-provoking suggestions. The orientation of human remains at one Hopewell-era site in Ohio, he argues, indicates that the Indians there may have organized themselves into social "halves" (or "moieties"). Such large binary groups would have helped draw potentially rival families and clans together. Coon also believes that some of the Ohio Hopewellians' engravings show human beings wearing animal masks, and he notes that masks would have improved social harmony by allowing lower-ranking people to disguise themselves while they publicly criticized their ruling elite. His hypotheses help answer one of the most fundamental questions facing any large society with a governing class: why do the governed give their allegiance to the governors? In the case of some of the Hopewell communities, the answer may lie in the formation of large groups that increased social solidarity and in the development of mechanisms for criticizing rulers.[12]

The Hopewell era coincided with the spread of a new crop, Meso-american maize (Indian corn), through the Ohio valley. It is likely that maize agriculture led to population growth in the region. A carbohydrate-rich diet lowers the risk that pregnant women will have miscarriages, and the development in the fifth century CE of thinner pottery that one could use to heat food more efficiently allowed women to turn maize into gruel, which they could use to wean their children at an earlier age. Women who stopped lactating would then resume their menses and their fertility. Population growth, which provided the labor force for the Hopewellians' mounds and earthworks, may have eventually produced social conflicts and stresses that the Hopewell culture's institutions could not contain. Perhaps this helps explain that culture's disappearance after 500 CE. Only a few centuries would pass, however, before new "mound-builder" cultures would take Hopewell's place.[13]

One of these cultures, the effigy mound builders of modern Wisconsin, emerged during the Late Woodland period (500–1200 CE) and began building their distinctive mounds around 700 CE. The Wisconsin mound builders lived in an ecologically diverse region rich in food resources: forests harboring game animals, marshes full of fish and birds, and flat prairies suitable for raising corn, which local Indians adopted around 900. They constructed their mounds, numbering over three thousand by 1200 CE, at places where large numbers of people gathered to hunt, fish, and hold religious ceremonies. The mounds

themselves apparently formed a vast symbolic map of the effigy builders' cosmology. Some of the effigies, concentrated in southeastern Wisconsin, represented long-tailed water spirits from the builders' watery
underworld, similar to the manitous in the Odawas' creation and flood
story. Some, concentrated in southwestern Wisconsin, represented bird
spirits from the builders' Upper World, akin to the thunderbirds from
Ojibwa mythology. Some, located in a band across the present southern
border of Wisconsin, represented bear and other animal spirits from the
Middle World (that is, the physical world). A few represent a horned
human who may have been a precursor of Red Horn, a culture hero of
the Ho-Chunks, whose cosmology resembled that of the effigy builders.
The finished mounds were probably ceremonial centers—some contain
concentrations of stones that archaeologists believe are the remains of
altars—and they certainly served as burial mounds, though the sparse-
ness of grave goods suggests that the effigy builders had an egalitarian
society, certainly more so than their Mississippian neighbors.[14]

The Mississippians would become the most famous of the post-
Hopewell mound-building cultures. Their society arose around 900 CE
and flourished in the greater Mississippi valley and the southeast until
1500 CE. The Mississippian people practiced intensive agriculture,
lived in large towns or cities, built large temple mounds, and organized
themselves into a hierarchy of social classes. Of the urban centers that
the Mississippians constructed, the largest was Cahokia, a city built
on the bottom lands near present-day Saint Louis. Cahokia's establishment was more a revolutionary than an evolutionary event: its builders
erected much of the city in a single surge of construction that began
around 1050 CE. Archaeologist Timothy Pauketat speculates that the
Cahokians may have drawn inspiration from the Crab Nebula super-
nova of 1054, which produced a bright new star visible everywhere in the
world. Cahokia was centered on a massive, terraced platform mound,
known today as Monk's Mound, which stands over one hundred feet
high and is comparable in size to the stone pyramids of Mesoamerica.
The city featured several other platform temple mounds, a vast public
plaza, several wooden "henge" structures used as astronomical calen-
dars, and the dwellings of about fifteen thousand residents. No other
city north of Mexico would reach this size again until the 1700s.[15]

The Mississippians' hierarchy comprised a small elite of priests and nobles, a large class of commoners and warriors, and a population of slaves at the bottom. Mississippian slaves were generally war captives, and like slaves elsewhere in the world they were (to borrow sociologist Orlando Patterson's term) "socially dead," not part of any kin group or patron-client relationship. Slaves at Cahokia sometimes became more permanently dead: archaeological excavation of one of Cahokia's mounds uncovered the remains of more than eighty men and women killed at the same time and interred with two high-status men. The eighty victims were almost certainly slaves sacrificed to "accompany" the two priests or nobles into the grave.[16]

Life in Cahokia was marginally better for commoners, but even they suffered from dietary deficiencies and hard labor, which raises the question of why they would remain in Cahokia and other Mississippian settlements if life was so difficult. Some Mississippians, like the nearby farming villagers who provided Cahokia's food supply, may have feared attack or enslavement if they didn't move into the region. Others probably remained in Cahokia and other Mississippian towns for security: there was safety in numbers, and warriors protected commoners from becoming another Indian community's captives and sacrificial victims. Moreover, there were positive benefits to living in Cahokia that compensated commoners for their other hardships. Based on remains found in a massive midden, or trash heap, at the Cahokia site, archaeologists believe that the city's elite held periodic feasts in which the whole populace gorged itself on meat and corn and smoked huge quantities of tobacco. These feasts created a collective state of euphoria and torpor that would have boosted public morale. With its public feasts, dramatic sacrificial ceremonies, and protective warriors class, the city of Cahokia offered ample compensations to Indian commoners who might otherwise have led easier lives, had they lived in a smaller town or village.[17]

Cahokia reached its peak of population and development during the first century after its founding. By 1150 CE, the city's population declined to about half of its peak level, and by 1300 Cahokia and most of the other Mississippian towns in the Great Lakes region stood empty. Some of this decline one can attribute to a series of droughts that hit the mid-continent during the twelfth and thirteenth centuries, depopulating the farming settlements that had previously fed Cahokia. Cahokia and its neighboring villages were also experiencing shortages of firewood by 1150, as the region's many city dwellers and farmers cut down the trees in the vicinity. Modern scholars detect a rise in individualism and war making among Cahokia's leaders, demonstrated by their display of increasingly exotic and unique "prestige goods" like shell cups and copper ornaments, and by a shift from the construction of temple mounds to the building of protective palisades. Cahokia's decline was not merely demographic but cultural: at a time when resource shortages were already placing a strain on the populace, the priest/aristocrat class who ruled the city devoted more resources to warfare and individual display than to collective well-being. Since Cahokia's elite derived its legitimacy from its mediation between their people and the spiritual world, and since poor harvests and drought indicated that supernatural forces had become more than a little angry, it is unsurprising that the city's commoners would desert their leaders.[18]

Other Mississippian centers in the Great Lakes region included Angel Mounds in Indiana and Aztalan in Wisconsin, the latter a fortified Mississippian colony with four large platform mounds. These communities joined Cahokia in decline in the thirteenth and fourteenth centuries. Their depopulation probably resulted from a combination of resource depletion and colder temperatures accompanying the beginning of the Little Ice Age, a global cooling period that began in 1300 CE and lasted half a thousand years. One of the more robust Mississippian offshoots, the Fort Ancient culture of present-day Ohio and Kentucky, lasted somewhat longer than its predecessors. Beginning around 1000 CE, the Fort Ancient people built settlements similar to those of other Mississippians, grouping their dwellings around central plazas with posts that served as solar calendar markers to indicate corn planting and harvest days. Perhaps as a response to the regional droughts that afflicted Cahokia, they developed and dug efficient storage pits for their surplus corn in the thirteenth and fourteenth centuries. Like the Hopewellians and Mississippians, the Fort Ancient people constructed geometric burial mounds, such as Serpent Mound in the Scioto River valley and Alligator Mound near present-day Granville, Ohio. Some of the artifacts they left behind, like stones from the game of chunky and shell-tempered pottery—pottery made with burned shells, to lighten and strengthen the clay—were also typical of Mississippian peoples, and one could find them in the southeast well into the eighteenth century.[19]

After 1450 CE, a changing (drier, cooler) climate caused the Fort Ancient people partially to disperse. They retained their core settlements but spent much of the year traveling the tributaries of the Ohio, hunting and gathering and trading. The other post-Mississippian cultures of the Great Lakes region decentralized or dispersed at the same time. The former residents of Cahokia abandoned the American Bottom altogether, while the people of Angel Mounds remained near the Ohio-Wabash confluence but resettled in small villages, grouped into a loose confederacy that archaeologists call the Caborn-Welborn culture. The native peoples of Wisconsin split into two groups of settlements, one on the Mississippi River and the other southeast of Green Bay, both belonging to what archaeologists now call the Oneota culture. The Oneotas made shell-tempered pottery like the Mississippians' and decorated it with bird and water-spirit images reminiscent of the Wisconsin effigy-mound culture, but they themselves did not build mounds and instead buried their dead in small cemeteries. They also spent less of the year in fixed settlements, devoting several months to hunting the bison that had begun moving into the eastern prairies (modern Illinois and Wisconsin) in the fourteenth century. Some of the old "moundbuilder" culture did remain: the trade networks that earlier elites had created, and recognition that the old mounds and earthworks in the region still had spiritual value even if few people visited them.[20]

The Indian cultures that dominated the Great Lakes region in the post-Mississippian period consisted of hunters, farmers, and traders, but no aristocrats or monument builders. European travelers of the eighteenth and nineteenth centuries considered this a devolutionary change. When they first discovered the mounds and earthworks of the Adena, Hopewell, Mississippian, and Fort Ancient cultures, Europeans assumed that the "Mound Builders" had been a single advanced civilization. They speculated that this predecessor race had descended from Old World migrants—Phoenicians, Vikings, the Ten Lost Tribes of Israel, even refugees from the mythical continent of Atlantis—unrelated to their more "primitive" Indian successors. (Joseph Smith, founder of the Church of Jesus Christ of Latter-Day Saints, incorporated this belief into the Mormons' religious doctrine.) It was not until the late nineteenth century that American ethnographers and archaeologists concluded that the Mound Builders represented several different cultures, all of them Native American. And it took scholars until the late twentieth century to begin working out the social and environmental causes of these different cultures' rise and fall.[21]

In the meantime, early European and American explorers persisted in viewing the Great Lakes region as a marginal country. French travelers and traders called it the *pays d'en haut* or "Upper Country," while English-speaking Americans used the term "Western World." It is evident, however, that the lands around the Great Lakes had been a center of human culture and development for thousands of years. Indians had been hunting in that region since the Pleistocene, had there learned to mine copper and domesticate dogs earlier than any other people in North America, and had built some of the largest towns and cities the continent would see prior to the eighteenth century. Far from a wild periphery, the Lakes region was long-settled, lay at the center of a continent-wide trading network, and for many centuries hosted highly sophisticated Native American cultures.[22]

The various "Mound Builder" cultures had almost all dispersed by the sixteenth century, but if their 2,500-year-long history makes one thing clear, it is that their disappearance need not have been permanent. The decline of one complex culture did not preclude the rise of a successor culture in the future. Hopewell succeeded Adena, the Mississippian and Fort Ancient cultures succeeded Hopewell, and there was no reason to assume, from the vantage point of 1600 CE, that the Indians of the Great Lakes region would not eventually create another complex, urban culture. Certainly there was still a large Native American population in the region, along with trading networks that could supply enough prestige goods to enrich and empower a future elite.

What prevented such a revival from occurring was the introduction of a new group of migrants who—largely inadvertently—decimated the region's Indian population and introduced a new supply of exotic goods too large for the region's surviving elite to control. The new migrants called themselves by several names; collectively, we would call them Europeans. Their invasion of the Midwest began the most revolutionary charge the region had seen since the rise of Cahokia, and possibly since the end of the Ice Ages.

2

The European Disruption

A MOSAIC OF HUMAN SOCIETIES ADORNED THE GREAT LAKES country in the era of European colonization. There were Algonquian speakers and Iroquoian speakers, patrilineal and matrilineal cultures, people who resided in longhouses and those who built smaller dwellings or temporary shelters. The Native American nations of the region also had much in common. The majority of them, or more precisely the majority of Lakes Indian women, practiced agriculture, and most of the region's people lived in settled villages and towns. All of the Lakes Indians traded with one another, and their commercial networks extended hundreds of miles to the north, east, and west. All gave young men the responsibility for becoming warriors, and all fought internecine wars with their neighbors for glory and captives. The Lakes Indians even shared some of the same mythologies, with several attributing their origins to divine or celestial realms, many describing the material world as a great island supported on the back of a giant turtle, and most believing that they shared the world with powerful manitous that

influenced human affairs. These similarities were not merely coinciden-
tal: they demonstrated that the contact-era Lakes Indians had been interacting with one another and sharing goods and ideas for centuries.[1]

The web of interaction that Native Americans created would later
magnify the destructive impact of European colonization. Trade routes
carried new diseases, which decimated the Huron-Wendat and Iroquois
confederacies at the eastern end of the Great Lakes. Old warpaths now
provided passage to Iroquois raiders and Illiniwek slavers armed with
European guns. French intruders found that, with a little help from their
Indian allies, they could employ Native American paths and waterways
to penetrate to the center of the continent. Having initially come to
North America to trade and evangelize, the French would by the end of
the seventeenth century use these routes to build and supply churches,
forts, and settlements. All of these became instruments of an empire
with which most Lakes Indians felt compelled to align themselves.

◆ ◆ ◆

The first Europeans to encounter the Great Lakes Indians came from
France, a western European kingdom with roughly the same popula-
tion as fifteenth-century Mexico. France was an old land, colonized by
modern humans long before the first Paleo-Indians arrived in North
America, but its culture and institutions developed much more recently.
The kingdom's principal language and its bookish, bureaucratized
Catholic faith derived ultimately from the Romans, who had blood-
ily conquered Gaul (as France was then known) in the first century
BCE and ruled it for five hundred years. The agricultural staples that
fed the French people, grain and livestock, had been domesticated several millennia earlier, but the productivity of early-modern France's
farms, and thus the subsistence of its twenty million people, depended
on medieval innovations like crop rotation and the horse collar. The
machinery (mine pumps and powered bellows) that allowed French
smiths to manufacture cheap metal wares, the goods most desired by
France's Indian trading partners, came into use even more recently, in
the fifteenth century. Even France's ruling class experienced significant
change, with the old warrior-aristocracy of the Middle Ages losing
power to wealthy merchants and guild masters, who used their money

to buy land, educate their children, and acquire honorable offices in the royal government. France was still a rural, parochial, and often violent society, but its people increasingly devoted themselves to industry, commerce, and exploration.[2]

The first Frenchmen to spend significant time in North America and trade with its Native peoples were humble fishermen from marginal coastal provinces, like Brittany and the Basque country. Early in the sixteenth century, these men began outfitting voyages across the Atlantic Ocean to the Grand Banks, a region of shoals off the coast of Newfoundland. There, currents deflected by the steep banks churned up nutrients that sustained huge quantities of plankton, which in turn fed millions of codfish. Cod was a protein-rich fish that fishermen could preserve for months, and for which there was a considerable demand among Europe's protein-starved working population. Cod became North America's first profitable transatlantic export, and by the 1550s hundreds of fishing vessels from France and other nations were plying the Grand Banks.[3]

To dry and salt their catch, cod fishermen landed on the coasts of Newfoundland, Labrador, and Quebec and spent weeks or months at temporary encampments. There some encountered Miqmaq and Montagnais Indians, who from an early date began to barter with these uninvited guests, exchanging food and animal furs for knives and glass beads. The Indians' furs, particularly the wooly pelts of American beaver, proved valuable to French hatters, and Canadian furs became the second significant North American export to Europe. Even while a series of religious wars (1562–98) disrupted the French economy, French mariners continued to catch cod and purchase beaver pelts, and around 1600 some established a semipermanent trading rendezvous on the Saint Lawrence River.[4]

Since American furs were a luxury item with a low production volume and high value, French merchants believed it possible to establish an effective monopoly over the fur trade, and in the early 1600s several companies of courtiers and merchants asked the king to grant them such a monopoly. In 1607 one of these partnerships asked mariner Samuel Champlain to help them find an appropriate site in Canada for a trading base and settlement. Champlain persuaded his sponsors to choose the narrows of the Saint Lawrence River, a site relatively secure from attack and closer than Tadoussac to the homelands of the region's principal Indians. The result was the outpost of Quebec (1608), which grew into both a successful trading center and the nucleus of French settlement in North America.[5]

Quebec occupied the land of the Montagnais Indians, but its principal trading partners, who accounted for over two-thirds of the furs sold to the Company of New France, belonged to a Great Lakes nation, the Hurons. The Hurons were members of the Northern Iroquoian cultural and language group, whose progenitors, according to archaeologist Dean Snow, probably migrated to the Great Lakes region after 900 CE, at the beginning of the Medieval Warm Period (900–1300) that preceded the Little Ice Age. By the seventeenth century CE, there were about twenty thousand Hurons residing in a cluster of towns east of Lake Huron and Georgian Bay. Huron towns consisted of several dozen wooden longhouses, each housing upwards of thirty people; their largest communities had two thousand inhabitants. Like other Iroquoians, the Hurons were matrilineal, tracing familial descent through the mother's side of the family, and they were also matrilocal, which meant that married men resided in their wives' households. The latter development helped avoid rivalries and civil discord by separating brothers from one another, making it harder for them to form factions of male kinsmen. It was a useful enough survival mechanism that even some of the patrilineal Great Lakes Indians, peoples like the Potawatomis and Mesquakies who traced descent through the father's line, were also matrilocal or bilocal.[6]

The Hurons' matrilineality and matrilocal dwelling customs probably reflect the importance of women, who did all of the Hurons' farming, to the nation's survival. While the Hurons also practiced hunting and fishing, agriculture provided about 80 percent of their calories. Even though they lived close to the 120-frost-free-day line that marked the northern limit of maize cultivation, the Hurons grew such a large surplus of corn that they could trade it with the Ojibwas and other Indians of the northern Great Lakes. In the early seventeenth century, Huron traders learned that the thick pelts of northern beavers and other mammals were valuable to Europeans, and they initiated a multiparty exchange of Huron corn for Ojibwa furs for European goods. The merchandise they obtained from French traders gradually improved the Hurons' standard of living without altering their basic lifeways. Durable iron axes and blades made it easier to fell trees, build longhouses, and improve the Hurons' bone- and wood-carving practices; light metal cooking pots made it easier to prepare food; and firearms gave Huron warriors an advantage in their periodic wars with the Iroquois.[7]

While individual families owned the Hurons' crops and trade routes, the nation avoided gross inequalities of wealth and promoted social stability with regular rituals of redistribution. Huron men and women expected their leaders to hold feasts and dances for them, some to serve as displays of hospitality and some to help heal the sick. All Hurons participated in a massive redistributive ceremony known as the Feast of the Dead, held every twelve years in the town of Ossossane, during which families dug up, skinned, and reinterred their deceased relatives. They accompanied these last rites with the display and distribution of thousands of presents. (The Hurons reinterred their dead after their relatives' "second souls," which they believed to remain with the body after the initial physical death, had passed on.) Hurons also redistributed goods as part of their legal culture: the families of those accused of murder had to pay sixty gifts to the victim's family, unless they wanted to invite violent retribution, while thieves' victims could confiscate their attackers' possessions.[8]

The Hurons' social cohesion began to break down in the 1630s, however, because of two additional imports from Europe: Old World diseases and Catholic Christianity. Europeans had acquired the former from their domestic animals or via overland trade with eastern and southern Asia, and over the centuries many Europeans had acquired immunity to diseases like smallpox and measles, usually after surviving a bout with them in childhood. Isolated from Eurasian disease pools and lacking domestic animals, Native Americans had no familiarity with crowd diseases. When they caught them, everyone in the community became sick at once, leaving no one to care for the afflicted, gather firewood, or bring in crops. Traders and travelers carried imported diseases to Huron towns, and the results proved deadly: in 1635, 1636–37, and 1639–40, epidemics of scarlet fever, influenza, and smallpox spread through the Hurons' longhouses and killed thousands of people. Neither the Hurons nor the Jesuit missionaries residing with them could fight either illness. Huron medicine, prescribed by holy men like the hunchbacked Tonneraouanont and the reclusive Tehorenhaegnon, focused on treating the sick with feasts, dances, herbal remedies, and enchantments. The Jesuits, who considered such healers demonic "sorcerers," prescribed instead palliatives (like sugar), Masses, and bleeding of the sick. None of these treatments drove away the demons or divine disfavor to which sorcerers and missionaries ascribed illness. Some, like communal gatherings and bloodletting, probably worsened patients' condition or infected others. Lacking effective medicinal techniques, nearly half of the Huron people died by the mid-1640s.[9]

The Hurons experienced further stress in the 1640s when a minority adopted Christianity, a faith brought to Huron country by Jesuits in the previous decade. The Jesuits, a new order of teachers and missionaries, sought to convert the non-Christian peoples of the world to Catholicism—and to European moral norms—during an era in which Catholic reformers also sought to wipe out superstition and disorder among European peasants. The techniques of conversion resembled those employed by other Catholic missionaries in Europe, relying heavily on visual images, music, and charitable gifts of food and medicine. Jesuit missionaries had a lasting impact on those Hurons who converted; two hundred years later, travelers to Huron-Wyandot communities in northern Ohio noted that some Huron words had apparently been adapted from Latin.[10]

However, by requiring converts to avoid traditional marital customs and religious observances, the Jesuits segregated Christian from non-Christian Indians. Most Hurons disliked Jesuits' separation of the "saved" from the unsaved, which broke the traditional bonds of community and kinship. One, referring to the missionaries' offer of heaven to those who broke from their unconverted kinsmen, said in 1637, "For my part, I have no desire to go to heaven; I have no acquaintances there, and the French who are there would not . . . give me anything to eat." Some converts faced mistrust or persecution from "pagan" kinsmen who opposed the Christians' abandonment of their old social

obligations. This growing division within Huron communities, combined with the confederacy's losses from disease, made them more vulnerable to external attack, which came with great force in the form
of the Iroquois.[11]

Residing in the Finger Lakes country on the southern shore of
Lake Ontario, the Five Nations of Iroquois strongly resembled their
Huron rivals. Their ancestors had developed "Three Sisters" agriculture (beans, maize, and squash) around 1000 CE, at roughly the same
time as the Hurons. They used the output of their fields, fisheries, berry
patches, and hunting territories to sustain a substantial population,
roughly twenty thousand people in 1600. They maintained large fortified towns, whose heavy palisades caused some European observers
to call them "castles," and therein dwelled in large multifamily longhouses. They organized their society around matrilineal families and
clans, and they even had a creation story resembling that of the Hurons, focusing on the Sky Woman—which probably reflected the social
importance of Iroquois women. One critical difference distinguished
the two groups, however: the Iroquois traded less with their Indian
neighbors and fought them much more frequently. In the sixteenth century, the Iroquois had developed a sophisticated mechanism for preventing conflict among themselves: the League of Peace. The chiefs of
this ceremonial body, whom Iroquois matrons appointed to their positions, used elaborate rituals of condolence to settle grievances between
Mohawks and Oneidas, or between Cayugas and Onondagas. Neighboring nations like the Hurons and Montagnais, however, remained
outside the league and thus remained enemies.[12]

French firearms and iron weapons gave the Hurons an early military advantage over the Five Nations, but in the late 1620s the Iroquois
began buying guns from the Dutch at Beverswyck (present-day Albany). Having leveled the military playing field, in the 1640s Iroquois
raiders intercepted Huron trading parties and robbed them of their
furs, wherewith they purchased more weapons and ammunition. The
primary goal of Iroquois warfare in this period, however, was to obtain
captives, to replace the population losses they suffered because of epidemic disease in the 1630s. (Ethnohistorians call this kind of warfare
"mourning war.") In 1648 and 1649, two large Iroquois war parties

invaded Huronia, destroyed several of the Hurons' towns, and killed
or captured about two thousand people. The Iroquois tortured and
executed a few captives, but they adopted most of them into their extended families and made them part of the Five Nations.[13]

The Hurons who evaded death or capture burned their remaining
towns to prevent the Iroquois from plundering them, then dispersed
from the ruins of their homeland. Some joined with a neighboring
Iroquoian nation, the Petuns, which had also come under Iroquois
attack, and moved west. These emigrants initially (1651–52) settled
at Sault Sainte Marie, a plain adjacent to the Bawating Rapids on
the Saint Mary's River, which several Ojibwa clans used as a fishery
and gathering place. Some settled at Michilimackinac ("The Great
Turtle"), the district south of Mackinac Strait. In these places of refuge, they became the progenitors of a new Indian nation, the Wyandots, who would play a significant role in the region over the next two
centuries.[14]

+ + +

The Huron/Wyandots first took refuge in the homeland of the Odawa[15]
and Ojibwa Indian nations, who along with the Nipissings and
Potawatomis made up the confederacy of Algonquian-speakers known
as the Anishinaabeg, or First People. The Anishinaabeg had resided
in the Great Lakes region for several centuries before the Hurons and
other Iroquoians moved into the eastern Lakes country. By the seventeenth century they probably numbered thirty or forty thousand,
divided into kinship groups that traced descent from totemic animal
ancestors—beaver, otter, pike, catfish, crane, moose, or heron. Residing on the northern Great Lakes, at or above the climatic boundary for
farming in the region, they relied on fishing, hunting, and wild plant
foods for their subsistence. The Potawatomis and some of the Odawas
raised corn in fields they visited seasonally. The Ojibwas traded with
the Hurons for agricultural produce, supplying their trading partners with most of the furs they resold to the French at Quebec and
receiving in return maize and French goods. The Ojibwas would later
become Huron/Wyandot allies against the Iroquois, who found the Anishinaabeg formidable adversaries. Ojibwa warriors defeated several

Iroquois war parties between 1653 and 1662, nearly annihilating the raiders in the last of these battles.[16]

The Anishinaabeg, particularly the Ojibwas, Odawas, and Nipissings, covered great distances to hunt, fish, and trade. Nipissing families traveled as far north as James Bay, while the Odawas ("Trading People") would range up to fifteen hundred miles in a season, using large birch-and-cedar canoes that could cross open waters out of sight of shore, carrying up to four tons of cargo and passengers. One could not, however, call any of these nations nomadic. All spent a large part of the year in sedentary farming or fishing villages, and when hunting or trading, several bands usually kept their camps within one to two days' travel of one another, so that they could pool resources or help other bands in an emergency. The northern Anishinaabeg bands also used an arc of rendezvous sites, including Michilimackinac, Manitoulin Island, and Lake Nipissing, to gather during the summer months. Like the Hurons, the Anishinaabeg held at their gatherings periodic Feasts of the Dead, in which hundreds of people interred their relatives' bones and helped other families, some of them from other nations, lay their dead to rest. Participants in these feasts also performed military and social dances, elected new chiefs, and received gifts from their leaders, reaffirming the social bonds that held bands together. These were not the only institutions that united the Anishinaabeg. Intermarriage joined the members of different clans in bonds of kinship (since women had to marry outside of their clan), and medicinal and lore-keeping societies known as *midewiwin*, founded sometime before the arrival of Europeans, tied together different kinship groups and different nations.[17]

Strong and cohesive as the Anishinaabeg clearly were, the Huron/Wyandots feared that their new homes in the Huron-Michigan-Superior confluence region remained vulnerable to Iroquois attack. In 1652 they moved west to Green Bay, Wisconsin, where they lived on several islands near the mouth of that inlet. Several years later the refugees moved onto the mainland and into the valley of the upper Mississippi River, settling for three years on an island in Lake Pepin (sixty miles south of present-day Minneapolis) and for another year near the headwaters of Wisconsin's Black River. Much of the region through which they passed had fertile soil and an abundance of wild animals, the latter drawn to the resource-rich ecological boundary separating the Illinois-Wisconsin prairie from the northern Lakes forests. Approximately twenty thousand Indians from a half-dozen nations dwelt together in the Wisconsin country in the mid-seventeenth century: the Ho-Chunks, known to their adversaries as the Winnebagos; the Mascoutens, or Fire People; the Mesquakies or Red Earth People, known to the French as the Fox Indians; and the Menominees, or "Folles Avoines." The Menominees' French name referred to wild rice, an abundant aquatic grain that many Native American women harvested in the northern Lakes country. Throughout the region, women produced and provided most of the food Indians consumed: wild rice, maple sugar, strawberries and other wild fruits, and crops like maize and pumpkins. Native American women also collectively owned the local resource sites that sustained their kinfolk: rice lakes, maple groves, berry patches, and fields. Indian men in the region worked as hunters and fishermen, and, as the local Indian nations were patrilineal, they passed their familial and clan identities to their children.[18]

In the Wisconsin country, Indians from different nations often lived together in the same settlements. It was not always a land of peace, however. In the early seventeenth century, the Illinois, Odawas, and Mesquakies fought with the Ho-Chunks, whom warfare, smallpox, and other disasters (like the sinking of one of their canoe fleets on the eve of a military campaign) dramatically weakened. In 1655, an Odawa and Huron refugee community near Green Bay repelled an Iroquois raiding party, whose warriors the Illiniwek and Ojibwas subsequently captured or killed. And in the 1660s, after traders Pierre Radisson and Medard des Groseilliers introduced them to the European fur trade, the Dakota Sioux expanded into the lands bordering Lake Superior. Numbering around thirty-eight thousand, the Sioux dwelt for part of the year in fixed settlements in the upper Mississippi valley but spent most of the year in mobile camps hunting deer, elk, and beaver. The prospect of trading with the French became an alluring one for the Dakotas, not only because French traders offered metal wares and firearms (which the Sioux initially called "sacred iron"), but because they offered potential marriage partners for single women in a society with strong incest taboos.[19]

In the process of extending their hunting and trading eastward, the Dakotas came into conflict with the Wyandots, who in 1662 had moved to Chequamegon (or Shagwaamikong) Bay, off Lake Superior in northern Wisconsin. The Chequamegon Bay settlement had been founded the preceding year by the Wyandots' Odawa allies, who wanted access to the beaver-hunting grounds in northern Wisconsin and refuge from the Iroquois. Instead they and the Wyandots found themselves in a new war with the Dakotas, an on-again, off-again fight for captives and hunting territories that lasted a decade. In 1671, the Wyandots retreated to Michilimackinac, where they would remain for three decades, while the Sioux continued to hunt and fish in the upper Great Lakes for half a century.[20]

The Wyandots' French allies had by now begun to establish their own tentative presence in the upper Great Lakes region. As early as 1634, the explorer Jean Nicolet had landed by Green Bay and met with the Ho-Chunks, whom he impressed with an embroidered mandarin robe he had brought in case he discovered a passage to China. French traders were slow to follow, as the Iroquois-Huron war had disrupted the fur trade and as the Odawas and Ojibwas were willing to bring furs to the new town of Montreal. Eventually, some traders began traveling to the upper Lakes, and Jesuit missionaries followed them into the *pays d'en haut,* establishing missions at Point Saint Esprit in 1665 and at Sault Sainte Marie in 1668. They began another mission at Green Bay, where several Indian nations had settled to defend themselves against the Iroquois, in 1669.[21]

One of these missions, Point Saint Esprit by Chequamegon Bay, the Jesuits established to preach to the Odawas and to the Huron/ Wyandots, but they also received Indian visitors from further south, including trading parties from the Illinois confederacy. Some of these Illini travelers expressed interest in receiving Jesuit missionaries in their homeland, and in 1673 a priest from Saint Esprit, Jacques Marquette, accompanied other French explorers through the Fox-Wisconsin River portage and down the Mississippi River to the Illinois country. He and subsequent French explorers wrote detailed accounts of how the people of the powerful Illini confederacy lived in the seventeenth century.[22]

The Illinois or Illiniwek ("The People") resided between the Illinois, Ohio, and Mississippi Rivers, with outliers in present-day Indiana and Arkansas. Their contact-era homeland occupied the ecological

borderland between the tallgrass prairies and the forested region south
of the Great Lakes. The rich farmland and ample fish and game of their
domain—the latter including bison, which lived on the Illinois prairie
in herds of four hundred or more—sustained an Illinois population of
more than ten thousand. Like the pre-Columbian cultures of the Ohio
valley, the Illinois lived in dispersed towns but gathered periodically
in their "Grand Village" (really a small city) to attend feasts, lacrosse
games, and religious ceremonies. Their religious pantheon had at its
apex the sun, which Illinois men saluted at the start of their dances
and invoked in diplomatic proceedings. Below this supreme deity lived
a multitude of manitous, spiritual beings associated with totemic animals and powerful humans. The Illinois initially identified the Jesuits
and their secular companions as manitous because of their cultivated
aura of other-worldliness and the powerful goods that they sold. One
did not have to be European to be a manitou: Illinois berdache, men
who dressed as women and assumed cross-gender identities, were also
regarded by their kinsmen as manitous—"spirits or persons of consequence," as Marquette put it.[23]

The Illinois people displayed great friendliness toward Frenchmen
but had also devised for themselves a fearsome military reputation.
The confederacy's warriors fought routinely with the Indian nations
residing to their west, north, and south, using firearms obtained from
French trading partners. The principal aim of Illinois warfare, as with
many other Native North Americans, was to acquire human captives.
Some of these the Illiniwek tortured to death, while many others they
turned into slaves, whom they referred to as "dogs." The Illiniwek used
their slaves as laborers, working in the fields under women's supervi-
sion or hewing wood and drawing water for their masters. Some elite
men exploited slave women's reproductive labor, coercing them into
sexual relationships as their second or third wives—in the Illinois language, "other wives," a term of contempt. The threat of violence hung
over all slaves, but the Illiniwek periodically returned captives to their
kinfolk to restore peace. As often, they traded slaves to other nations,
including the French, to solidify alliances in advance of future wars.[24]

Even one of the confederacy's ostensible rites of peace, the calumet
ceremony, had an underlying military purpose. The calumet was a long,

stone-and-wood tobacco pipe that the western Lakes Indians had adopted from the Plains Indians, with the first examples probably entering the region via Wisconsin around 1350 CE. The Illinois and their neighbors decorated calumets with feathers and ceremonially presented them to the sun, thereby consecrating the pipes and infusing them with celestial power. They employed the calumet like a baton in a balletic dance, which they performed to honor and ceremonially adopt esteemed visitors. However, they also used the calumet dance to seal alliances and to show off their warriors' prowess. Before the calumet dance the Illinois displayed their warriors' weapons, and during the ceremony warriors performed war dances and recited their martial exploits. The calumet served as a military instrument as much as the war club or gun.[25]

If the Illinois seemed militaristic, it was probably because they believed it best, while living on a flat floodplain accessible to potential enemies, to cultivate a strong military reputation. This did not prove helpful, however, when the Five Nations of Iroquois struck into Illinois country in the 1680s. During the previous two decades the Iroquois had been preoccupied with fighting the French and the Susquehannock Indians, but in 1666 French troops had coerced the Five Nations into signing a peace treaty, and in 1676 the Iroquois absorbed the Susquehannocks, who had survived a bitter war with English colonists. Soon thereafter the Iroquois were ready to resume their western campaigns for hunting territory and captives.[26]

In two devastating attacks in 1680 and 1681, Iroquois war parties killed or captured between 1,700 and 2,700 Illiniwek and Illini slaves, or 17 to 27 percent of the confederacy's population. By themselves, or even with the help of one or two Native allies, the Illinois could not punish or deter the Iroquois invaders. To do so, Illinois captains would need a large supply of firearms and a military ally capable of assembling a regional Indian alliance against the Five Nations. That ally would turn out to be France, which was about to convert its thin commercial and ecclesiastical presence in the Great Lakes into a more formidable imperial establishment.[27]

The transformation came too late to help some of the region's Indian peoples, in particular the precursors of the nation later known as the Shawnees. These Algonquian-speaking people were known in the

seventeenth century as the Monytons and Ouabashe, and they probably, along with the Miamis of present-day Indiana, descended from the
Fort Ancient culture. Most resided in farming settlements in present-
day Ohio, Kentucky, and West Virginia, though early seventeenth-century
European maps identify "Shawnees" living on the Susquehanna and
Delaware Rivers. Certainly the Monytons and Ouabashe had trading
connections with the Indians of present-day Pennsylvania, who sold
their furs to Dutch and English traders and supplied them with beads,
knives, and other European wares. The subdual of the Susquehannocks,
however, cut this east-west trading connection, and in 1669 Iroquois war
parties began raiding Monyton and Ouabashe towns for captives. By
the mid-1680s, the two nations had lost several hundred people to the
raiders, as well as others to epidemic disease. Seeking refuge and new
trade links with Europeans, the proto-Shawnees dispersed, many of
them moving south to present-day Tennessee, Alabama, and Georgia.
A few moved to the English colonies of Maryland and Pennsylvania,
whence they began recolonizing the Ohio country in the late 1720s. By
then the entire social and political landscape south of the Great Lakes
had changed once more—perhaps as much as it had changed during the
half century before the Shawnees' initial departure.[28]

✦ ✦ ✦

The people of the Lakes country displayed considerable diversity when
Europeans first encountered them shortly after 1600. Numbering about
125,000 or 150,000 people, the Lakes Indians grouped themselves into
more than a dozen nations and confederacies and spoke languages belonging to three distinct linguistic families. Like most human beings,
however, they did not live in isolation; the human landscape of the
Great Lakes region was not a mosaic of distinct tribes but a network
of relationships, sustained by trade, warfare, and intermarriage. Since
people who interact with one another tend, over time, to share cultural traits with one another, it is unsurprising that the region's Native
Americans had many features in common. With the exception of the
Ojibwas, all of the Lakes Indians were farmers, relying on squash, corn,
and beans for a large portion of their calories. Some, like the Hurons
and Illiniwek, had agricultural surpluses that contemporary European

MAP 1. Native Americans in the Great Lakes region to 1700 CE. *Map by Brian Edward Balsley, GISP*

peasants would have envied. All were traders to one degree or another, and their networks extended for hundreds of miles; the Hurons' and Ojibwas' into northwestern Canada, the Illiniweks' to Lake Superior and the Missouri valley, the Monytons' to the Dutch and English colonies on the Atlantic seaboard. And all had ceremonies and institutions, like redistributive feasts, that allowed them to maintain harmony within their communities, while some had developed rituals, like the calumet ceremony, that helped them forge alliances with other nations.[29]

While the Great Lakes Indians were used to adopting outsiders' culture and had developed mechanisms for promoting social harmony, the stresses and changes that Europeans brought to America proved too profoundly unsettling to manage, at least in the short term. The French came to the Upper Country in the seventeenth century neither to make war on the Indians nor to found permanent settlements, but they brought disruption and death all the same. French goods intensified rivalries among the region's Indian peoples, as they struggled for access to furs and French trade goods. New diseases weakened some Indian nations, such as the Hurons, Ho-Chunks, and Monytons, and drove others into destructive "mourning wars" for captives. By the 1680s the human landscape of the Lakes region had changed considerably, with the eastern districts (Huronia and the upper Ohio valley) depopulated, the powerful Illinois confederacy besieged and damaged, and northern Michigan and Wisconsin full of refugees. In the eastern Lakes country, the land itself experienced "rewilding," as Indians' timber-clearing burns ceased and oak and maple spread into abandoned fields and towns. (Drawing more carbon dioxide from the atmosphere, these new trees contributed to the fall in global temperatures that characterized the century.) In the upper Lakes, the newcomers' crowded settlements placed pressure on their localities' thin-stretched food supply.[30]

Meanwhile, as their European homeland entered a long period of imperial rivalry with Britain, French officials hoped to treat the much-altered Lakes region as a tabula rasa on which they could inscribe a new pattern of alliances that would sustain a French claim of territorial sovereignty. They found that the region's Native peoples were ready to form such partnerships, modeled on the alliances they had earlier made with one another. What the French would learn in the eighteenth century, however, is that whatever losses the Lakes Indians suffered in the 1600s, and however much they had come to rely on French goods and whatever offers of fealty they tendered, Native peoples still held the balance of power in the Upper Country. If the French wanted to claim the region as part of their empire—that is, if they wanted to exclude other Europeans from the Great Lakes—they needed first to learn how to weave themselves into the social fabric of what remained an Indian country.

3

France's Uneasy Imperium

DURING THE SECOND HALF OF THE SEVENTEENTH CENTURY, THE first Europeans to encounter the Great Lakes Indians shifted the emphasis of their colonial project from commerce to empire. The new goal of French officials in Canada was to hold territory, with the aid of Native American allies, and use it as a barrier against English expansion. A secondary goal, projected into the long term, was to persuade those allies to become French subjects, less through force than through voluntary religious conversion and intermarriage with French colonists. The new empire had little place in it for independent Indian nations, and French flags, forts, and soldiers demonstrated both France's imperial goals and its willingness to pursue them with violence. At various times between 1680 and 1750, the Iroquois, Mesquakies, and Chickasaws felt the sharp end of French imperial policy. Yet many, if not most, of the Native peoples of the Lakes country would later recall the era of French dominion as something of a golden age.

When they waxed nostalgic for the era of French rule, the Lakes Indians observed that the French, unlike their British and American successors, never coveted their land nor destroyed their settlements. The nineteenth-century US historian Francis Parkman attributed this to differences between English and French views of Indians: where the English "scorned and neglected" the Indians, the French "embraced and cherished" them. Parkman's comparison would have puzzled France's Native American adversaries, and the understanding of European motives that it displayed was shallow, but it does oblige one to ask why the two colonial powers had such different relationships with Indians and leads one to find answers in the empires' differing goals. What drove most English colonists to North America was *colonialism,* the desire to subjugate indigenous peoples and seize their land and resources. Furs and converts drew the French into the North American interior, but what kept them there was *imperialism,* the desire to assert sovereignty over the continent and deny other empires the use of its resources.[1]

Imperialism was hardly a peaceful or benevolent motive, but since it resulted from conflict with other European empires, it prevented France from concentrating on the subdual of Native Americans. On the contrary, France depended absolutely on its Indian allies to help protect the remote forts and settlements where the French flag waved and contain the expansion of England's fast-growing colonies. French officials could not afford to alienate the Indians of the Great Lakes region. The French regime in Canada went to some trouble to accommodate its allies' demands and expectations, to provide them with regular gifts and regulated trade, to set aside their own standards of justice in favor of the Lakes Indians' customs, and even, through intermarriage, to tie Frenchmen to Indians' kinship networks.[2]

Accommodation did not always bring peace. Maintaining alliances with some Indian nations could create enmity between the French and other Native American groups. Moreover, France's reliance on Indians, whose motives they did not always understand, did not make French officials feel especially secure. Indeed, with the passing decades they grew increasingly worried about their "subjects'" reliability and were prone to view every sign of disaffection or discontent as evidence of an anti-French conspiracy. In these fears lay the seeds both of French warfare against some of its Indian neighbors and ultimately of another radical change in policy that helped wreck the fragile edifice of French rule.

That edifice lasted for approximately seventy years, however, and the Indians of the Great Lakes region did not find it a terrible place in which to dwell.

◆ ◆ ◆

France's shift to an American military empire arguably began in the 1660s, when Louis XIV royalized and garrisoned New France, and when Quebec's governor used royal troops to invade Iroquoia and coerce the Five Nations into a peace treaty. Initially this change had little impact on New France's policies or the Upper Country; Louis informed his new governors that he still intended Quebec to function as a trading colony and preferred it should remain compact. In the 1680s, though, the Iroquois's devastating raids into Illinois provoked French military intervention in the Great Lakes region and shifted that region's balance of power and alliances.[3]

In 1684, one of the Five Nations' war parties plundered French voyageurs and attacked a trading post, Fort Saint Louis, in Illinois. The Iroquois probably viewed France's shipment of weapons to the Five Nations' western adversaries as a hostile act, and decided to respond in kind. The attack provoked a similar response from the French. New France's governor, Joseph-Antoine de La Barre, had already begun to station troops at the Lakes trading posts, and in retaliation for the 1684 raid he organized a punitive expedition against the Hodenosaunee. Influenza crippled La Barre's army, however, and he essentially capitulated to Iroquois emissaries' demands without firing a shot. Three years later La Barre's successor, the Marquis de Denonville, organized a more successful strike: twenty-one hundred gunmen, including four hundred Indians, landed in Seneca country and destroyed several towns and four hundred thousand bushels of corn. This did not prove a knockout blow, and its main effect was to strengthen a budding alliance between the Five Nations and the English colony of New York.[4]

The outbreak of war between England and France in 1689 placed New France on the defensive. Louis XIV declined to send reinforcements to Canada while he needed them in Europe, and England's American colonists and Indian allies launched a powerful offensive. In the summer of 1689 over fifteen hundred Iroquois warriors raided the French village of Lachine, near Montreal, killing or capturing one hundred residents, while in 1690 a Massachusetts naval expedition under William Phips attacked the French colonial capital of Quebec. When garbled news of the Lachine raid reached the upper Lakes, some of the Native American chiefs there believed the French had lost Montreal and would soon abandon their Indian allies. A peace party emerged among the Odawas, Hurons, and Mascoutens, and the new governor of Canada, Louis de Frontenac, feared that the dissidents would form their own separate alliance with the Iroquois. To forestall this possibility, Frontenac sent emissaries to Michilimackinac to meet with the disaffected nations. The diplomats told the Hurons and Odawas that France remained still powerful and able to punish its adversaries, but the haste with which they had traveled to Michilimackinac (a journey that included fighting their way through an Iroquois ambush) and the boatloads of presents they brought indicated the extent of their masters' anxiety. France could neither defeat the Iroquois nor maintain its regional power without the Lakes Indians' cooperation.[5]

The crisis passed, and the French and their allies resumed their offensive against the Five Nations. War parties from the Anishinaabe, Illini, Miami, and Wyandot nations raided the Senecas and Onondagas, two of the more important Hodenosaunee nations, allegedly taking over four hundred scalps. French troops also undertook two more expeditions against the Iroquois, accompanied by a knowledgeable and formidable ally, the Kahnewakes. This nation originated with the Franco-Iroquois peace treaty of 1666, which allowed French Jesuits to establish a mission in Iroquoia. Several hundred Iroquois men and women, chiefly Mohawks, became Christian converts, and in the 1670s French officials persuaded many of them to move to Kahnewake, a mission settlement adjoining Montreal. The converts, who collectively took the name of their new home, retained many of their old lifeways. They continued to hunt, raise corn, and wear their hair in Iroquois fashion, and they found continuities between their new faith and indigenous traditions, substituting the Mass for sacrificial feasts and using mortification of the flesh (flagellation) to evoke the stoicism of a warrior undergoing torture.[6]

If the Kahnewakes' cultural transformation had been partial and carefully managed, not so their political alignment. Christian Mohawks had come to the Saint Lawrence valley in pursuit of French spiritual power, and now they aligned themselves with French military power as well. Kahnewake warriors helped French soldiers attack the Five Nations Mohawks in 1693 and the Oneidas and Onondagas in 1696. The attackers burned towns and killed or captured several hundred English-aligned Iroquois. The Hodenosaunee could not replace these losses through capture and adoption, and by the end of the decade the Five Nations had lost nearly half of their male fighting population. They also lost a substantial part of their territory. The Mississaugas (People of the River's Mouth), an Anishinaabe people closely related to the Ojibwas, drove the Iroquois from the northern shore of Lake Ontario. The region became the Mississaugas' homeland, the place where they dwelled, fished, harvested crops, and held their festivals. The Five Nations now had a dynamic and powerful Native adversary at the threshold of the Longhouse.[7]

The war between France and the Iroquois's principal ally, England, came to an end, and the Iroquois lacked the manpower to continue fighting on their own. They chose now to stop. Following a preliminary ceasefire in 1700, the Five Nations sent delegates to a peace conference in Montreal, the cramped, palisaded French trading town at the rapids of the Saint Lawrence. There two hundred Iroquois joined Governor Louis-Hector de Callière and over one thousand Lakes Indians and spent the summer of 1701 feasting, returning captives, and exchanging wampum belts and words of condolence for the departed. At length the delegates affixed their marks or clan totems to a formal treaty, establishing peace between the signatory nations and admitting all parties into one another's homelands to trade. It might have represented the apex of French power and prestige in North America.[8]

◆ ◆ ◆

Shortly after the conclusion of the Treaty of Montreal, trader and adventurer Antoine Laumet de La Mothe Cadillac received approval to establish a multiracial settlement, Detroit ("the Strait"), on the river connecting Lake Huron with Lake Erie. The new outpost would slow Iroquois commercial expansion into the upper Lakes (though Cadillac did encourage Iroquois hunters to trade there), discourage English expansion into the region, and concentrate the Indians of lower Michigan in one more easily governable place. While Detroit would include a French garrison and Jesuit missionaries, its principal settlers would be Native Americans: Odawas and Huron/Wyandots from Michilimackinac, Potawatomis from the Saint Joseph River in southwestern Michigan. These communities' leaders expressed reluctance to emigrate, but their people began moving in small groups to the Detroit River in 1702, and by 1710 over eighteen hundred Lakes Indians resided there.[9]

In 1706, an incident at Detroit demonstrated both the limits of French power and the need for Frenchmen and Indians to accommodate one another's differences if they wished to continue living in the same settlements. A party of Odawas, believing that the Miamis planned to attack their village, preemptively struck the Miami settlement near Fort Pontchartrain and killed five people; subsequently, Odawa warriors killed two French soldiers and a Jesuit outside of the fort. Normally, the Odawas compensated the families of murder victims by giving them valuable gifts, a ritual known as "covering the dead" or "covering the grave," but Governor Philippe de Vaudreuil told Odawa leaders that "French blood is not paid for by beavers or belts." Instead, the attackers must throw themselves on his mercy. In the fall of 1707, the Odawa captain who led the previous year's attack, Le Pésant, surrendered to the French at Detroit. Cadillac, after briefly imprisoning Le Pésant (registering thereby his submission to French authority), quietly allowed the captain to escape from custody.[10]

This "drama" of submission and reprieve synthesized both French and Lakes Indian judicial cultures. Where the French, like other Europeans, believed in retributive justice, most of the Native peoples of the Great Lakes region favored redemptive justice: the forgiving of criminals and their payment of presents to their victim's family. In a similar episode two decades earlier, French trader Daniel Greysolon Dulhut blended the two legal cultures himself: he executed a Menominee man and an Ojibwa man for killing two Frenchmen, but then he gave compensatory gifts to the Ojibwa man's father and accepted wampum belts from Anishinaabe leaders to "cover the [French] dead." In another case, sixteen years after the killings at Detroit, officials in Illinois freed a Frenchman accused of killing another Frenchman because an Illinois chief intervened on the killer's behalf. Even in conflicts involving only their own countrymen, French officials could not behave exactly as they pleased; in Native country, they had to adhere to Indians' rules, so long as they wished to keep living and doing business there.[11]

This principle applied not only to France's administration of justice in the Upper Country but also to everyday economic and social relationships between colonists and Indians. The Franco-Indian fur trade, in particular, depended on large concessions the French made to Lakes Indian needs, sensibilities, and expectations. These included fixed, *bon marché* ("good deal") prices for furs and European merchandise, and the obligation of French traders and officials to give their Indian clients regular presents of ammunition, clothing, and tobacco. "All the nations of Canada," observed Governor Beauharnois in 1730, "regard the governor-general as their father, who as a result in this capacity . . . should give them something to eat, to dress themselves with and to hunt." Such gifts annually cost the Crown 20,000 livres (about $180,000 in 2016 US dollars) per year by 1716, and they imposed additional costs on traders, insofar as Lakes Indians treated preseason advances as gifts and often declined to repay the loans in full. The French had to understand, or pretend to understand, that for Native Americans the fur trade was not a rationalized exchange of goods but a display of reciprocity and solidarity between French "fathers" and Indian "children."[12]

French traders and officials also had to understand what the term "father" meant to the Lakes Indians. If the newcomers hoped that metaphorical "fatherhood" gave them the ability to command their dutiful Indian progeny, they hoped in vain. In the Great Lakes region, Indian families usually traced descent through the father's line, but many patrilineal nations (like the Potawatomis) adopted matrilocal dwelling customs, and over time authority in matrilocal households tended to shift to the mother's line. Moreover, some Lakes Indians applied the kinship term "father" to a range of male relatives. The

Kickapoos used "father" (*mo'sa*) to describe a person's biological father, paternal uncles, and all the male relatives in his/her mother's family. Native speakers thus might—indeed, commonly did—use "father" not to describe a dread authority figure but to evince a jolly avuncular relative, who dispensed gifts and settled arguments between his children. Fathers did not rule; they indulged.[13]

If the French did not meet these expectations, their Native American trading partners had other options. After the 1701 peace conference gave them access to the trading center of Albany, they could do business with the English. Odawa leaders made this clear to French officials when Governor Callière announced he would let French traders lower the prices they paid for furs: many objected to the announcement, and Le Pésant declared that his people would henceforth trade with the English. (The governor backed down.) The Lakes Indians could also go without European goods for several years, having retained the ability to make hide clothing, stone blades, and other traditional wares. As late as 1718, the former commandant of Detroit noted that French merchandise diffused but slowly through the Lakes Indian population: the Ho-Chunks and Mesquakies near Green Bay and Illiniwek and Miamis south of the Lakes still wore skin clothing (women in Wisconsin wore some cloth garments), and Illinois men still commonly used bows and arrows. When in 1697 the French Crown tried to restrain unruly traders by suspending trading licenses and obliging Indian hunters to come to Montreal, those hunters stayed home, dealt with smugglers, or came no further downstream than Detroit. Fur exports from Canada fell dramatically, and in 1714 New France's governor began efforts to return French traders to the Lakes country.[14]

Following the War of the Spanish Succession (1702–14), with France facing a fur shortage after decades of glut and with British access to the Canadian interior (via Hudson Bay) now guaranteed by treaty, the French government enlarged the support it gave the Lakes fur trade. Governor Vaudreuil and French traders opened new posts at Green Bay, at Kaministiquia on Lake Superior (near modern Thunder Bay, Ontario), and at Ouiatenon (modern Lafayette) on the Wabash River. The Crown authorized new trading licenses and temporarily took over the fur trade at unprofitable posts like Fort Niagara, which France had established earlier in the century to let Lakes Indian hunters bypass Albany. The French government also installed smiths at many of the Lakes trading posts to repair Indian visitors' guns and metal wares. This concession made Indians less dependent on the French but probably more willing to do repeat business for nonmetallic merchandise, particularly clothing. Thanks to this new government support of the fur trade, and traders' increasing use of large "master canoes" that could carry up to two tons, the volume of French trade goods shipped into the Great Lakes doubled from the 1690s to the 1720s.[15]

The enlargement of the French trade also furnished the Lakes Indians with new ways to buy European goods. French voyageurs traveling into the Lakes country faced an arduous journey, requiring them to cover twelve hundred miles or more (the distance from Montreal to Illinois) in fourteen-hour days of paddling, and to carry up to three hundred pounds each over portages. To increase the manpower available to them and minimize their need for heavy supplies, fur traders hired Native Americans as porters and purchased food, warm clothing, and other equipment from Lakes Indian women. The Senecas at Niagara, the Potawatomis and Wyandots at Detroit, the Odawas at Michilimackinac, and the Ho-Chunks and Odawas in Wisconsin became not only suppliers of furs and peltries but part of New France's trading infrastructure.[16]

The relationship between French traders and their Indian partners was never merely an economic one, and in some cases French men and Native American women agreed to make that relationship familial and biological. Some Lakes Indian nations, like the Odawas and Huron-Wyandots, had developed a female-to-male gender imbalance after their wars with the Iroquois. Liaisons with Frenchmen provided single women from these nations with an alternative to remaining single, of which their kinsmen would have disapproved, or becoming junior wives in a polygynous marriage, which might well prove abusive. (Jesuit missionaries were, in any case, discouraging the Anishinaabeg and Hurons from practicing polygamy.) They also provided both Indian women and French traders with some of the benefits of a more formal marriage: sex, companionship, access to resources like European goods or food and clothing, language instruction, and children who would legitimately belong to at least one society (their mother's).[17]

Some traders also gained entry into prominent Indian families through "country" marriages. The Frenchman Sabrevois Descaris married a very prominent Ho-Chunk woman, Hopoekaw (1711–ca. 1770), in the late 1720s, presumably to improve his business relationship with his wife's relatives. Descaris later deserted his spouse and children, but his breaking of his marital alliance did not injure the larger political alliance he and his fellow countryman sought to build. By midcentury, Hopoekaw had become the Ho-Chunks' principal chief, and in this capacity she counseled her countrymen to fight as French allies in the Seven Years' War.[18]

French officials and Jesuit priests generally did not approve of marriages "à la façon du pays" (in the custom of the country), but they did recognize that, as in Hopoekaw's and Descaris's case, Indian-white intermarriage could strengthen alliances and promote cultural conversion. In the 1660s, French finance minister Jean-Baptiste Colbert advised colonists to bring Indians into their own settlements and convert them to French customs and Catholic Christianity. The first royal charter of New France (1663) made intermarriage a means to turn Indians into Frenchmen, extending French identity and privileges to any child of mixed parentage who became a Catholic. Conversion to Catholicism proved appealing to a substantial minority of the Lakes Indians in the seventeenth and eighteenth centuries: several thousand Hurons, a number of Anishinaabeg, and about two thousand Illiniwek adopted the new faith. Part of Catholicism's appeal lay in the techniques of the Jesuit missionaries who introduced the faith to the Lakes Indians. The Jesuits moved into potential converts' communities, learned their languages, and encouraged them to blend indigenous and European religious practices; they were not dismayed but pleased to see Illinois converts giving propitiatory offerings of tobacco to a crucifix or claiming when they died that they would "take possession of paradise in the name of the whole nation."[19]

Catholicism proved especially appealing to single women in societies with a reduced male population, both because the Catholic faith honored celibacy among the female laity and because conversion made it easier for Indian women to contract sacramental marriages with French traders. Catholic women like Marie Rouensa-Oucatewa,

a Kaskaskia chief's daughter, could use the option of celibacy to negotiate with their parents regarding an unwanted marriage. They could
employ the Church and its saints, like Margaret and Bridget (both pa-
tronesses of married women), as sources of personal spiritual power.
Missionaries sometimes encouraged fur traders to marry Catholic Indians in the expectation that convert wives would make their unruly
husbands better Catholics. This influence sometimes extended beyond
the home; among the Illiniwek, female converts worked as lay teachers (as Rouensa did) and church bell ringers. French traders who married Catholic Indian converts, meanwhile, might find those marriages
harder to dissolve than a "country" partnership, but they became more
thoroughly part of their wives' kinship networks and usually also
gained an introduction to their spouses' new religious "kinsmen"—
their Catholic godparents.[20]

Intermarriage became particularly common in southwestern Illinois, near the confluence of the Mississippi and Missouri Rivers, where
Frenchmen and Illiniwek had established two bicultural villages, Cahokia and Kaskaskia, in the early eighteenth century. During the first
few decades of the 1700s, about one-fifth of the sacramental marriages
in the province were between French men and Indian, usually Illini,
women. The inhabitants of these settlements created what on the surface resembled European farming villages, complete with churches,
mills, herds of livestock, and wheat fields. In many respects, however,
their inhabitants' lives resembled those of Lakes Indians: the white male
settlers were usually fur traders and militiamen (warriors, of a sort),
while their Illini wives worked in the fields and tended the livestock.
Some Lakes Indian women became well-to-do through their marital
alliances. Marie Rouensa left behind a large material estate, including several houses and barns and several dozen head of livestock. Her
near-contemporary, Marie Réaume, acquired a different but equally
important "estate": a social network that tied her, through her godpar-
enting of Indian converts and the marriage of her daughters to French
traders, to prominent families in Michilimackinac and Saint Joseph.[21]

Illinois's bicultural and accommodative character began to change
in 1717, when the French government annexed the territory to Louisiana and commandant Pierre de Boisbriant began issuing land grants to

French settlers. By the 1750s there were six French towns in the region, with 750 free inhabitants and 600 slaves, most of them African. The region was by then annually producing one million pounds of flour, which its farmers sold to the French garrisons and settlements in lower Louisiana. The French settlements in Illinois still retained some Native American features: several dozen of their free inhabitants were Catholic Indians or their biracial children, about 25 percent of the villages' slave population was Native American, and the French male *habitants* still avoided field work, preferring to leave this to their bondsmen. However, segregation and conflict were becoming more the order of the day in the province. Local officials had ordered many of Kaskaskia's original Indian inhabitants to leave the town, and by the 1730s both French settlers and their Indian neighbors were squabbling over straying cattle and French encroachment on Illini lands. By the 1740s interracial marriages had become vanishingly rare in the province.[22]

As Illinois's experiences show, while the French and the Lakes Indians generally sought mutual accommodation, they did not always succeed. Rivalry and conflict periodically disrupted peaceful human relations in the region. The bloodiest disruption, the "Fox Wars," lasted two decades and pitted the Mesquakies (Foxes) and their allies against the Anishinaabeg, Huron-Wyandots, and Illiniwek. Both of the Fox Wars grew out of internecine rivalry between these adversaries, and the French tried to stay out of both conflicts. In each case, however, France's Indian allies compelled the Europeans to fight.

The Mesquakies had intermittently fought their Lakes Indian rivals for several decades, and a brief period of peace, during which the rival nations united to fight the Iroquois, had ended with the 1701 Montreal treaty. French and Mesquakie relations had become strained at about the same time, when some of the Foxes blocked the Wisconsin-Fox River portage in order to deprive their Dakota rivals of trade. In 1710, Sieur de Cadillac invited the Mesquakies and their Mascouten allies to Michigan, hoping thereby to clear the portage and build up Detroit's trading population. About one thousand people accepted his invitation, but war captain Pemoussa's band of Mesquakies alarmed the French by settling directly adjacent to Detroit. Meanwhile, the Mascouten migrants became embroiled in a war with the Odawas and, in

1712, lost over two hundred people to an Odawa attack. The surviving Mascoutens took refuge with their Mesquakie allies at Detroit. The increasingly agitated French commandant ordered both nations to leave their settlement and called on his own Native allies for reinforcements. In May 1712 a large Anishinaabe, Huron, and Illinois war party attacked and dispersed the Fox settlement, then pursued the fleeing Mesquakies and killed or enslaved more than one thousand of them.[23]

Such massively disproportionate violence is difficult to explain, but most likely France's allies wanted to make a show of force that would impress and intimidate the French. The attack had quite a different effect on Pemoussa's Mesquakie kinsmen, who in retaliation raided Anishinaabe and other Indian towns around Lake Michigan. Eventually, Governor Vaudreuil had to launch a punitive expedition, which in 1716 attacked the principal town of the Wisconsin Mesquakies, forcing the defenders to capitulate. Casualties proved so light, however, that at least one historian suspects the French attack was a "sham," intended less to punish the Foxes than to pacify them and reopen the faltering fur trade. Certainly the peace terms that the French imposed on the Mesquakies included the payment of furs and Indian slaves to repay the costs of the war, and the expedition's commander boasted that his efforts yielded "an extraordinary abundance of rich and valuable peltries."[24]

Peace between the French and Mesquakies lasted for a decade, but the Foxes resumed fighting their Native rivals soon after 1716. French slave traders played a role in reigniting the conflict, encouraging the Mesquakies' enemies to raid Fox settlements for captives. In retaliation, the Mesquakies destroyed two Illini towns, driving the remaining Illiniwek southward, and made war on the Ojibwas. Fox warriors tortured and executed their own captives: a French priest visiting the Mesquakie homeland observed the racked and burned bodies of Fox victims outside their towns. French officials, hoping to preserve the slowly reviving Lakes fur trade, tried to keep their nation out of the internecine war, but the conciliatory Governor Vaudreuil died in 1725 and his successor feared the Mesquakies would endanger the new French settlements in Illinois. Negotiations between that new governor, Charles de Beauharnois, and Fox chiefs broke down when the Illiniwek refused to return Mesquakie slaves. In 1728 Beauharnois initiated the final phase of the

Fox Wars, sending sixteen hundred warriors and French troops to ex-
tirpate the Mesquakies. The governor's adversaries did not lack allies
of their own, however, and from one of these, the Six Nations of Iroquois, the Foxes received warning of the attack. When the expedition
reached Green Bay in the summer of 1728, the attackers discovered that
their quarry had retreated westward. The French consoled themselves
by burning the Mesquakies' abandoned towns and fields.[25]

The allies changed tactics. Smaller Anishinaabe, Ho-Chunk, and
Menominee war bands harried Mesquakie settlements and travelers.
By the summer of 1730, these raiders had killed or enslaved five hundred Fox Indians, and the surviving Mesquakies decided, for their own
safety, to seek refuge with the Six Nations. To reach Iroquoia the Foxes
had to cross the territory of their Illini enemies, and neither Illini nor
French military leaders would give the Foxes free passage. The Illiniwek and their allies assembled thirteen hundred warriors and colonial
militia to intercept the Mesquakies. After a brief siege of the Foxes'
camp on the Sangamon River, and a failed parley, the attackers killed
about six hundred Mesquakies and enslaved most of the survivors.
Only a few hundred Foxes survived to take refuge over the Mississippi
River. In less than twenty years the Fox Indians lost over 80 percent of
their population.[26]

In their duration and ferocity, the Fox Wars evoked the Iroquois
wars of the previous century. In both of these conflicts, the intense
desire for captives turned ordinary internecine fighting into wars of
annihilation. While the Iroquois primarily wanted captives to replace
their own losses, however, the Mesquakies' adversaries intended to
sell most of their prisoners as slaves. New France became the primary
destination for these bondsmen, and hard labor and degradation their
lot. Most of the eighteen hundred Indians whom French Canadians enslaved became construction and field workers in French towns or found
themselves forced into concubinage in an *habitant*'s bed. If the Fox
Wars proved anything, it was the diversity of French motives in North
America: French traders and officials might want peaceful relations
with the Lakes Indians, but French settlers wanted land and laborers,
and their desires made peaceful coexistence difficult if not impossible.
The wars also showed that the desire for vengeance, prestige, captives,

or a combination thereof could push virtually any group of people, Native American or European, into a war of annihilation. It could even, as in the case of the Iroquois wars, push them into a war hundreds of miles from their homeland. Prosecuting such a war to a successful conclusion, however, was another thing, as the French learned during their other major conflict with Native Americans in the continental interior: the Chickasaw War.[27]

Although the Chickasaws resided in present-day Mississippi, their hunting ranges extended north to the Ohio River, and since the late seventeenth century they had been fighting a desultory war with the Illiniwek, whose towns they raided for plunder and slaves. (The Illiniwek periodically returned the favor.) By 1730, however, Chickasaw leaders had become alarmed by French Louisiana's campaign against the neighboring Natchez Indians, and they sent emissaries to Illinois to organize a Native American defensive alliance against France. French officials instead arrested the three diplomats and sent them to New Orleans, where the governor burned them alive. Subsequently the Chickasaws gave asylum to Natchez refugees and began raiding French shipping in the Mississippi River. Governor Jean-Baptiste Le Moyne de Bienville of Louisiana decided that he could not preserve his government's credibility with its Indian allies—protect "the honor of the French name"—unless he extirpated the Chickasaws, and thus at great expense he organized two military expeditions against the Chickasaws' towns.[28]

Bienville's two expeditions drew on both Louisiana and the Great Lakes region for manpower. The first army, dispatched in 1736, included Illini and Miami warriors, who participated in a failed assault on a fortified Chickasaw town; the Illiniwek fled the field after their French commander was wounded, and Bienville's army took over sixty casualties. Bienville spent three years organizing another army, but his second expedition essentially collapsed in the field, depleted by desertion and illness. The governor's mutinous officers forced him to sign a truce with the Chickasaws before his soldiers ever reached Chickasaw country. The truce itself was short-lived; in the early 1740s, Chickasaw warriors raided French shipping on the lower Ohio River, and their nation's war with France lasted nearly two more decades. The Franco-Indian expeditions of 1736 and 1739 had proven so expensive, however, that Bienville decided to rely henceforth on his southern Indian allies, particularly the Choctaws, to harry and raid the Chickasaws.[29]

◆ ◆ ◆

The "Great Peace" of 1701, which marked the end of the Iroquois wars in the Lakes country, did not inaugurate a peaceful epoch in that region's history. For three decades Lakes Indian warriors and French officers and paymasters preoccupied themselves with two protracted, expensive interethnic wars. Both of these conflicts, and to some extent the final phase of the Iroquois war, were consequences of the French alliance with the Lakes Indians. New France wanted to hold onto its thinly dispersed empire in the *pays d'en haut* and their Mississippi River communication line with Louisiana. They needed their Indian "children's" good offices, but they particularly needed their military services, without which they could neither intimidate France's North American adversaries nor protect their own frail outposts.

The Lakes Indians were not mercenaries, however. They entered into their alliance expecting the French not only to supply them with goods and blacksmiths but also to marry into their families, adhere to their customs, and respect their autonomy. "You who are great chiefs," an Illini chief told French officials during a 1725 visit to France, "should leave us masters of the country where we have placed our fire." Most of all, they expected the French to fight for them. The Anishinaabeg and Illiniwek used this mutual obligation to push the French into a war with the Fox Indians; when it appeared New France might make peace, these Indian nations used slave raiding to reignite the conflict. West of the Lakes country, one might note, the Cree and Assiniboine sold Sioux slaves to French traders in order to sow discord between the French and the Sioux, checking New France's commercial expansion. The Franco-Indian alliance was not one that the French controlled, nor was it based solely on peaceful commerce.[30]

While some of the Lakes Indians tried to prevent the French from allying with their own Native adversaries, so too did French officials worry about their Indian allies uniting against them. New France needed strong Indian defenders, but not too strong. Fear of an Iroquois alliance with the Odawas and Wyandots had produced a risky and expensive anti-Iroquois diplomatic mission in 1690 and probably helped motivate Governor Frontenac's offensives against Iroquoia later that decade. Fear of a Chickasaw alliance with the Illinois and other southern Lakes nations helped ignite and sustain the Chickasaw war of the 1730s and '40s. The French might periodically fret about inter-Indian conflict, but they preferred to let such fighting occur, and even to participate in it themselves, to keep their allies separated and weak. The Franco-Indian alliance wasn't merely a violent one: it also generated mutual suspicion. This would only grow as French officials contemplated both the fragility of their North American dominion and their growing inability to separate their Indian "children" from the greatest threat to their empire: the rapidly expanding colonies of Great Britain.

4

The Hazards of War

IMPERIALISM USUALLY FEEDS OFF EMPIRE BUILDERS' FEARS: FEAR
that their own empire is weak; fear that an end to expansion will bring
economic collapse; fear that if one's own empire doesn't seize a prized
territory, some rival surely will. This last fear weighed heavily on the early
modern imperial mind, and it drove the French to build their tenuous and
economically unproductive North American empire. Tens of thousands
of Indians supported that empire, partly with furs and food and slaves,
partly by their profession of kinship with the French and their monarch,
and partly with their military labor, their willingness to fight France's adversaries. Fear of British competition for those Native allies drove officers to build forts hundreds of miles from the nearest French settlement,
and to mount showy and expensive military campaigns from New York
to Mississippi. Fear eventually drove the French to initiate the war that
brought down their extensive and expensive North American empire.[1]

French officials particularly feared the potential consequences of Native Americans' autonomy. The Indians in their empire were not subjects

but allies, independent nations who manipulated the French to their own ends, and who might at some future date "defect" to the British. In point of fact, only a small minority of Lakes Indians sought to break with the French by the mid-eighteenth century. While many traded with the British colonists, they also continued to buy goods from and pledge their loyalty to their French fathers, and during the Seven Years' War (1754–1760), most demonstrated that they preferred the French as allies. Lakes Indian warriors raided Britain's settlements, besieged its forts, and helped the French oppose its armies. Their aid, ultimately, did not suffice to save the French empire, for Britain had resources that neither Louis XV nor his Indian supporters could match: a huge navy, ample money and credit, and an American colonial population fifteen times larger than French America's. When the war ended, however, the Lakes Indians would demonstrate quite clearly that they retained their independence and power, and that Britons could not safely belittle or ignore Native peoples.[2]

✦ ✦ ✦

The European kingdom that would become France's principal colonial rival, England, paid little attention to the North American interior in the seventeenth century. Like its French neighbor, England—after 1707, part of the Kingdom of Great Britain—had been in past centuries a province (a marginal province) of the Roman Empire, then a cluster of tribal kingdoms unified in the eleventh century CE by the Danes and Normans. It remained an unstable realm for another seven hundred years, experiencing a major rebellion or civil war once or twice each century. The seventeenth century brought to England a bloody civil war and a royal coup d'état, which (not surprisingly) distracted its royal government from goings-on in the new overseas settlements. The English colonies on the Atlantic seaboard functioned as chartered companies or family properties with substantial local autonomy; as long as they sent valuable exports back to England and served as dumping grounds for vagrants, criminals, religious malcontents, and unplaced younger sons of the aristocracy, the Crown usually left them alone. Despite this neglect, and thanks to "push" factors like a stagnant English economy that drove hundreds of thousands of people across the North Atlantic, the English American colonies' settler population steadily grew. By 1700 it reached 250,000 colonists, sixteen times as many whites as one could find in New France, and their numbers would quadruple during the next half-century.[3]

Though the English colonists had little interest in the country west of the Appalachians, their influence already extended there. The Dutch colony of New Netherland and its successor colony of New York sold the Iroquois the weapons they used to disperse the Hurons, fight the Anishinaabeg, and harry the Illiniwek. New York later became an alternative trading center, if a somewhat remote one, for Lakes Indians dissatisfied with French goods or prices; hunters could canoe to Lake Erie or Lake Ontario and traverse Iroquoia, stopping along the way to pay respect and gifts to the Five Nations. Some French traders came to Albany and bought English textiles for resale to their own Indian customers. Meanwhile, the colony of South Carolina became the center of the English Indian slave trade, which ensnared thirty thousand to forty thousand people by 1715. While this trade mainly occurred in the southeast, it extended into the southern Lakes country: one of Carolina's principal slave-trading partners, the Chickasaws, sent war parties into Illinois in search of captives, and French settlers sold Illini and Kickapoo slaves to Carolina traders.[4]

Albany stood distant from the Lakes Indians' settlements, and Carolina's Indian slave trade collapsed after the Yamasee War of 1715–16. Shortly thereafter, though, two other British colonies began to pose a more serious challenge to French authority. Both played a part in igniting the conflict that ultimately destroyed the French empire in North America. The first was Pennsylvania, established in 1681 as a refuge for Quakers and other religious dissidents, and as a real-estate venture by founder William Penn. Pennsylvania's Quaker-controlled government refused to create a provincial militia, instead cultivating good relations with the colony's Delaware Indian neighbors, trading them weapons and using them to defend the colony's borders. After it became clear that the Pennsylvanians wanted peace and that their government had legally restricted the purchase of Indian lands, Native peoples from other regions began relocating to Pennsylvania's river valleys. The Indian settlers included a faction of the Five Nations Iroquois, known to their detractors as "Mingoes" (here we will refer to them as "Ohio Iroquois"), and some of the Shawnees.[5]

Pennsylvania's white settler population also grew rapidly, rising to 160,000 by 1760. As the colony grew, the Penn family used land cession treaties, some of them fraudulent, to push their Indian neighbors and allies westward. Their main targets were the Delawares, an Algonquian-speaking nation known sometimes by the names of their divisions, the Lenapes and Munsees. Both of these Delaware groups distinguished themselves by their fluid gender boundaries: Lenape and Munsee men and women both dressed alike and both sexes could serve as sachems and religious leaders. The Iroquois derided all of the Delawares as "women," but the targets of their scorn did not take this as an insult; to them, women were spiritually equal to men and often served as intercultural mediators. For the Lenapes and Munsees, "woman" served as a metaphor for diplomat.[6]

The Penn family chose to view the Delawares' predilection for diplomacy and gender egalitarianism as signs of weakness. In 1737, the Penns and their allies drove the nation entirely out of the valley that bore its name. Pennsylvania officials presented Delaware leaders with an old (and fake) deed of cession to tribal land on the Delaware River, with one of the cession's boundaries extending as far as a man could walk "in a day and a half." The Penn family then hired runners to cover fifty-five miles of ground on the days allotted to mark the boundary. When the Delawares protested the so-called Walking Purchase, the Penns brought in the Iroquois, with whom they had been cultivating an alliance for several decades, to bully their smaller Indian neighbors into leaving. At a 1742 conference, Onondaga chief Canasatego declared that "we [the Iroquois] conquered you; we made women of you; you know you are women, and can no more sell land than women," and ordered the Delawares to "remove immediately." Canasatego's tone and threats made it clear that he used "women" as a label for subjugation, and the Iroquois continued to use gendered language to shame and belittle the Delawares into the 1750s. For its victims, the Walking Purchase became a bitter experience and a cautionary tale to Lakes Indians with whom they subsequently resided. Pierre-Joseph Céloron reminded the Allegheny Delawares of their mistreatment when he visited them in 1749, and four decades later a Wyandot chief recounted the colonists' perfidy to an American governor.[7]

The Delawares driven from their homes after the Walking Purchase sought a new homeland in the upper Ohio valley, joining there Shawnees and Ohio Iroquois who had begun moving to the region in the 1720s. The migrants established farming settlements centered on communal longhouses, where they held religious ceremonies like the Delawares' annual *gamwing* rite—twelve days of singing, vision dances, and thanksgiving to the Creator. They extended their winter hunting trips to the southern shore of Lake Erie, a region notable for its "abundance of game," including bison. There men shot beaver, deer, waterfowl, and other animals, which provided their families with meat and with peltry exchangeable for European goods.[8]

The Indian communities in western Pennsylvania established ties to those living on the southern Great Lakes. The Odawas, Potawatomis, and Wyandots residing near Detroit and Sandusky regularly traded with the Delawares, whom the Odawas called Wapanachki (Easterners), and with the Shawnees. Men and women from all of these nations used the southern shorelands of Lake Erie as a common range. Hunting and fishing in shared country, the Anishinaabeg and Wyandots shared campfires and stories with the newcomers and developed a common identity with them. They saw themselves not as French or British allies, or as members of wholly distinct nations, but as an autonomous regional alliance—as Ohio Indians. Their confederacy eventually became one of the nuclei of larger pan-Indian movements in the region.[9]

Reinforcing the Ohio Indians' autonomy was their willingness to trade and negotiate with both of the European empires that claimed the region. Fur traders from British Pennsylvania followed the Ohio valley migrants west to their new homeland. By the early 1740s, one of the most prominent, George Croghan, had pushed into modern Ohio, building a trading post for the Delawares and Ohio Iroquois on the Cuyahoga River. Concurrently, the Pennsylvania provincial government developed diplomatic ties with the southern Lakes Indians. In 1747–48, Pennsylvania commissioners invited Ohio Iroquois and Miami deputies to Philadelphia and Lancaster and there signed with them treaties designed to detach them from the French alliance. More ominously, they also interviewed the Miamis on the principal river routes and

French forts in their homeland, demonstrating Pennsylvanians' interest in expanding even further westward.[10]

France had always maintained a tenuous sovereignty over the Lakes Indians. French officials needed their Native American allies more than the Indians needed them, and the Lakes Indians saw the French kings and governors not as their rulers but as their fictive "fathers," men who gave gifts and resolved disputes but had no command authority. France also found it difficult to govern the Lakes Indians because none of the Lakes nations comprised a politically consolidated whole. Individual towns had headmen and war parties had captains, but the region's chiefs played ceremonial and diplomatic roles and could govern their kinsmen only through persuasion. Political factions formed easily in the region's Native American communities, and often those factions opposed an exclusive relationship with the French or favored an alliance with Britain.[11]

One such faction emerged within the Miamis, an Indian nation descended from the Fort Ancient culture and loosely affiliated with the Illiniwek. Residing chiefly in the Wabash and Maumee River valleys, to which they had migrated from Illinois in the mid-seventeenth century, the Miamis had in 1718 around eight thousand people, gathered into a half-dozen towns with extensive fields and access to rich beaver and bison-hunting grounds. Their population and productivity as hunters gave the Miamis leverage over their French trading partners, whom they obliged to build convenient trading posts at Fort Miami (present-day Fort Wayne) and Ouiatenon. During King George's War (1744–48), however, the British navy blockaded New France, and French goods became scarce in the Lakes country. So too did the generosity of French traders, whom many Lakes Indians suspected of cheating or exploiting them. By 1747 a faction of Miamis under Memeskia, or La Demoiselle (as the French called him), had begun diplomatic communication with the English, and the following year this group moved their homes to Pickawillany (modern Piqua, Ohio), where George Croghan had constructed a trading post.[12]

Another disaffected group came from the Huron-Wyandots, who had settled near Detroit earlier in the century. Some of the Hurons had come to dislike French traders' goods and attitudes. Others had come

to distrust the neighboring Odawas, whom the Wyandots, as farmers
and Christians, considered a primitive, pagan people. In 1738 a faction of disaffected Wyandots moved to Sandusky Bay, fifty miles from
Detroit. During King George's War their principal chief, Orontony, put
out diplomatic feelers to Pennsylvania, and in 1747 he helped organize
an anti-French "revolt" in the lower Lakes region. Among other incidents, Wyandot warriors slew five traders at Sandusky, while Miamis
plundered another eight French traders at Fort Miami. The following year,
Orontony and his kinsmen burned their settlement and relocated to the
Muskingum River, where they continued to trade with the British.[13]

French officials found the Pennsylvanians' presence in the Ohio
country and the growing disaffection among the southern Lakes Indians deeply troubling, as it threatened to create a salient of British
influence between Canada and Louisiana. Some feared that Britain had
even more ambitious goals, that it would use the Ohio valley as a base
to seize Louisiana, then advance from that province to conquer Spanish
America, thereby giving Great Britain mastery of the hemisphere. Such
fears impelled French officials to an energetic and violent response,
similar to Governor Bienville's response to the Chickasaws' challenge
in the 1730s.[14]

First, the governor of New France in 1749 sent a party of soldiers
under Pierre-Joseph Céloron to descend the Ohio River, post or bury
metal plates proclaiming the renewal of French rule over the region,
and inform the Ohio valley Indians that their lands came under Louis
XV's authority. Céloron visited several communities of Iroquois, Shawnees, Delawares, and Miamis, warned them not to trade with Britain,
and told them that British colonists only wanted their lands. Most of
his hosts responded with politeness and flattery, raising French flags,
greeting the emissaries with "pipes of peace," and assuring Céloron
and the governor of New France of their friendship. However, some
Ohio Indians fled at the French party's approach, and others allegedly
planned to attack Céloron and his companions. Still others argued,
as bluntly as protocol permitted, that French traders could not supply
them and that they needed English goods and blacksmiths to survive.
One Delaware spokesman told Céloron that without British aid, "we
shall . . . be exposed to the danger of dying of hunger and misery on

the Beautiful River. Have pity on us, my father, you cannot at present minister to our wants." When the French emissaries returned to Quebec, their report only confirmed what their superiors already feared.[15]

A more violent assertion of French authority soon followed. In 1752, the biracial trader Charles Langlade received French approval to attack La Demoiselle's base at Pickawillany. Langlade, an Odawa relative by virtue of his Odawa mother, assembled two hundred Anishinaabe warriors and destroyed the Miami settlement. Other French-allied war parties attacked or threatened British traders in the Ohio country, forcing them to withdraw east of the Allegheny Mountains. The following year, Governor Duquesne led twenty-two hundred French soldiers to build a chain of forts from Lake Erie to the Ohio River. The undertaking proved costly in money and lives, but Duquesne and his superiors in the Ministry of Marine (France's colonial bureaucracy) considered the forts essential to block English expansion and control the upper Ohio valley. For their part, the Ohio Indians initially regarded the French incursion as an opportunity rather than a threat. The previous winter had been a lean one, and the Delawares, Ohio Iroquois, and Shawnees were happy to feed the French soldiers and hire out their horses. This set the new pattern for French-Indian relations in the eastern Lakes country: not a sovereign-subject relationship but a marriage of convenience, which Native Americans would abandon once it became inconvenient.[16]

Arguably, the Franco-Indian offensive against British traders and the Indian-assisted French occupation of the upper Ohio valley marked the beginning of the "French and Indian War," the British colonists' name for the Seven Years' War. It took the British government a while to detect a threat to their own interests, but one of the British American colonies saw France's move into the upper Ohio valley as an immediate and intolerable challenge. That colony was Virginia.[17]

Virginia, the oldest and largest of Britain's North American colonies, had by the eighteenth century developed a robust plantation economy, maintained by a rapidly growing African slave population and headed by a cohesive planter elite. Virginia's gentry made their fortunes from tobacco, but by the second quarter of the eighteenth century many wanted to diversify their sources of income, and speculation in frontier land seemed the most respectable alternate investment for gentlemen.

Moreover, Virginia's officials worried about threats to the colony by the French and their Native American allies, or by runaway slaves who might be able to establish refuges on Virginia's western frontier. To prevent such threats, they encouraged Scottish and German immigrants to move to Virginia and settle in its western counties, providing the province with a security buffer of white settlers and giving speculators a chance to enrich themselves through frontier land sales.[18]

By the early 1740s most of the land within the modern boundaries of Virginia had been purchased by speculators or opened to white settlement. However, Virginians' territorial ambitions did not stop at the Blue Ridge Mountains or the Potomac River. The colony claimed a substantial part of North America under its charter, and in 1744 colonial commissioners purchased from the Six Nations of Iroquois all of their territorial claims west of the Appalachian Mountains, including the Ohio valley. (The Iroquois claimed this area by virtue of having "conquered" the Indian inhabitants, a claim more politically useful than accurate.) Five years later the British Privy Council granted three hundred square miles around the forks of the Ohio River to a group of Virginia speculators, the Ohio Company, on the condition they bring white settlers into the region. The company advanced its project slowly, but by 1752 the partners' agents had secured Delawares' and Shawnees' permission to settle in the region and had begun building blockhouses on the path between the Potomac River and the Ohio forks.[19]

When French troops reached the forks of the Ohio in 1754, they expelled a detachment of Virginia troops from the site and began building a log-and-earth fort that they named for Governor Duquesne. Governor Robert Dinwiddie of Virginia had the year before sent a diplomatic party, headed by militia officer George Washington, to order the French out of what Virginia considered its territory. When French commanders politely refused, Dinwiddie sent Washington back, this time accompanied by provincial militia, to compel the "intruders" to leave. What then transpired was midway between a tragedy and a farce: Washington and his men got into a firefight with a party of French soldiers sent to parlay with them, retreated to an indefensible encampment at Fort Necessity, and surrendered to a seven-hundred-man French and Anishinaabe force after another short fight. The following year, both of the kingdoms whose men had stumbled into one another sent reinforcements to North America and prepared for a protracted fight.[20]

Leading Britain's 1755 campaign against the French was Edward Braddock, an experienced but (as it turned out) incompetent general responsible for coordinating a massive attack on New France's defenses, from Nova Scotia to the Ohio. This broad offensive failed, and Braddock's own part of it, an attack on Fort Duquesne, destroyed both him and his army. Leading his troops on an exhausting march from Virginia, Braddock and his advance column of twelve hundred men ran into three hundred French infantry and six hundred Anishinaabe, Delaware, Kahnewake, and Shawnee warriors near Fort Duquesne. The Franco-Indian force quickly recovered from their surprise, took cover, and proceeded to pick off the British officers, including Braddock. By day's end (July 9, 1755), they had killed or wounded two-thirds of the enemy column and routed the survivors.[21]

Braddock's defeat initiated two more grim years for British American settlers, and two profitable years for the French and their Native American allies. The governor of Canada, Pierre de Rigaud de Vaudreuil, began furnishing supplies, militia reinforcements, and advice to Indian war parties willing to attack British settlements. Many warriors proved willing. Military raids would provide some Indian groups, like the Delawares, with payback for past British crimes (like the Walking Purchase), and young men from others, like the Anishinaabeg, with the chance to obtain glory, plunder, and captives. For the French, Native American raids had the beneficial effect of wrecking British backcountry settlements and diverting colonial militia from offensive operations to defensive ones. In Virginia, an observer reported that "our frontiers are daily ravaged by savages, and worse than savages, papists [i.e., French Catholics]," and the provincial government began building a four-hundred-mile line of stockades just west of the Blue Ridge Mountains. Pennsylvania's government, while it did agree to create a militia in 1755, could only adopt a policy similar to Virginia's, building fortifications and watching helplessly while refugees streamed into older settlements. Until 1758, defensive preparations took both of these populous British colonies out of the war.[22]

The Indians' offensive, meanwhile, brought considerable short-term benefits to Lakes and Ohio Indian communities. One was plunder, which supplemented the supplies that war parties were already receiving from the French. From British farmsteads and blockhouses warriors took clothing, hardware, and cattle, as well as horses—thirteen hundred of the latter animals in one season alone—which increased the range and mobility of war parties. More valuable "spoils" of war were the two-thousand-plus captives whom the Lakes Indians took during the mid-1750s. To terrify their enemies, the captors executed and mutilated a few of these captives. The majority, however, were taken by the raiders back to their towns as captive laborers, or for adoption into Native families, or to exchange with the French or British for ransom. Two Ohio Seneca sisters, for example, adopted captive Mary Jemison (whom they renamed Dehgewanus) to replace their deceased brother, while a French priest ransomed Charles Stuart and his wife and obliged them to work off their debt. Some of the captives remained with their adoptive families—Jemison never returned to her old life—but most gladly returned home after their captivity. James Smith, despite adoption into and several years' good treatment by an Ohio Iroquois family, still escaped to the French when he heard they might send him home to Pennsylvania.[23]

Overall, the raiders managed to kill or capture about one percent of Virginia's and Pennsylvania's population and turn thirty thousand civilians into refugees. Over the longer term, however, the offensive of 1755–57 proved counterproductive for the Lakes Indians. The availability of plunder and captives decreased with each farmstead burned or abandoned, and the fear that Native American attacks wrought in white communities turned very quickly into hatred of Indians. British American newspaper editors stoked anti-Indian sentiment by developing a genre that Peter Silver calls "the anti-Indian sublime," one that evoked the violated innocence of white settlers' bodies and families and emphasized the wickedness and savagery of their attackers. Such stories spread quickly throughout British North America, thanks to a vibrant network of colonial newspapers and a literate populace. Legislators contributed to colonists' perception of Indians as subhuman barbarians by offering bounties for scalps, akin to the bounties some colonies paid for killing wolves.[24]

Lakes Indian warriors eventually even alienated some of their French allies, though the alienation proved mutual. French officers commanded some raiding parties early in the war, guiding them in attacks on British colonial forts and blockhouses. In the summer of 1756, one of the French generals in America, Louis-Joseph Montcalm, led a successful attack on British-held Oswego with three thousand French troops and several hundred Indians, including Nipissings from Lake Huron and Menominees from Wisconsin. A year later, in August 1757, Montcalm led an even larger army and war party, comprising six thousand French and two thousand Indians (Miamis, Odawas, and others), in an equally successful attack on Fort William Henry, near Lake Champlain. Indian warriors fought in both battles, and in the 1757 campaign Odawa canoeists severely weakened Fort William Henry's defenders by defeating a large English raiding party on Lake George. French artillery, however, played the primary role in compelling the surrender of the two garrisons. In both battles, Montcalm insisted on following European military protocol, refusing to allot his Indian allies captives or plunder. And in both engagements, Lakes Indian warriors took prizes from their adversaries despite French orders. Most famously (or infamously), after the surrender of Fort William Henry, warriors killed and robbed prisoners in the hospital and attacked a column of French soldiers and British prisoners leaving the fort. Altogether, Montcalm's allies killed sixty-nine people and captured over one hundred in what the British inevitably called the Fort William Henry "massacre."[25]

The outcome of the siege of Fort William Henry increased General Montcalm's determination to win the war in America without Native American assistance, an unlikely prospect given Britain's huge advantages in a conventional European-style war. Had Montcalm and other French generals wanted Indian assistance, however, the aftermath of the siege severely curtailed Native Americans' ability to offer it: some of the thousands of men concentrated at Fort William Henry had been sick with smallpox, and Lakes Indian warriors brought the disease home with them after the battle. It is hard to tell how many people died in the ensuing epidemic, but smallpox reportedly "laid waste" the Odawa towns at Arbre Croche and the Potawatomis on Saint Joseph's River, and it killed at least three hundred Menominee men. For another year or so, the "French and Indian War" would have to remain a strictly European affair.[26]

Unfortunately for the French, the epidemic came just as Britain's military fortunes began to prosper. Britain and France had formally declared war on one another in 1756, and in 1757 Colonial Secretary William Pitt, with George II's blessing, took control of the British war effort. Pitt, in turn, let his homeland's European allies fight a holding action in Europe, while Britain's armed and naval forces conducted a general offensive in North America. Over the next couple of years, Britain sent thirty thousand troops to its American colonies and paid colonial governments to raise another twenty-three thousand volunteers. Meanwhile, the Royal Navy began attacking French ships in the Atlantic, depriving the French of reinforcements and provisions. New France continued to receive communications and Indian trade goods, but it received few soldiers and less food, a serious problem in a colony already suffering wartime shortages.[27]

In 1758, in quick succession, British forces captured the French fortress of Louisbourg, which guarded the approaches to the Saint Lawrence River (July 27), followed by Fort Frontenac, the principal supply depot for the Lakes forts (August 27), and then the site of the war's earliest fighting, Fort Duquesne (November 25). The evacuation of Duquesne came partly in response to the approach of a British army under John Forbes but also from the decision by France's Indian allies in the Ohio valley, especially the Delawares, to drop out of the war. The Delawares' participation in the conflict had depended on their desire for vengeance against Pennsylvania and a steady supply of French goods, and by 1758 they had satisfied the former and lost access to the latter. At this opportune moment, the governors of Pennsylvania and New Jersey convened a treaty council with the Ohio valley Delawares and secured a promise from them to quit the war; they also agreed, on behalf of King George, to reserve the lands west of the Appalachian Mountains for Indians. Reassured by this Treaty of Easton (26 Oct. 1758) and having nothing further to gain from the war, in November 1758 the Delawares refused a request for aid from the commandant of Fort Duquesne. The commander then abandoned the indefensible post.[28]

France's position had become equally untenable. In 1759 British troops, building on their earlier successes, captured the French colonial capital of Quebec. A British naval force also destroyed France's Atlantic squadron off the coast of Brittany, ensuring that New France would receive no more reinforcements. In the summer of 1760, with British and colonial troops converging on him from three directions, Governor Vaudreuil surrendered Montreal to General Jeffery Amherst. Shortly thereafter, French garrison commanders in the Great Lakes region turned over their isolated forts to British officers. Britain now ostensibly controlled three million square miles of North American territory, and her climactic victories had almost all come without direct Indian assistance. Perhaps this helps explain why Amherst decided he could safely govern Britain's "conquests" without accommodating their Indian inhabitants.[29]

Amherst's policy toward the Lakes Indians differed radically from the old French policy. With a curious mixture of thrift, arrogance, and paranoia, the general banned the regular distribution of gifts by garrison commanders to Indian visitors, arguing that the practice would lead Native American men to idleness, and that idle hands would do the devil's work. Oblige the Lakes Indians to hunt for furs and skins, rather than giving them presents, Amherst argued, and they would have less free time to plot mayhem. Similar concerns caused Amherst to restrict the sale of muskets, powder, and ammunition to the Indians, and to ban the sale of alcohol, whose consumption would, he believed, lead only to more idleness.[30]

Amherst's policy seemed calculated to alienate nearly everyone in the Lakes country. Gift giving had been the marrow of the old French alliance, a demonstration of mutual loyalty, reconciliation, and goodwill; as late as 1758, officials had given the Lakes Indians one million livres' worth of presents, consolation for the recent smallpox epidemic and a pledge to renew their alliance. The end of the gift policy suggested Britain had no need of Indians' friendship and considered them a foe. One Ojibwa chief, Minavavana, said as much to a British trader: as long as Britain did not provide the Lakes Indians with gifts to "cover . . . the bodies of the dead," the British necessarily remained at war with them. And alcohol, though it could sicken, befuddle, or enrage those who consumed it, had also been a symbolically important French gift, metaphorically analogous to food ("milk") that a parent gave to children. Finally, Amherst's curtailment of gunpowder sales made it harder for Lakes Indians to hunt for the furs they needed to buy goods Britain would no longer give them.[31]

Had Britain found the Lakes Indians broken and starving in 1760, Amherst's parsimony would have injured them but not incited them to revolt. The region's Indian peoples did not consider themselves broken or conquered. In 1759 they had in fact contributed more warriors to the defense of New France than they had raised in 1757. In 1760 Anishinaabe and Miami warriors told French officials at Montreal that "they would never recognize the King of England as their father," an easy enough pledge to keep so long as the British refused to behave paternally. Jeffrey Amherst and his superiors in London suspected that the Lakes Indians harbored such unfriendly sentiments, but the commander assumed that his curtailment of gifts and ammunition would make it harder for them to act on these sentiments. He was wrong.[32]

✦ ✦ ✦

The French and Indian War, as historians would call the American phase of the global Seven Years' War, brought France's empire in North America to an end. It is ironic that the war grew out of French fears that Britain threatened their alliance with the Lakes Indians, for despite all the damage that the conflict inflicted on New France, the Franco-Indian alliance emerged from the war as strong as ever. France's Native American allies generally saw the war as an opportunity, a chance to obtain presents, plunder, and captives. While smallpox and French arrogance weakened the alliance in 1757–58, French officials patched up their relationship with their king's Indian "children," and thousands of Indian warriors turned out in 1759–60 to pledge their support and join in the last-ditch defense of New France.

The British victors of the war knew little about this revived alliance. Having deployed over fifty thousand troops in North America, and having defeated France's armies and occupied its settlements, generals like Jeffery Amherst assumed that a few thousand "savages" posed no threat, and that they could impose whatever terms on the

Indians they liked. For their part, the Lakes Indians, many of whom had traded with the British before the war, decided to give accommodation a chance, but they considered the peace that followed the fall of Montreal as a truce. The truce was contingent on British officials' and colonists' behaving as brothers and allies, rather than treating their Indian neighbors as enemies. When the British failed to live up to this implicit obligation, several thousand Lakes Indians proved more than willing to return to war. What followed became both the final phase of the French and Indian War and the beginning of a new cultural movement that changed the way the Lakes Indians, and many other Native Americans, perceived themselves.

5

Nativists and Newcomers

UNLIKE THE FRENCH, WHO PEACEFULLY INSINUATED THEMSELVES into the Upper Country decades before they began building an empire there, the British began their imperial reign in the American interior with the behavior of a conqueror. General Jeffery Amherst and his subordinates planted the flag and garrisoned a dozen posts around the Great Lakes, and they told the region's Indians that henceforth Britain would value them only for their labor, not for their allegiance. The friction generated by this abrupt shift from French alliance to British arrogance ignited combustible elements that had built up in Native communities since the 1740s: nativists' stories of an uncorrupted past to which the Master of Life wanted Indians to return, civil and military leaders' nostalgia for the era of French rule, and widespread Native American suspicion of British officials and settlers. The ensuing explosion killed over two thousand whites and Indians and spread destruction from Pennsylvania to Illinois. Historians would call it Pontiac's War (1763–65).[1]

The conflict did not entirely expel British forces from the Great Lakes. It did sufficiently chasten British officials that they began adopting a more enlightened policy toward the Lakes Indians—a program of regulated trade and respectful treatment that bore some similarity to the old French regime. This was, to some extent, the insurgents' goal: turning back the clock to the earlier era of French accommodation. Britain, however, faced a very different political situation in 1765 than did France in 1680. The Seven Years' War had left it with a financially and militarily overstretched empire, and its government found itself unable to govern Britain's own fractious American colonists, let alone police new territories that extended from Canada to Florida. The British government implicitly acknowledged its limits with the royal Proclamation of 1763, a ban on new white settlements and land purchases west of the Appalachians. France, with its much smaller settler population and greater reliance on its Indian allies, had never needed or wanted such a restriction. Britain's American colonies had a large and rapidly growing settler population, totaling over one million people in 1750, and doubling (as Benjamin Franklin observed) every quarter-century. Those settlers eagerly sought land and wealth and despised Native Americans. Once Pontiac's War had ended, they moved into the western Ohio valley (western Pennsylvania) by the thousands, seeking quick profits from illicit trading and hunting or land they could take for their own. British officials lacked the resources to stop them, and within a few years many sought to encourage or benefit from these incursions, establishing companies to profit from Indian lands and taking those lands by fraud or force.[2]

Before the 1760s, effective control of the Great Lakes region still rested with the Native peoples who had lived there for centuries. The French claimed the American interior as part of their empire, but the huge expense of running an empire and their limited settler population meant that their so-called Indian subjects called the shots. Pontiac's War represented, in part, an attempt to turn back the clock to this era of Native American autonomy under a benevolent and pliable European sovereign. The Indian combatants also looked ahead to future threats: the growing dependence of Indians on European goods and the seizure of their lands by Anglophone settlers. Nativists viewed all of these as dangers against which they had to fight. Few people viewing the events that followed Pontiac's War would have gainsaid them.[3]

+ + +

In 1761 the British trader Alexander Henry, meeting with some of his future trading partners at Michilimackinac, heard a startling declaration from the Ojibwa chief Minavavana. British troops had captured Montreal the year before and were now taking France's posts in the Lakes country, but the king of France remained undefeated, or so Minavavana insisted. "He is fallen asleep . . . but his nap is almost at an end," and "I hear him already stirring and inquiring for his children." When the French king awoke, he would surely destroy the English.[4]

Minavavana was mistaken, but this became obvious only in hindsight: in 1761 Britain and France remained at war and French troops still occupied posts in Illinois and the Mississippi valley. More important, the chief's prediction, accurate or not, clearly illustrated the Lakes Indians' allegiance and understanding. The Anishinaabeg and their neighbors, Minavavana reported, remained loyal to their French "father" and at war with the British as long as Britain refused to make a specific and separate peace with them. His people peacefully coexisted with British troops and traders at the moment, but the truce could end at any time.[5]

The armistice lasted for two more years, until British officials imagined that it had become a lasting peace and evidence of Britain's mastery of the Lakes country and its inhabitants. In May 1763, many of the region's Native Americans suddenly and violently disabused the British of this assumption. Miami warriors surprised and overwhelmed the garrisons at Fort Miami that guarded the portage between the Maumee River and the Wabash, and at Ouiatenon on the Tippecanoe River. Wyandots hit Sandusky, at the mouth of the eponymous waterway that flowed from Lake Erie to within a few miles of the Scioto River. Anishinaabeg captured the British post on the Saint Joseph River, which Indians used to cross Michigan's lower peninsula or travel from Lake Michigan to the Wabash. A large Anishinaabe war party under the leadership of Odawa captain Pontiac tried to take the British-held fort at Detroit; failing in the attempt, the warriors besieged the town for six months. In early June, the very post where Minavavana had delivered his warning, Michilimackinac, fell to an Anishinaabe ruse. Warriors playing lacrosse outside the fort "accidentally" hurled their ball into the stockade, then rushed into the fort to retrieve the ball—and the guns that their female relatives had cached there. Further east, Delaware, Shawnee, and Ohio Iroquois warriors besieged Fort Pitt, while Senecas besieged Niagara and destroyed British-held forts at Presque Isle and Le Boeuf along the carrying path from Lake Erie to the Allegheny River. On the borders of Pennsylvania and Virginia, raiders from several nations attacked frontier settlements, killing hundreds of whites.[6]

The attackers' targets adjoined and guarded the principal avenues of communication in the Great Lakes region: the straits through which the lakes flowed into one another, and the portages separating the Lakes watershed from the tributaries of the Ohio and Mississippi. Britain's occupation of forts at these vital points helped persuade officials that they controlled the region, but the rivers and paths that intersected there allowed the Lakes Indians rapidly to mobilize war parties by foot and canoe. By their lightning attacks and widespread military success, the warriors demonstrated, to anyone on the other side clear-headed enough to understand their message, that Native peoples remained the dominant regional power.[7]

British officers and some later historians assumed that the impetus for such a powerful and concerted attack, which involved several thousand warriors and killed twenty-four hundred British soldiers and civilians, must have come from the French, from *habitants* in the Lakes region or officers in Louisiana. Little evidence supported this. One could find French civilians nervously meeting with the insurgents and Indians flying the white flag of the French royal dynasty in their towns. However, French officials apparently did not support the uprising; indeed, the last French garrison commander in Illinois rejected Pontiac's plea for assistance and helped induce him to end the siege of Detroit. There is instead overwhelming evidence that Pontiac's War grew from strictly indigenous sources, with little European input.[8]

Moreover, while British actions ignited the war, they do not explain why so many Lakes Indians were willing to unite and attack across such a large region. To understand the scope of the 1763 insurgency, one must look at the ideas that inspired and united the insurgents, particularly a new ideology that historians have called *nativism* (which one should not confuse with the later American anti-immigrant movement). Nativists believed that all Indians were products of a separate creation, that a single creator god had bestowed their lands on them in perpetuity, and that Europeans and their customs represented spiritual dangers. This belief system became noteworthy for its longevity. The material causes of Pontiac's War did not persist after the end of the conflict: Britain modified, by choice or necessity, the most egregious of its policies. The ideas that inspired Pontiac and his allies, however, lasted for decades after the war ended, and the idea of pan-Indian resistance contributed to another backcountry war less than ten years after Pontiac's associates signed their peace treaties.

✦ ✦ ✦

After the last governor of New France surrendered his colony to British forces, some Indians still wanted to continue fighting on behalf of their French father. Miami and Anishinaabe warriors reaffirmed their support for the French king, and French-allied Senecas circulated war belts among the Wyandots and Delawares, trying to rally their brothers-in-arms for another campaign. However, most Lakes Indian leaders preferred to seek accommodation with the victorious British. They took heart from a promise made by Sir William Johnson, who at a Detroit peace council (1761) promised the Lakes Indians a relationship with Britain similar to its "covenant chain" with the Iroquois. This venerable alliance had grown out of an Anglo-Iroquois military and commercial pact inaugurated in the previous century. Within it, the Six Nations had enjoyed steady trade with British North America and a presumption of authority over other Indian nations. Johnson, who for the previous two decades had lived among the Iroquois as a trader, agent, and consort of two Mohawk women (Elizabeth Brant and Molly Brant), had fashioned himself into a small link in the chain. Now, as Britain's Superintendent of Indian Affairs for the Northern Department, he offered to draw the Lakes Indians into the covenant-chain league as equal members. In affirmation of the new state of coexistence and

mutuality, Native American hunters began doing business with British traders like James Kenny, manager of Pennsylvania's public trading
post at Fort Pitt, while Indian women began selling supplies to the British garrisons in their homelands and entering into liaisons with some
British soldiers.[9]

During this period of fraternization, however, the Lakes Indians
steadily accumulated grievances against British soldiers and colonists.
In 1761–62, British troops built a new fort at Sandusky and occupied
several French posts they had not previously taken, like Michilimackinac. They made no payment for these or any of the other forts Britain
held. Nor did British officers furnish the Lakes Indians with customary
gifts of food and clothing during the hard winter of 1761–62. Hunger
and exposure increased the death toll from an outbreak of "ague," most
likely influenza, that afflicted several nations in 1762. British soldiers
and officials called themselves the Indians' allies and brothers, but they
actually behaved much more like intruders. Additional intruders—
namely, British settlers—exacerbated this ill behavior by squatting in
the upper Ohio valley on land reserved to the Delawares and Shawnees
by the Treaty of Easton. The promises that had secured Britain's truce
with the Lakes and Ohio Indians now became empty ones.[10]

This would not have surprised the adherents of a new movement,
known to modern historians as "nativism," that had germinated in
Pennsylvania twenty years earlier and that now slowly spread into the
Lakes country. Nativism began as a religious awakening, but since Native Americans did not separate religion from other aspects of their
lives, it quickly became a cultural and political movement as well. Early
nativist leaders were prophets and seers who held direct communion
with the Master of Life, much as Shawnee and Anishinaabe shamans
communed with wind spirits and other unearthly beings. They declared that the Master of Life had created the white and "red" races
as separate peoples and bequeathed to these different peoples different
customs and separate lands. Delaware seers of both genders began to
spread the new gospel in the 1740s and '50s, telling their followers that
their declining numbers and brushes with famine and illness resulted
from their forsaking of ancestral ways and their blurring of the line of
separation between whites and Indians.[11]

Neolin, the Delaware prophet who most directly inspired the 1763 rising, told his adherents he had made an eight-day dream journey to see the Master of Life, whom he could not reach until he shed his European-made clothing and possessions. When Neolin finally reached the Master's dwelling, the deity told him that he had made America for Indians, not Europeans, and that Indians should "live just as you lived before you met" the whites. Similar separatist views were spreading into the upper Lakes country by the early 1760s; Minavavana demonstrated this when he told Alexander Henry that the Ojibwas did not depend on Europeans for sustenance, for "the Master of Life has provided food for us in these spacious lakes and on these woody mountains."[12]

Nativism could engender considerable distrust for Europeans, whose lifeways Neolin and other prophets considered not only inappropriate for Indians, but potentially poisonous. The Pennsylvania nativist prophets all identified alcohol as particularly dangerous and urged their followers to avoid it. Delaware and Shawnee nativists instead advised Native Americans to imbibe "bitter water," a reference to an herbal tea known as "black drink," which southeastern Indians used as an emetic. Some nativist leaders also warned their adherents to avoid Christianity and its ritual artifacts, like the Christian Bible. Neolin included firearms in his list of proscribed tools, though he suggested Indians should take a few years to relearn archery before they gave up guns. The Master of Life told Neolin that whites themselves were toxic, particularly the British—"those who come to trouble your lands." Frenchmen the Indians should treat as "brothers," but Neolin and his followers should "drive [the British] out, make war on them."[13]

Nativism became a powerful unifying force in the 1763 uprising, but it was not the only bond of union between the insurgent nations. The Indians of the Great Lakes had traded with one another for centuries— Huron/Wyandots with Anishinaabeg, Shawnees with Delawares— and their exchanges of goods regularly renewed ties between different nations. Migration also brought distant Indian nations within the Lakes region together. The Anishinaabeg routinely traveled hundreds of miles by canoe to trade, hunt, fish, and gather, and the Wyandots, Delawares, and Shawnees had moved away from (and sometimes back to) their old homelands to escape Iroquois raiders or English settlers.

Several of the Lakes region's major trading centers, like Green Bay and Michilimackinac, were multitribal settlements whose inhabitants shared resources across ethnic boundaries, and different nations also shared land and resources in regions like the southern shorelands of Lake Erie. The adoption of captives and intermarriage between Indian men and women further blurred ethnic divisions. Nicholas Perrot, a French trader and translator, claimed that the Potawatomis had so heavily intermarried with the Sauks and Mesquakies that the "tribe is half Sakis." Some Illiniwek, like Marie Réaume's son Louison, also married Potawatomis, and Iroquois, like the adopted Seneca captive Mary Jemison, sometimes took Delaware husbands and wives. These interethnic alliances bound different nations together by blood and made it easier to learn one another's languages and customs.[14]

When they did not easily speak their allies' language, Lakes Indians had by the 1760s adopted another form of symbolic communication that made it easier to share ideas and plans: the wampum belt. Wampum were shell or (increasingly) glass beads, manufactured in light or dark colors, which northeastern Algonquians and Iroquois drilled, strung together, and wove into belts. By the eighteenth century, Lakes Indians and their European partners had begun to use wampum as trade goods and diplomatic currency, to make peace or seal alliances. The French, for instance, used wampum in 1759 to invite the Ohio valley Indians back to their alliance. Many Indians also used wampum belts as mnemonic transcripts of speeches or concepts. Pontiac had one belt, reportedly made in the 1720s, that "described" 210 Indian towns and probably symbolized pan-Indian alliance, while in the early 1760s the nations seeking to organize a war against Britain sent wampum belts to potential allies.[15]

The Lakes Indians had developed a powerful sense of unity, an equally powerful pan-Indian network, and a collective set of grievances against Great Britain by the onset of Pontiac's War. It is, however, easy to overstate the cultural distance between the British and their Indian neighbors. The Lakes forts saw considerable fraternization between British traders and soldiers and Lakes Indian men and women, interaction that both contributed to the uprising's success and limited its range. Fort Miami, for example, would not have fallen so quickly if a Miami woman had not lured away the British sentry, her *façon du pays* husband, with a request to help a sick relative. The ruse that took Michilimackinac similarly depended on a close relationship between the Anishinaabeg and the British soldiers at the fort: Anishinaabe men planned their lacrosse match for George III's birthday, when they knew the redcoats would be off duty and likely to attend the game, and Anishinaabe women could hide firearms in the fort because they often entered the stockade to sell provisions or fraternize with British soldiers. The British post at Sandusky fell after one of its ensigns invited Odawa and Wyandot warriors inside to smoke, presumably not a unique request, and the ruse by which Pontiac planned to take Detroit involved moving men into the town under the guise of hunters come to trade. Conversely, some Lakes Indians protected Britons with whom they had developed a close relationship. A party of Ojibwas gave refuge to Alexander Henry during the insurgency, and another group of Anishinaabeg warned the garrison at Green Bay of the uprising to give the soldiers time to evacuate.[16]

Fraternal sentiment played no part in British commanders' reaction to the Indian attacks. General Jeffery Amherst, the commander of North American forces, demanded that "no mercy whatever be shown to these perfidious barbarians" and wondered whether his officers could give the insurgents smallpox. The general did not know that the commandant of besieged Fort Pitt, Simon Ecuyer, had already given blankets from the fort's smallpox hospital to some of the besieging Delaware, Iroquois, and Odawa warriors. Pox did in fact break out among the besiegers and their kinsmen, killing several hundred people in 1763–64, and while Ecuyer's blankets may not have been the cause, certainly he intended the result.[17]

More conventionally, Amherst sent several hundred reinforcements to Fort Pitt and Detroit. The Detroit expedition failed to break through the warriors besieging the town, sustaining 60 casualties at the Battle of Bloody Run. The Fort Pitt relief expedition enjoyed slightly greater success: Lakes and Ohio Indian insurgents attacked Henry Bouquet's column at Bushy Run, but Bouquet and his men rallied, feigned a retreat, then enfiladed the warriors who gave chase. The battle had, however, so depleted Bouquet's force (110 British to 60 Indian casualties) that he could contribute little to Fort Pitt's defenses. The siege continued until disease and depleted supplies forced the Indians to lift it.[18]

By the end of 1763, the insurgency had run its course. Its participants had destroyed most of the British-held forts in the Great Lakes region, delivering a sharp blow or "coup" that they no doubt hoped would teach the redcoats to respect their Indian neighbors. The sieges of Fort Pitt and Detroit actually lasted a long time, given their low probability of success—it was difficult to take a large fort without the advantage of surprise or without artillery to batter down the walls—but by late fall the insurgents, sick or hungry or demoralized by the absence of French aid, had given up both operations. The following year, British generals John Bradstreet and Henry Bouquet went on the offensive, more or less. Bradstreet took twelve hundred troops to Presque Isle and Detroit and met there with Shawnee, Wyandot, and Anishinaabe emissaries, with whom he negotiated peace treaties that his superiors later repudiated. He also sent a subordinate, Thomas Morris, to make peace with the Illiniwek, but abuse and death threats kept him from advancing beyond the Miami towns at Kekionga. Bouquet took a more confrontational approach: he led fifteen hundred soldiers to the Scioto valley, obliged Delaware and Ohio Iroquois villagers there to surrender captives, and demanded their attendance at a later peace conference.[19]

The British had not won the war. Few of the empire's forts in the Lakes region still stood, and most of the Native insurgents had achieved their (limited) goals. When chiefs and officials met in 1765, the former clearly indicated that they were making peace with equals, not surrendering to a conqueror. At Fort Pitt the Shawnees returned their remaining captives to British Indian Superintendent William Johnson, but they called the returnees "flesh and blood," the same formula the Illiniwek had used when giving slaves to their allies. Redeeming captives, they implied, created a bond of blood and kinship between the Shawnees and their new British allies. The same year, Miami, Mascouten, and Odawa insurgents (including Pontiac) met and exchanged wampum with George Croghan, now working as a diplomat for the Crown. They also reminded Croghan that if their new British "father"

FIGURE 1. The 1765 Fort Pitt conference featured the same dynamics and protocols as this 1764 meeting between Shawnee chiefs and Henry Bouquet. Benjamin
West, "The Indians Giving a Talk to Colonel Bouquet in a Conference at a Council Fire Near His Camp on the Banks of the Muskingum in America, in October
1764." *Courtesy of the Paul Mellon Collection, Yale Center for British Art*

wanted continued peace and harmony, he would have to accept terms: gifts for Indian emissaries, charitable treatment for Native American hunters, and above all no British seizure of their lands, which their people had never sold or surrendered to the French.[20]

The British imperial government had already begun, on its own initiative, to make temporary reforms that addressed a few of the Indians' postwar demands. In the fall of 1763, King George III had by royal proclamation halted white settlement and land sales west of the Appalachian Mountains, subject to future modification by the king and his agents. The following year the British Board of Trade, a council created by Parliament to regulate relations with Britain's colonies, issued its "Plan of 1764" regarding colonial Indian affairs. The plan provided for the appointment of agents empowered to settle disputes between Indians and whites, and it placed restrictions on trade: only licensed traders could deal with Native Americans, and then only at specified posts like Detroit. These restrictions did not prevent British traders from renewing the pre-1763 fur trade at a high volume. Pack traders like Matthew Elliott were heading to the Shawnee towns on the Scioto River as early as 1764. Nearly fifty British entrepreneurs, most of them former army officers, moved to Detroit by 1775 and took over the local Indian trade, while a well-capitalized firm of Quaker merchants and London investors, Baynton, Wharton, and Morgan, sought to monopolize the Illinois fur trade, spending nearly £75,000 on goods and transport during their first two years of operations.[21]

Lakes Indian hunters soon found that white traders honored the strictures of the Plan of '64 only in the breach. In the 1760s, imperial licenses proved hard to obtain, as violent colonial protests against the Stamp Act (1765) resulted in a shortage of the stamped paper on which officials had to print the licenses. Traders went into Indian country without license or oversight. Frenchmen from the new town of Saint Louis did business in the western Lakes region, and unlicensed peddlers from Detroit, known there as "Liberty Boys," took their wares directly to Indian towns, rather than obliging Indians to come to them. Some Native Americans became traders themselves. Sally Ainse, of the Oneida nation of Iroquois, went into business among the Mississaugas in 1766 and at the trading hub of Michilimackinac the following year.

By 1774 she had joined the mercantile community in Detroit, where she commanded several thousand pounds' worth of commercial credit and a respectable share of the town's fur trade.[22]

While Ainse's customers left no significant record of complaint, unscrupulous trading practices abounded in the Lakes country, generating friction and even violence between white traders and Indian hunters. Iroquois and Lakes Indian chiefs reported to Superintendent William Johnson that unscrupulous white peddlers cheated their male relatives and befuddled them with liquor; indeed, some less well-capitalized traders carried no trade goods but rum, recognizing that Indians would almost always buy it. General Thomas Gage observed that Lakes Indian men did not always confine themselves to complaints. In 1767 Potawatomis from Saint Joseph killed two traders, and by the early 1770s "scarce a year passe[d] that the Potawatomis [were] not guilty of killing some of the traders." Odawa and Kickapoo hunters occasionally also put those who abused them to death. While not condoning such killings, Johnson attributed them to abusive, no-account whites who "when they have obtained credit for a little goods . . . rambled into the back country." Yet even licensed traders from Detroit and other posts often, in the eyes of Indian men, displayed unconscionable stinginess or dishonesty.[23]

Violent disputes between European traders and their Indian trading partners had occurred in the past, but French garrison commanders had developed mutually acceptable protocols for handling them. British garrison commanders and officials labored under comparative disadvantages that made it much more difficult for them to keep the peace. Their authority in the region was very new, and the government that paid for their upkeep struggled to meet its expenses in the aftermath of the costly Seven Years' War. After Parliament's efforts to impose new taxes (like the infamous stamp tax or the 1767 Townshend duties) on the American colonies resulted in riots, the British ministries embarked on a program of retrenchment. In April 1768 the new colonial secretary, Lord Hillsborough, voided the Plan of 1764 and returned responsibility for fur-trade regulation to colonial governments. In the same year the British army began closing its frontier forts, both to save money and to move their soldiers to the rebellious city of Boston. By

1772, apart from a tiny garrison at Kaskaskia, British troops occupied only three posts in the Lakes country: Niagara, Detroit, and Michilimackinac. Without clear legal authority or the means to enforce their orders, imperial officials like William Johnson had to cede authority to the local population.[24]

Increasingly, that local population consisted of British colonists, who viewed the Lakes country and Ohio valley not as Native American homelands but as the spoils of war. White farmers followed military roads to the upper Ohio valley, where they settled near Pittsburgh; by 1773 their population had reached about ten thousand. A council of Lakes Indian chiefs reported in 1773 that they "could not help being alarmed" by the colonial surge, which appeared to them unauthorized and unrestrained by any government. Others, like Daniel Boone, sought the quicker profits of commercial hunting on the Kentucky grasslands, south of the Ohio River. The territory they began infiltrating in 1766 belonged to the Shawnees, who had resumed using it as their hunting preserve earlier in the century, and who now resided for up to half the year in Kentucky hunting camps. The Shawnees allowed the newcomers to hunt in their territory for food, but not for profit, and they confiscated pelts from whites whom they caught hunting for commercial gain. In one case Shawnee men took over one thousand deerskins from a party of whites they found guilty of poaching.[25]

Though Lakes Indian chiefs complained of these intrusions to British officials, William Johnson and other British leaders were now aligning their personal interests with the expansion of colonial settlement. In 1768, at a conference in Fort Stanwix, New York, William Johnson and officials from New Jersey, Pennsylvania, and Virginia met with two thousand Iroquois (and a few hundred Delawares) and obtained from them title to all of the lands south and east of the Ohio River, including most of Kentucky. The Iroquois claimed the territory by "right of conquest," the same justification they had used to sell land to Virginia a quarter-century earlier. The Treaty of Fort Stanwix gave cover to the white farmers and hunters then moving into the upper Ohio valley, though the Shawnees denied the legitimacy of the cession.[26]

Meanwhile, white speculators were staking a claim to Indian lands north and west of the Ohio River. In the mid-1760s, a coalition of investors, including Superintendent Johnson, Benjamin Franklin, George Croghan, and the Baynton & Wharton partners, began promoting a prospective colony in the Ohio valley. After 1770, they renamed their project "Vandalia" and obtained the backing of a well-connected Englishman, Thomas Walpole. Britain's Privy Council rewarded their persistent lobbying with its endorsement of the Vandalia colony in 1772. Other colonial land companies pursued schemes even further afield: in 1773, a partnership called the Illinois Company bought tracts on the Illinois and Wabash Rivers from eleven Illini chiefs, and in 1775 the Wabash Company purchased two tracts in Illinois and Indiana from the Piankeshaws. Parliament did not immediately approve any of these ventures, but in 1774 it did create a civil government for the Great Lakes region, placing European settlers and traders there under the jurisdiction of the province of Quebec while preserving the validity of earlier colonial land claims.[27]

The Indians in the southeastern Lakes country knew that both imperial and colonial expansionists conspired against them. Some decided to resist, and chief among the resisters were the Shawnees. Their lands in Kentucky lay under the most immediate threat, and they had been the last to lay down their arms in Pontiac's War; a Shawnee captain, Charlot Kaské, had helped drive a British infantry detachment out of Illinois in 1765. The Shawnees also numbered among the first Lakes Indians to begin renewing their former confederacy. In 1767 Shawnee and Miami leaders began discussing a new alliance with the Delawares, Ohio Iroquois, and Mascoutens, and by 1770 the Scioto Shawnees had built a council house for potential confederates.[28]

As it turned out, the Shawnees' preparations for armed resistance played into the hands of a leading British expansionist, who would use it to shore up his province's claim to the Ohio valley and his own flagging political popularity. That expansionist was John Murray, Earl of Dunmore and royal governor of Virginia, a man growing increasingly unpopular with his subjects. Colonial leaders had reached the point of open rebellion against the British Parliament in the wake of the Coercive Acts (1774), which closed the port of Boston and imposed a more authoritarian government on Massachusetts, and Dunmore faced the unpleasant task of maintaining order in Virginia and preventing a sympathetic uprising there. The outbreak of a brushfire war in the Ohio valley offered Dunmore the chance to distract white Virginians from divisive imperial politics by redirecting their attention toward expansion of their own territory. At the same time, he could boost his political prestige, in the time-honored fashion of both European executives and Native American war captains, with a quick military victory.[29]

Relations between Indians and white sojourners in the Ohio valley had been worsening for several years, and in April 1774 a party of Cherokee warriors attacked a group of British traders there. Lord Dunmore blamed the attack on Shawnees and Ohio Iroquois, and white settlers in retaliation killed as many as forty Indians; in one particularly gruesome incident, Pennsylvania frontiersmen invited a party of Ohio Iroquois to their camp for drinks and a shooting contest, then butchered eight of their guests. The victims included the family of Ohio Iroquois chief Logan, who later that year killed a dozen whites in retaliation. Shawnee leaders disavowed any responsibility for this wave of violence and promised Virginians they would remain peaceful, but the opportunistic Governor Dunmore decided not to give them that chance.[30]

Dunmore mobilized twenty-four hundred militia, more troops than Virginia had raised in the Seven Years' War, and in the fall of 1774 he marched them northwestward to subdue the Indian communities of the Ohio valley. His offensive would have a transformative effect on one of the principal waterways in the Lakes region, the Ohio River. For centuries, the "Beautiful River" had served the Shawnees and Delawares and other Indian nations as an avenue of commerce and a symbol of home. Now it became a vector of Anglo-American conquest and expansion.[31]

Dunmore sent one detachment across the mountains into present-day West Virginia, toward the middle Ohio valley, and led a larger force to the head of the Ohio River, pausing at Pittsburgh to assert his province's claim to western Pennsylvania. While the governor proceeded down the Ohio, his other militia force, under Andrew Lewis, ran into a small army of Shawnees, Delawares, and Ohio Iroquois at Point Pleasant, near the confluence of the Kanawha and Ohio Rivers. The group's war captains had resolved, at a conference on the Scioto

River, to resist any Virginian attack on their homeland; their reso- lution now resulted in a heated battle with Lewis's army, which the Shawnees wanted to neutralize before it joined with the governor's main force. In the fight at Point Pleasant (October 10, 1774), the In- dian allies, led by Shawnee captains Cornstalk and Blue Jacket, killed or wounded about 140 Virginians, withdrawing from the field only after Lewis received reinforcements.[32]

While the Battle of Point Pleasant was essentially a draw, the Shaw- nees and their allies could not stop Dunmore's advance thereafter. The governor sent a militia detachment to destroy the towns on the Muskingum River, while he himself marched to the allied Indians' base communities on the Scioto and compelled the Shawnees to sign a pu- nitive treaty. Under its terms, Shawnee leaders gave Virginia their na- tion's claims to Kentucky, a cession they may have viewed as temporary but which Dunmore considered permanent. There were already in 1774 a few white surveyors and land speculators in the Bluegrass country, staking claims for companies organized after an earlier (1770) Chero- kee cession of Kentucky, but the Shawnee treaty persuaded Virginians that the territory had fully opened for white settlement, and it opened the Ohio River route to emigration. By 1776 over one thousand white and black colonists lived in central Kentucky. Their outposts became an important cause of the continuation war that would shortly erupt between the Ohio valley Indians and white Americans.[33]

Dunmore himself returned to Williamsburg in triumph, accompa- nied by several Shawnee hostages to betoken his victory. "Dunmore's War," as historians came to call it, had inflicted far worse casual- ties and consequences on the Shawnees than British forces had done in Pontiac's War. The war also distracted white Virginians from the governor's earlier dissolution of the colonial assembly and from the debates in the concurrently meeting Continental Congress. Dunmore's own popularity did not last long, however: in the spring of 1775, Vir- ginia's political leaders branded him a public enemy after he took gun- powder from the arsenal and armed his Shawnee hostages, whom he now hoped would help defend him from his own Virginian subjects. Dunmore and the Virginia rebels had come to the conclusion that they were greater enemies of one another than of the Indians. In their violent divergence of interests lay both opportunity and danger for the British colonies' Indian neighbors.[34]

◆ ◆ ◆

The era of British rule in the Great Lakes region began, like the French imperial epoch, with a violent conflict, in this case a war between the British and the Lakes Indians. After a brief probationary period, Native people concluded that Britons were inhumane intruders who merited violent "correction." Some of the Indians were also nativists, who believed that British traders, soldiers, and settlers brought only spiritual poisons to Indian country. Others were political nostalgics or conservatives who wanted to restore the old French alliance while strengthening the bonds—marital, commercial, and communal—that already existed between the various Lakes Indian nations.

This variety of motives ensured that Pontiac's War would spread widely and attract thousands of Indian participants, but it also helped ensure that the war would end quickly and that some sort of peace could follow it. Indians who wanted merely to chastise the British had done so by the end of 1763, and both "conservatives" and nativists discovered a way to neutralize Britons' cultural toxicity: by transforming them, essentially, into Frenchmen. Native American men and women had already been interacting and trading with Britons before the insurgency, and in the peace conferences that ended Pontiac's War, some leaders created a symbolic blood tie with the British, while others secured from them the same kind of protective guarantees that France had once extended to them.

These guarantees did not last. The British imperium in North America proved significantly weaker, from Native Americans' perspective, than the French one. After the Seven Years' War, Britain's resources stretched thinly throughout a worldwide empire whose North American colonial subjects became dangerously rebellious in the 1760s. Focused on riots and tumults in the American seaboard colonies, British officials and soldiers could not prevent thousands of white colonists from settling in the upper Ohio valley, nor white hunters from invading Kentucky. By 1770, in fact, many imperial officials had decided to abandon restrictions on white settlement west of the Appalachians and instead profit from colonial expansion—hence, the Treaty of Fort Stanwix, the proposed Vandalia colony, and John Murray's war of conquest in the Ohio country.[35]

Ultimately, British officials could not bribe the American colonists with plans for expansion because those colonists came to see the political rift between themselves and the mother country as unbridgeable. By the 1770s, colonial activists had come to fear that Britain wanted to turn them into a non-English "Other," deprived of self-government and the other "rights of Englishmen." After the Boston Tea Party and the Coercive Acts, rebellious colonists began to behave like political outsiders, creating their own intercolonial government and army and terrorizing white colonists loyal to the old regime. They thereby turned their rebellion into a war, which both they and the British imperial government fought the same way European empires had always fought one another in America: with armies and fleets, of course, but also with indigenous allies. Britain's brief empire in the Great Lakes region ended as it began: with a war in which Native Americans would be key participants, and with another reminder to British officials, who perhaps had begun to forget, that they could not take the Lakes Indians for granted.[36]

6

Revolutionary Stalemate

THE IMPERIAL CRISIS OF THE 1760S, WHICH BEGAN IN THE MARITIME communities of the Atlantic seaboard, did not take long to spread into the Great Lakes region and affect the lives of Native Americans there. The British Empire was an integrated bureaucratic system, and events in one colony could easily affect other provinces, even distant ones. Spending cutbacks in London obliged the imperial government to close several western forts and withdraw their garrisons; the transfer of forces helped ensure that the Crown would remain weak in the Lakes country, even as it lost authority in its seaboard colonies. The lack of a civil government in the Great Lakes region became one of the problems that inspired the Quebec Act of 1774, whose provisions, particularly its authoritarian frame of government and establishment of the Catholic Church, so angered New Englanders and Virginians that they labeled it an "Intolerable Act" and indicted it in the Declaration of Independence.[1]

The most important reason that the revolution spread into the North American interior, however, was that both British officials and colonial leaders forgot the limits on political power that exist within an empire. If an empire comprised of different ethnic groups, each with its own leaders and sources of power, wishes to function smoothly, some power must flow between the imperial capital and the peripheral provinces, and between provincial capitals and the provinces' peripheral peoples. This cannot happen when one part of the empire says, "I am absolutely sovereign and you must surrender." The result is usually war, or rebellion, or both. The Coercive Acts of 1774 constituted Parliament's declaration of absolute sovereignty, or close to it, and they triggered the final stage of the colonial revolt that led to the Revolutionary War. Meanwhile, the 1768 Treaty of Fort Stanwix, which ceded the Ohio forks and environs to Pennsylvania, and Dunmore's War, which ceded Kentucky to Virginia, essentially constituted those colonies claim of absolute sovereignty over the southern Lakes Indians. "Surrender your lands and we shall take them and ignore you," said Pennsylvania; "surrender your lands or we shall destroy you and take them anyway," said Virginia. The Shawnees, Delawares, and Iroquois disagreed, and their Native neighbors soon sided with them.[2]

Indians and white Anglophone colonists had begun drawing thick dividing lines between their cultures in the mid-eighteenth century, when "nativist" prophets identified Britons and their wares as poisons, and practitioners of the "anti-Indian sublime" described Indians as irredeemable savages preying on innocent white settlers. These lines thickened during the war, when many Indians aligned themselves with Britain against the rebel colonists. The Lakes Indians' determination to recover lost land and retain their autonomy, and the rebel settlers' perception of Indians as a subhuman, enemy race, ensured that the Revolutionary War would become a desperate and destructive conflict on the frontier. By 1782, the smoldering remains of fields and towns darkened the landscapes of New York, Pennsylvania, and Virginia, as well as the future states of Kentucky and Ohio, and several thousand whites and Indians there lay dead. If the conflict did not become a general war of extermination, or end in a decisive victory for one side or the other, this primarily resulted from the technical limits on the combatants' military strength: supply shortages, limited manpower, and their inability to persuade the few neutralists in the region (like the

French *habitants*) to support them. The American Revolution certainly had consequences for the Great Lakes country: in addition to the physical destruction of the war, the revolution ended British control of the American colonies, increased American migration to the Ohio valley, and accelerated the Lakes Indians' loss of demographic and political strength. What it did not produce was a decisive outcome on the frontier, and so peace would prove elusive in the years to come.[3]

❖ ❖ ❖

At the outbreak of the Revolutionary War, the American Continental Congress pursued an ambivalent strategy toward the neighboring Indian nations. In October 1775, the rebel assembly urged the Iroquois and Lakes Indians to remain neutral, a diplomatic maneuver that some historians believe was an attempt to reprise the more successful negotiations at Easton in 1758. Representatives of the Congress at Philadelphia and of the rebel government of Virginia met with Delaware, Iroquois, Odawa, Shawnee, and Wyandot diplomats at Fort Pitt. All paid careful attention to protocol. Indian diplomats politely referred to their white counterparts as "Brothers Onas and Long Knife," the Iroquois titles for the old colonies of Pennsylvania and Virginia. This reference acknowledged continuity between the old colonies and the new rebel assemblies and also reflected the Iroquois practice of "requickening," bestowing the titles of the deceased on their successors after a condolence ceremony. For their part, the rebel commissioners condoled with and gave gifts to some of the Indian conferees, returned the Shawnee hostages whom Virginians had taken during Dunmore's War, and advised everyone to stay out of "the dispute between us and some of our Father's evil commissioners beyond the Great Water."[4]

At the same time, the United Colonies wanted to recruit Indian auxiliaries for their war against the redcoats, and British officials and army officers were doing the same. The Continental army had in the spring of 1775 welcomed a party of Mohican scouts from the town of Stockbridge, Massachusetts, and later that year Congress sent an agent, Silas Deane, to Paris to buy trade goods for potential Indian allies. On the other side, British officers and officials followed Lord Dunmore in recruiting Indian warriors to assist the Crown: Sir Guy

Johnson, for example, recruited forty Kahnewake Mohawks for service in Canada in mid-1775.[5]

The most effective recruiters of Native American warriors, however, were other Indians. At least in the early years of the conflict, when Indians fought in the Revolutionary War they generally did so in pursuit of agendas that predated the fight between Britain and the rebellious colonists. Just as they had been doing since 1769, the Shawnees took a leading role in organizing resistance to American settlers. They had over the past twelve years suffered defeat on the battlefield, invasions of their communities, and the loss of their seasonal home of Kentucky. In August 1775, the Shawnee leader Kishanosity complained that Virginians were not only building settlements in Kentucky but hunting north of the Ohio River. American commissioners retorted that the colonies had fairly purchased Kentucky and now expected to "enjoy" the territory in peace, and they warned the Shawnees that Virginians would take "ample satisfaction" for any "injury" they received. Unfortunately for the blustering rebels, the Shawnees had developed a network of allies extending throughout the Ohio and Tennessee valleys. In the spring of 1776, several Shawnee captains activated this alliance, traveling south to meet with Cherokee captains and urge them to strike a blow against intruding American settlers. Cherokee warriors angered by their chiefs' land cessions took up the war belt proffered by the Shawnees, and they fought an intense—and, for the Cherokees, intensely devastating—war with the rebel states of Virginia, North and South Carolina, and Georgia. The American Congress would in its Declaration of Independence blame the Cherokees' raids on British instigation, but the Cherokee war of 1776 actually just extended and continued the territorial conflict Virginians had begun two years earlier.[6]

Most of the eastern Ohio valley Indians, who shared the Shawnees' alarm about the expansion of colonial settlements, entered this conflict a few months later. In December 1776, a party of Ohio Iroquois warriors crossed the Ohio River and raided McClelland's Station, north of present-day Lexington. (Their captain, Pluggy, died in the attack.) A few months later, Shawnee warriors initiated what white Kentuckians would call "the year of the Bloody Sevens," a campaign intended to drive the thousand or so American intruders out of Kentucky. Shawnee warriors raided Harrodsburg and Boonesborough, burning cabins and taking horses. Further up the Ohio River, Indian war parties attacked farms in western Pennsylvania, and in September two hundred Ohio Iroquois, Shawnees, and Wyandots attacked the stronghold of Fort Henry (modern Wheeling, West Virginia), ambuscading the fort and destroying crops and livestock.[7]

The raiders did not engage in violence for its own sake. Their primary goal was to kill or terrorize isolated whites, destroy the food supplies of the larger settlements, and thereby compel the intruders to withdraw. One might call their strategy "purgative," insofar as Lakes Indian warriors wanted to expel a dangerous mass of intruders from territory they considered part of their homeland, part of their own nation. While they did succeed in driving remote settlers into the larger fortified towns, the warriors did not succeed in regaining control of the Ohio valley. They did terrorize white frontiersmen into starting a cycle of vengeance and reprisal that intensified the border conflict, chiefly because those seeking vengeance turned neutral Indians into their targets. Since the Seven Years' War, when practitioners of the "anti-Indian sublime" had raised whites' fears of Indians (and their belief in their own innocence) to new heights, many white settlers had come to see Native Americans as an innately predatory race seeking to kill or enslave white Americans. Even nominally friendly Indians might turn on their allies at any time. Thus, in the fall of 1777, Virginia militia arrested and killed three neutral Shawnee emissaries who had come to Fort Randolph. Their victims included Cornstalk, a signer of the Treaty of Fort Pitt, whose death ensured that more of his kinsmen would range themselves against the Americans. Soon thereafter, in January 1778, a regiment of Pennsylvania militia killed four Delaware women and children in northwestern Pennsylvania. Their victims were relatives of Konieschquanoheel, the principal war leader of the Delawares' Wolf clan, known as Captain Pipe by his American allies. He would not remain their ally for long.[8]

The war in the Ohio valley intensified in 1778, the pivotal year in the conflict. In January a Shawnee war party under Black Fish captured twenty-seven Kentucky settlers, including the militia officer Daniel Boone, and brought them to Chillicothe. The Shawnees adopted half of the captives, flogging them through a gauntlet and then plucking their hair and dressing them as warriors. Boone offered to make a permanent peace by taking Boonesborough's inhabitants to the Shawnees' towns and incorporating them into the Shawnee nation as adopted kinfolk. When in September Black Fish led 350 warriors south to accept the settlement's surrender, he found the gates closed to him; Boone's fellow settlers had rejected his proposal that they give up their cultural identity and had determined to fight. The warriors mounted a desultory siege of the fortified village but departed ten days later. Without surprise or artillery, Indian warriors continued to find it difficult to take fortified strongholds. A Wyandot and Ohio Iroquois war party had failed in a similar attempt to capture two forts on the Kanawha River five months earlier; the 300 warriors killed the settlers' livestock but could not compel the forts' defenders to surrender.[9]

The year 1778 also saw the first major rebel campaign in the Great Lakes region, consisting of offensives at both ends of the Ohio valley. In the summer, George Rogers Clark led 175 militia to Illinois, where he occupied Cahokia and Kaskaskia. Meanwhile, commissioners of the Continental Congress persuaded Delaware captains to sign a treaty of alliance with the United States. Under its terms, the Delawares let the rebel army march into and build forts on their territory, and that fall General Lachlan McIntosh, at the head of 1,200 troops, established a fort and garrison on the Tuscarawas River, near the Delaware town of Coshocton. He ordered the region's Shawnees, Wyandots, and Odawas to come to the new Fort Laurens to make peace, and he planned an expedition against British-held Detroit.[10]

The shared goal of these offensives was to neutralize the Lakes Indians by seizing the British posts they depended on for military supplies. McIntosh and Clark differed in their assumptions regarding Indians' wartime motives. General McIntosh assumed that Native Americans merely did Britain's bidding and that defeating their British bosses would keep the warriors home. He thus made no serious attempt to conciliate or impress the Delawares, whom he would depend on to secure Fort Laurens and guide his troops to Detroit. He tried to cover up his militia's murder of George White Eyes (Quequedegatha), a prominent Delaware leader and American ally, and he ordered the Delawares

to provide Fort Laurens with food, a directive that emphasized the outpost's isolation and dependency. The southern Lakes Indians laughed
at McIntosh's demand that they come to a peace conference. Delaware
warriors shot at the Fort Laurens garrison or pillaged their supplies,
and they stood by while British-allied warriors besieged the post in
February 1779. The siege failed, but it so clearly demonstrated the difficulty of maintaining Fort Laurens that General McIntosh closed it.[11]

For his part, Clark also regarded Britain as the rebels' main enemy
and Detroit as an important target, but he did recognize that two other
populations held the balance of power in the southern Lakes country:
the Lakes Indians, and the several thousand French *habitants* who had
long traded and intermarried with them. Shortly after arriving in Illinois, Clark befriended some of the region's French traders and magis-
trates and persuaded them to invite Anishinaabe, Kickapoo, and Miami
diplomats to treaty conferences. At these conferences, Clark blended
conciliation with threats. He smoked the calumet and shook hands
with Lakes Indian chiefs and captains, and he gave them a somewhat
fictionalized economic history of the Revolutionary War, claiming that
the Virginians lived by "making corn, hunting, and trade as you and the
French your neighbors do," and that they had gone to war after Britain
refused to let them make their own goods. Clark also offered the Indian
visitors a choice between grasping a white wampum belt and a "bloody
belt," and warned that if they took the latter "we will try like warriors
[to] . . . keep our clothes the longest perfumed with blood."[12]

Clark continued this mixture of bloody threats and conciliation
after capturing Vincennes in early 1779. Shortly before commandant
Henry Hamilton surrendered his garrison, Clark arrested five Odawa
men who were traveling to the British-held fort and tomahawked them
within sight of the garrison. The execution served as an indirect blow
at Hamilton himself, who as lieutenant governor of Detroit had established a firm military tie between Britain and Lakes Indian warriors. In
1778 the governor had held a massive conference, where he distributed
gifts to nearly 1,700 Indians, and urged them to help him fight the rebels; when he marched to Vincennes that fall, 550 Odawas and Miamis
accompanied him. Nearly all of Hamilton's companions had returned
home by 1779, however, and none of the Indians residing in the lower

Wabash valley helped him fight the Kentuckians, ensuring that Hamilton would lack enough manpower to defend his post.[13]

After sending Hamilton to Virginia in irons, Clark invited the Weas and Miamis to another conference, where he praised them "for their manly behavior and fidelity." He sent a gendered threat to Britain's remaining Indian allies, telling them to come out and "fight like Men that the Big Knives may not be ashamed when they fight you, that the old women may not tell us that we fought only squaws." The addressees declined Clark's invitation, but the Kentuckian's speeches and behavior had a larger demonstrative point: the Big Knives were people much like the Lakes Indians and the French, and this made them more natural allies for Native Americans than the British. Clark wanted to invert the "Othering" process that had helped turn Lakes Indians and Kentuckians into such implacable enemies. He would not, however, give up the settlements in Kentucky that he had launched his expedition to protect, and he was unable to install permanent garrisons in the territories he had "conquered," and that meant he could not secure a permanent peace with the Shawnees or their allies.[14]

Clark's and McIntosh's offensives did not gain the rebels any territory. McIntosh evacuated Fort Laurens in August 1779, and Clark withdrew most of his troops from Vincennes the following year. The campaigns did, however, deflect Indian war parties from the Kentucky-Virginia frontier, as did a May 1779 militia raid on the Shawnee town of Chillicothe, which captured 180 horses and killed or mortally wounded several Shawnee leaders (including Black Fish.) The brief period of relative calm coincided with the Virginia legislature's passage of a land law for Kentucky, setting a nominal price of four shillings in Virginia currency for every one hundred acres of land, giving reduced rates to "actual" settlers. The commonwealth sold nearly two million acres of Kentucky land within a year of the law's passage. Cheap land and the prospect of greater security accelerated migration to Kentucky, whose adult white male population exceeded three thousand within a year.[15]

The other major rebel campaign in Indian country during the late 1770s had more spectacular tactical success but less durable strategic consequences than Clark's or McIntosh's expeditions. The rebels' target, the homeland of the Six Nations of Iroquois, lay at the far eastern edge of the Great Lakes region. Iroquois chiefs had agreed at the war's outset to remain neutral, but some warriors did participate in the British defense of Canada. In 1777 the English-educated war captain Thayendanegea (Joseph Brant), backed by British agents with ample presents, persuaded most of the Iroquois to fight for King George. The following year, war parties destroyed American settlements at German Flats, Cherry Valley, and Wilkes-Barre, killing several hundred militia and civilians. Unfortunately, the Iroquois offensive unfolded as the British army reorganized and redeployed southward, leaving the Continental army free to wreak havoc in Iroquoia. In the summer of 1779, General Washington sent John Sullivan and four thousand regulars up the Susquehanna River to knock this powerful Indian confederacy out of the war.[16]

Thanks to feints up the Mohawk and Allegheny Rivers, which forced the Iroquois defenders to divide their forces, the Continental soldiers defeated the small war parties sent to oppose them. They then laid waste the densely populated country they had invaded. As General Sullivan exchanged toasts with his officers and worked on a manuscript in praise of the Christian religion, his soldiers destroyed forty Iroquois towns, burned or consumed 160,000 bushels of maize, and girdled thousands of fruit trees. Many of the Iroquois took refuge in a vast encampment outside of British-occupied Fort Niagara, where more than three thousand survivors endured a hard, lean winter. The next year, the Americans learned that Sullivan's invasion had not driven the Six Nations to their knees—it had only driven them deeper into Britain's embrace. With British supplies and encouragement, Iroquois war parties struck the New York and Pennsylvania frontiers; by 1782 they had raided nearly a dozen towns and destroyed four times as much grain as had Sullivan's men.[17]

Sullivan's tactics, and later punitive campaigns by Daniel Brodhead and George Rogers Clark, drew on a long tradition of European counterinsurgency. European armies had long considered attacks on civilians acceptable and even necessary treatment of subject peoples in rebellion. Spanish troops had scourged rebellious Dutch cities in the sixteenth century, British soldiers repeatedly brought fire and sword to the Irish countryside, and the Duke of Cumberland inflicted rapine and plunder on the Scottish Highlands in 1746. Native Americans were not exactly rebels, but in wartime Europeans and white Americans did not recognize them as "civilized" combatants, since warriors did not fight under the same regimented discipline as European armies and since whites did not consider Indian chiefs coequal with European sovereigns. The "rules of war" that European and white American armies applied to one another they thus did not consider applicable to Indians. That Indian warriors often targeted civilians themselves, taking men and women as captives and destroying their food supplies, only strengthened Euro-Americans' commitment to anticivilian "pacification" tactics.[18]

The Lakes Indians in 1780 undertook just such an assault on white civilians in an attempt to dislodge the growing salient of American settlement in Kentucky. The difficulty of this task, exacerbated by the arrival of several thousand more white settlers and black slaves in 1779–80, did not prevent some of the Lakes Indians and their British allies from trying. In June 1780, a force of 700 Shawnees and 150 British troops captured Ruddle's Station and Martin's Station on the Licking River, south of present-day Cincinnati. The raiders took 350 captives, most of whom they ransomed in Detroit for British goods, though the Shawnees did keep many of the African American slaves they captured. The raid's presiding officer, Henry Bird, intended to divert the rebels' attention from a concurrent Indian thrust against the town of Saint Louis, whose sovereign, Spain, had declared war on Britain the year before. About 1,000 British-allied Dakota, Ho-Chunk, Menominee, and Sauk warriors assaulted Saint Louis in May 1780. Spanish artillery and a hastily built defensive tower repelled their attack. Before they withdrew, the attackers killed the French *habitants'* livestock and allegedly dismembered several captives, presumably to demoralize their adversaries.[19]

The Kentuckians, *habitants*, and Spanish then individually counterattacked. George Rogers Clark took militia and cannon across the Ohio River and attacked the Shawnee towns of Piqua and Chillicothe. The Virginians managed to defeat Shawnee warriors outside Piqua and to burn both towns, though a shortage of supplies forced Clark and his men to return home immediately thereafter. Such shortages plagued all of the armed forces fighting in the War for American Independence, particularly in regions like the Ohio valley where transportation was expensive and subsistence agriculture the norm. During his invasion of Illinois, Clark would not have been able to feed his militia if Fernando de Leyba, the commandant of Saint Louis, had not persuaded local merchants to supply him. By the summer of 1780, though, the *habitants'* patience had just about run out. Vincennes residents complained that Kentucky militia had bought up their limited food stocks with increasingly worthless Virginia paper money and taken flour and cattle at gunpoint. In 1781 the Kentuckians' credit ran out, and they had to withdraw from Kaskaskia.[20]

The disaffected *habitants,* however, had by then conducted their own offensive against the southern Lakes Indians, which proved one of the more quixotic episodes of the war. In 1780 about one hundred French gunmen under the command of French colonel Augustin Mottin de La Balme left Kaskaskia for Detroit, which they hoped to capture with the help of that town's French residents. La Balme may have hoped to capture Detroit for France, which had formally entered the war two years earlier. His companions hoped to neutralize the Miamis and Potawatomis, who had begun to raid Francophone settlements, and they planned after capturing Detroit to continue on to Philadelphia and there present their land claims to Congress. The *habitants* managed to occupy and plunder the Miami town of Kekionga, but on November 5 a large force of Miami warriors under Little Turtle ambushed them, killing La Balme and thirty of his men. Having previously lost forty men to desertion, the few survivors hastily retreated to Vincennes. The expedition primarily benefited one person: Little Turtle, whose prestige grew considerably after the Miamis' victory.[21]

A smaller *habitants'* expedition marched against the British post at Saint Joseph, Michigan, but Potawatomi warriors and Loyalist militia soon drove them out. Their attempt did not go unnoticed, however. Commandant Francisco Cruzat of Saint Louis decided that a follow-up attack on Saint Joseph would destroy an important British base and demoralize Britain's Indian allies. The Potawatomi chief Le Tourneau (Blackbird) also encouraged the Spanish to attack, as this would lower the prestige of Le Tourneau's British-allied Potawatomi rival, Little Corn. In January 1781, a party of 130 militia and Anishinaabe warriors started up the Illinois River for Saint Joseph, which they reached after six weeks of rowing and marching. The expeditionaries quickly captured the British post and its defenders, then withdrew with their plunder and prisoners. Crucial to the success of the raid was the cooperation of the local Potawatomis, whom the Spanish commander promised half of the plunder from the fort if they kept out of the fight.[22]

Plunder was an important consideration. The Lakes Indians were no more mercenary in the late eighteenth century than they had been in the French imperial era, but as the Revolutionary War continued, access to European goods and provisions became an important concern, one which impelled many Indians to fight for the British. Since British ships commanded the Atlantic and denied imported goods to the rebels, the Americans proved unable to supply their Indian allies, as Continental army officer Daniel Brodhead ruefully observed. While Britain's allies were "clothed in the most elegant manner and have many valuable presents made them, the captains I have commissioned . . . are naked and receive nothing but a little Whiskey, for which they are reviled by the Indians in general." British and French-Canadian fur traders did not suffer from the same constraint, but army officers sometimes commandeered ships on the Great Lakes, making it difficult for private traders to bring merchandise into the Lakes country. The rebels' destruction of the southern Lakes Indians' fields and food stores created additional scarcity. Many Native Americans would have found it difficult to feed themselves or obtain vital clothing and ammunition unless they received them as gifts from the British Indian department, which dispensed from the Lakes forts £15–30,000 (New York currency; $675,000–$1,300,000 in 2014 currency) of goods every year. "The warriors' cabin is generally empty," the Delaware war leader Captain Pipe reminded a British officer in 1781, while "your house is always full."[23]

By the time Captain Pipe made this remark, his Delaware kinsmen had particular need of British assistance. The American rebels' murder of Captain Pipe's relatives and of George White Eyes had spread disaffection and suspicion through the Delawares' Ohio communities, and this intensified in 1779 when American farmers and hunters, whom Clark's victories had emboldened, resumed encroaching on Delaware hunting grounds. The breaking point in the Delawares' relationship with the United States came shortly thereafter, when Continental army commander Daniel Brodhead proved unable to supply them, and British agents at Detroit promised to meet their needs instead. In 1781, after hearing reports that Delaware chiefs were planning to switch sides, Brodhead decided to terrorize them into neutrality. In early April, he and three hundred soldiers and militia burned the Delaware town of Coshocton, killed fifteen captive warriors—allegedly in retaliation for earlier Delaware attacks—imprisoned twenty women and children, and plundered a large quantity of goods and livestock. If the Delawares had been thinking of switching sides, Brodhead's treachery clinched their decision. The survivors of the raid sought refuge at Sandusky with the British-allied Wyandots.[24]

Some of the Delawares would have preferred to remain in eastern Ohio, had their kinsmen not compelled them to move. Earlier in the century, missionaries from a small central-European sect known as the Moravians had made a few converts among the Delawares, and in the 1770s those converts and their relatives had established two towns, Gnadenhutten and Salem, on the Muskingum River. Much like the Illiniwek at Kaskaskia, the Moravian Delawares wore European-style clothing, raised cattle, and had their own church decorated with religious paintings, where upwards of 150 Indians attended Sunday sermons and sang German psalms. While the Moravian Delawares were pacifists and would have preferred to remain neutral, other Delawares viewed them with suspicion, believing their Christian faith made them likelier to align with the Americans. After the Coshocton raid, Delaware warriors compelled the Moravians to move to Sandusky to isolate them from the American enemy. When food ran short at Sandusky, some of the evacuees returned to their abandoned towns to gather corn. There, in February 1782, disaster struck. Pennsylvania militia pursuing an Indian raiding party reached Gnadenhutten, arrested the Moravian Delaware workers, and accused them of assisting the raiders. After allowing their captives to spend the night in prayer, the militiamen took the prisoners in small groups to the town's slaughterhouses and beat them to death with mallets. Ninety-five Delaware men and women died in what historians now call the Gnadenhutten Massacre.[25]

Even in so long and destructive a war as the one that had been raging in the Ohio valley, the slaughter of the Moravian Delawares stood out for brutality. It demonstrated how white Pennsylvanians had moved from merely supporting the displacement of Indians (as in the Walking Purchase) to advocating their extermination. The shift had accelerated after 1776, when the new Commonwealth created what one scholar calls a "frontier government," dominated by backcountry districts, dedicated to military security, and regarding Indians as "permanent enemies of the state." Pennsylvania's government rewarded the murderous militia with commendations and promotions. Others did not consider the Gnaddenhutten murders heroic acts. The massacre shocked American officers in other states, and it infuriated the surviving Delawares and their allies. Later that spring, when Continental army officer William Crawford led an expedition to destroy the towns at Sandusky, the Delaware refugees took their revenge: after the American force broke up and retreated, the Delawares captured its commander and tortured him to death. Longtime associate George Washington was stricken by news of his friend's execution, but he understood the Delawares' motives.[26]

The Revolutionary War was winding down. Cornwallis had surrendered at Yorktown, and a new British government was negotiating with the rebels. In the absence of a formal armistice, however, Lakes Indian warriors continued to raid American settlements, and British agents continued to give them arms and encouragement. In the spring of 1782, war parties attacked farms and stations in northern and western Kentucky. A larger strike soon followed: in August three hundred Wyandot and Anishinaabe warriors hit Bryan's Station, north of Lexington. The war party killed the defenders' cattle and destroyed their crops, retreated when they learned more militia were on the way, then turned to fight their pursuers at Blue Licks (August 19, 1782). With a flank assault on the militia's line, the Lakes Indians routed their adversaries, killing or capturing seventy of them in the process. The warriors scalped or mutilated their fallen adversaries' bodies and, to terrify and demoralize any pursuers, executed their prisoners before crossing the Ohio River.[27]

Kentucky's militia officers believed they then had little choice but to counterattack. Their district's defensive forts stood in ruins, and none of the Lakes Indians had offered to negotiate peace terms with Virginia or the United States, probably because frontier militia had killed so many who might have negotiated. An offensive might at least "make a powerful impression" on the Lakes Indians and deter them from making additional raids. In the fall, George Rogers Clark assembled 1,050 Kentucky militia, a large part of the district's adult male population, and on November 10 the Kentuckians plundered and burned the Shawnees' settlements at New Chillicothe on the Great Miami River. Clark considered the raid a satisfactory victory, notwithstanding two significant problems: the Shawnees had played no part in the 1782 raids or the Battle of Blue Licks; and Britain, the United States, and the Lakes Indians had just agreed to an armistice.[28]

Clark's raid was less an embarrassment, however, than a harbinger of future events. The Revolutionary War had made the conflict in the lower Great Lakes more violent and intense, but it had not been the cause of that conflict—that had been Dunmore's campaign, and the 1768 Treaty of Fort Stanwix. Clark showed that the end of the Revolutionary War would not bring the fighting in the Lakes region to an end. Instead it would consume the Lakes Indians and their white neighbors for another twelve years.

✦ ✦ ✦

The War for American Independence had not affected all parts of the Lakes country equally. For some nations, like the Dakotas and Ojibwas, the war merely meant occasional supply shortages and new opportunities for warriors to earn glory and plunder. For the southern Lakes Indians, however, the conflict too often brought death and destruction. Captain Pipe observed in 1781 that many Indians had died and many "nations have suffered and been weakened." Native American losses are hard to calculate, but the Six Nations of Iroquois sustained hundreds of fatalities in 1779–80, while southern Lakes Indian casualties likely approximated those suffered by white settlers from Kentucky, which lost 860 adult white men between 1776 and 1782. Both sides also lost homes, fields, and livestock, and nearly all the surviving Native

Americans from eastern and central Ohio became refugees in other peoples' homelands.[29]

This bloody conflict grew out of political dynamics similar to those that had produced the war between rebel colonists and Great Britain. Colonial governments and white settlers had taken the sources of the southern Lakes Indians' livelihood and autonomy—namely, their lands—without consulting them, and they had threatened them with force if they did not accept. The Lakes nations rebelled, and like the rebel colonists they did so collectively, with the Shawnees bringing in the Cherokees, the Ohio Iroquois, and the Wyandots. British officials and Loyalist agents then encouraged other Lakes Indians, such as the Anishinaabeg and Miamis, to join the war. Their attacks left a swathe of burned-out farms and grieving families extending down the Ohio valley from Pittsburgh to Louisville and jutting deep into the Kentucky Bluegrass region. Damaging as these raids could be, Lakes Indian warriors found it nearly impossible to seize the fortified stations that white Americans used as refuges. They also found it difficult to stay on the offensive when rebel troops counterattacked their towns or established posts north of the Ohio River, as they did in 1778–79. Thus, the Lakes Indians could not dislodge the tiny white settlements from Kentucky or the upper Ohio valley, and during periods when their raiders stayed home, whites' numbers skyrocketed. By 1780 a stalemate was the best the confederated Indians could expect.

A deadlock they would have. The Lakes Indians' white adversaries had the advantage of growing numbers and martial enthusiasm, growing from Virginians' and Pennsylvanians' long-nourished hatred of Native Americans and association of Indians with the British foe. However, they suffered from many of the same problems the rebels faced on the eastern seaboard: limited manpower; shortages of money and supplies; and the difficulty of convincing the public, in this case the Indian and French population of the Lakes region, that the new American governments deserved their respect. The Ohio River marked the boundary of American power during the Revolutionary War: north of it the Americans could attack, but they could not hold the ground. Fort Laurens lasted less than a year before the Lakes Indians starved out the garrison, and Clark's garrisons in Illinois and Vincennes failed when the local populace ceased to supply them. The tendency of white frontiersmen to regard Indians as a single enemy race and to target neutral or allied Indians for vengeance made it even harder for the rebels to establish local control. American attacks on Cornplanter, George White Eyes, the family of Captain Pipe, the Coshocton Delawares, and the Moravians at Gnadenhutten showed that American friendship brought neither benefits nor protection. As of 1783, when Britain and the United States signed a peace treaty and Britain gave up its territorial claims south of Canada, there was little political authority and no stability in the southern Lakes region.

A revolution, in the modern sense of the word, is a fundamentally destructive event, one that wrecks an old social and political order and replaces it with a new one. In the Great Lakes region, the American Revolution destroyed more than lives and livelihoods: it ended an era in which Native Americans were the predominant regional powers. After the Revolutionary War, the Lakes Indians faced a rapidly swelling American settler population, which would equal their own by the 1790s, and a new "imperial" government, the United States, which proved more aggressive in its pursuit of land than its French and British predecessors. Britain's Native American allies had not suffered a defeat, but proving that point to their white adversaries meant that the war with the Americans was far from over.

7

The United Indians versus the United States

AT THE START OF THE REVOLUTIONARY WAR, THE LAKES INDIANS showed little interest in the rebels' general government. During the 1775 Fort Pitt conference, Indian diplomats referred to American federal commissioners as "Brothers Onas and Long Knife," the names they had long used for the colonies of Pennsylvania and Virginia. Other nations, borrowing a term from British agents, called the Americans "Bostonians," after the city that Britain considered the seat of the rebellion. To Native Americans the former colonists were at best subjects of old colonial governments with whom they had a long-established relationship, not part of a new, independent nation-state.[1]

Later in the war, the southern Lakes Indians encountered more officials and soldiers from the Americans' Continental government and probably began to realize they were dealing with a new political entity. If so, their experiences did not suggest that they should regard the United States as something different from the colonial governments and militias that had been taking their land and destroying their towns.

The Continentals could certainly destroy, as the Six Nations of Iroquois, still recovering from the 1779 Sullivan invasion, could readily attest. However, in the Great Lakes country they proved unable to hold territory, provide for their allies, or protect their friends.

The United States' power did not increase with the end of the war. Its representatives' rhetoric remained fiery, but Congress's military and financial power faded to a shadow. For a time in the 1780s, the southern Lakes country turned into a borderland, in which there were claimants to political power and authority—Kentucky settlers, British commanders in the Great Lakes forts, the local Indian nations—but no dominant group able to protect its constituents from attack. All of the local inhabitants tried to build their strength and influence in the 1780s and '90s, and Native Americans enjoyed some success in filling the political void. Many southern Lakes Indian communities built a new Native American confederacy after the Revolutionary War, a confederacy with a substantial body of warriors and numerous allies.[2]

The United Indians' confederation ultimately collapsed. Its internal cohesion depended on material support from Britain, whose government proved feckless; on the framing of a common territorial policy, on which different subregional factions could not agree; and on continued military success, which its warriors could not always achieve. The main reason for the confederation's dissolution, however, was that the Americans succeeded in building a stronger federation than the Lakes Indians, a consequence of the federal Constitution of 1787 and the replacement of the feeble Congress with a more powerful fiscal-military state. This new government had sufficient funds and manpower to emulate the old French and British regimes of the colonial era, but its intractable demand for Indian land meant that the United States would use the sword as often as the calumet. Despite some devastating early military reversals, the army that held that sword would soon prove a formidable foe.[3]

❖ ❖ ❖

The end of the Revolutionary War found the United States government behaving just as belligerently toward its Native American neighbors as France had done in the 1750s and Britain in the early 1760s. After

1783, Continental officials perplexed and alienated the Lakes Indians by asserting the United States had defeated Britain's Indian allies in battle and therefore had the right to dictate peace terms and take Native American land. At the 1784 Fort Stanwix treaty, conference federal commissioners called the Six Nations "a subdued people." A few months later, at Fort McIntosh, Pennsylvania, these commissioners informed 460 Anishinaabeg, Delawares, and Wyandots that the United States claimed their "country by conquest" and would destroy them if they didn't come to terms. During the 1786 Fort Finney conference with the Shawnees, war captain Kekewepellethe (Captain Johnny) declared that the Shawnees could not cede land because "God gave us this country." He gave American commissioners a monitory black wampum string, which Richard Butler contemptuously flung back on the table, warning the Shawnees to surrender, or else. The Lakes Indian leaders who attended these treaties might have found them merely insulting if the Americans had not brought soldiers to the negotiations, if they had not obliged the signatories to surrender hostages until they returned all their captives, and if they had not demanded a thirty-million-acre land cession north and west of the Ohio River. By the time the conferences had all ended, the Native American signatories had come to view the treaties as high-handed and unjust.[4]

They probably also found the treaties baffling because they asserted a level of coercive power the United States did not, in fact, possess. The US government's claim to sovereignty over the Lakes Indians grew out of the 1783 Treaty of Paris, whereby Great Britain ceded to the United States its claim to the lands south of the Great Lakes and east of the Mississippi River. The treaty did not mention, however, that Britain's authority over the Lakes region had always been nominal, that the Americans had never won a decisive victory over the Lakes Indians, and that the United States government, bereft of money and soldiers, had significantly weakened by 1783. The United States still owed more than $50 million to its creditors, and lacking the ability to collect taxes, it had only one asset it could sell to repay that debt: Native American land. Virginia and other states with western land claims transferred their claims between Kentucky and the Great Lakes to Congress by 1784. Congress named the region "the Territory North and West of the

River Ohio," and in two federal ordinances (1784–85) guaranteed eventual statehood for white residents and the orderly survey and sale of the territory's lands. These provisions would attract white settlers and, thus, customers at the land office. Congress then chose to take a large parcel of Lakes Indian land within the new territory for the benefit of its creditors. It claimed that this land was an indemnity "for the enormities which [the Indians] have perpetrated," giving them no compensation besides a nominal quantity of gifts and rations. There was a hint of desperation in the demand: the US government had to take the southern Lakes Indians' lands by force because it lacked the means to pay them, but it also lacked the means to raise an army to enforce the seizure.[5]

The US government did have one source of potential strength, but it was a troubling and dangerous one: the rapidly swelling population of the district of Kentucky, directly adjacent to Congress's Northwest Territory. In 1780 there were three thousand adult white men and an additional three to six thousand women, children, and African American slaves in Kentucky. By 1790, that number had swelled to seventy-nine thousand, more than the number of Native Americans in the Great Lakes region. They came through the Cumberland Gap and by flatboat down the Ohio River, whereon US Army officers observed up to four thousand settlers passing Fort Harmar every month. Their male leaders wanted to obtain farmland and the independence and dignity that came from holding real estate, crucial in a republic where voting often depended on land ownership. At least some of them were willing to fight Indians for that land, as wartime experiences and propaganda had persuaded them that Indians were an enemy race. In the event of armed conflict, they could serve the US War Department as a militia reserve.[6]

The problem for federal officials, though, was that white settlers in Kentucky, like their Indian neighbors, had little use for or fear of the federal government. They resented the United States' engrossment of the lands north of the Ohio River and some acted, extralegally, on their resentment. In 1785, Kekewepellethe informed American emissaries that there were squatters living north and west of the Ohio River, "drawing so close to us that we can almost hear the noise of your axes." Since federal troops seemed more interested in guarding federal land than protecting white settlers, Kentuckians gave them little respect; indeed, they were openly hostile to the commissioners sent to negotiate with the Shawnees in 1785–86. White settlers had no more respect for Congress, especially after Spain closed the Mississippi River, the outlet for Kentucky farmers' produce, to American shipping, and Congress considered signing a treaty that would have closed the river for another twenty-five years. While never ratified, the Jay-Gardoqui treaty triggered a bitter debate in Congress and persuaded some Kentuckians to consider secession from the Union.[7]

The Lakes Indians proved equally ill-disposed toward the American general government. In 1785 a British Indian agent noted that the region's Native Americans did not consider themselves conquered peoples and had "unanimously determined to support their right to the country." The following year, the Miamis and many of the Shawnees concluded there was no reason to maintain the 1783 cease-fire and began raiding flatboats on the Ohio River and farmsteads in Kentucky. Some of the warriors wanted glory or plunder or horses, but most also wanted to slow or stop the invasion of their homeland. Their leaders saw the raiding campaign as a "coup," a blow against the Americans that displayed the Lakes Indians' martial strength and united resolve. In the wake of that year's raids, leaders from several Lakes nations met near Detroit and drafted a message to Congress on behalf of the "United Indian Nations," offering the United States peace if they met certain conditions: suspend settlements north of the Ohio River, and conduct no more treaties unless representatives from all the Lakes nations attended them. "If fresh ruptures ensue," the confederates warned, "we . . . shall most assuredly, with our united force, be obliged to defend those rights and privileges . . . transmitted to us by our ancestors."[8]

The confederation's leaders probably drafted their speech with the aid of Mohawk war captain Joseph Brant. After the Revolutionary War, Brant persuaded the British Indian department to purchase a reserve for their Iroquois allies on the Grand River. The Grand River valley afforded its new residents a nearly idyllic refuge: abundant timber, a large freshwater fishery, and fertile farmland. By the late 1780s, over eighteen hundred Iroquois, Delawares, and Mohicans made their homes in the reserve, and its principal town, Ohsweken, featured a school, a church, and the spacious home of Brant and his family. However, neither Brant nor his compatriots turned their backs on their former kinfolk south of the Lakes, and some urged the southern Lakes Indians to maintain a united front against the Americans. Brant's British allies also provided aid and encouragement to the United Indians. Britain had refused to surrender eight forts on the American side of the new international boundary, declaring it would hold them until the United States fulfilled its obligations under the peace treaty. From these posts, including Detroit and Mackinac Island, garrison commanders distributed gifts and supplies to the Lakes Indians, to the tune of £20,000 (about $3.1 million in modern currency) annually.[9]

British and Francophone fur traders used the same posts as operational bases from which they could supply their Indian customers. One of the principal firms at Detroit, the Miamis Company, melded the capital of several British merchants with the labor and personal connections of French traders, who did business with the Sandusky Wyandots, the Shawnee towns on the Mad River, the Miamis at Kekionga, and the Weas and Piankeshaws near Vincennes. Business south of the Great Lakes flagged in the mid-1780s, as mild winters made it harder for Indian hunters to track their quarry, but the animal population prospered and the peltry and meat trade revived with colder weather by 1790. Some of the Miamis Company's partners buffered themselves against such temporary losses by building more extensive trading networks, covering a larger swath of the Lakes region. John Askin, in particular, opened stores at Mackinac and Sault Sainte Marie, and by the late 1790s he had a small fleet of ships on the Great Lakes. If Lakes Indian military leaders took a hard line against the United States, they did so in part because their British allies enjoyed more military power and commercial reach than the Americans did.[10]

They may also have calculated that the Americans, short of public funds and military resources, could not mount a very vigorous response to the 1786 offensive. George Rogers Clark did manage to organize a militia expedition against the Wea settlements at Ouiatenon, but his men mutinied shortly after leaving Vincennes. Benjamin Logan could raise troops only for an assault on the neutral Mekoche Shawnees, the principal signatories of the Fort Finney Treaty. His attack, designed to secure prisoners for exchange and exact vengeance for previous raids, succeeded in taking captives and destroying the Shawnee towns on the Mad River, but it also killed chief Molunthy, one of the Shawnees' principal peace advocates, cut down even after he gave the Kentuckians a flag and his copy of the treaty.[11]

Subsequent Kentucky militia offensives proved no more effective in distinguishing between neutral Indians and confederates. A 1787 raid destroyed the last Shawnee town on the Scioto River shortly after Daniel Boone had negotiated a truce, and two more expeditions in 1788 and 1789 killed Piankeshaw Indians from neutral towns. These raids persuaded many neutral Indians that the United States could not or would not protect them from its own citizens. "[We] doubt that you are carrying on a confederacy with these people that strike us every now and then," Delaware and Wyandot leaders told American officials in 1787. Some ex-neutrals joined the United Indian confederacy for their own protection. Others decided to seek the protection of Spain, moving (as some Miamis did) to the Arkansas valley or joining Shawnee and Delaware migrants in Missouri. Many more Lakes Indians would follow their example in decades to come.[12]

As Kentucky settlers and the confederated Lakes Indians fought their bitter war of raid and retaliation, the feeble United States government slowly insinuated itself into the Ohio valley. A small regiment of US troops set up forts on the Muskingum River (Fort Harmar) and at Vincennes and Cincinnati (Forts Knox and Washington), which served as de facto trading posts and diplomatic centers for Indian visitors. Army officers also on occasion visited nearby Indian encampments, dined with chiefs, watched young men play lacrosse, and joined Native American men and women in their ring dances. Meanwhile, in New York, Congress passed the 1787 Northwest Ordinance, thereby extending an offer of legal protection to all of the inhabitants of the Lakes country. The ordinance guaranteed the civil and property rights of whites and the land claims of Native Americans, excepting only Indian lands taken in "just and lawful wars authorized by Congress." It also, however, ensured that white settlers would dominate the judicial and political systems of the western territory, creating law-enforcement bodies—namely, juries and militias—that local whites would control, and creating territorial legislatures and independent state governments when particular territories reached threshold populations (sixty thousand free inhabitants for statehood). The ordinance was a practical consequence of the American Revolution, an event whose upheavals made whites wary of buying or settling land in regions without a local government, and unwilling to surrender republican self-government for long. It ensured, however, that the same frontiersmen who despised Indians would have considerable control over their lives and lands.[13]

Settler sovereignty still lay decades in the future. Initial control of the Northwest Territory's government and Indian relations lay in the hands of territorial governor Arthur St. Clair, who in the fall of 1787 accepted (at Congress's direction) the United Indians' proposal for a general treaty council. St. Clair took a year to stockpile supplies and send invitations to various Indian nations, but he and five hundred Iroquois and Lakes Indians finally kindled their council fire at Fort Harmar in December 1788. After several weeks of public speeches and private negotiation, the governor and leaders from Anishinaabe, Delaware, Sauk, and Wyandot communities signed the Treaty of Fort Harmar (January 9, 1789). The agreement extended the huge Fort McIntosh treaty cession, for which the new signatories would now receive $6,000 worth of goods, the right to hunt on the ceded lands, and the right to punish white intruders on their remaining territory.[14]

Despite its pretensions of friendship, the Fort Harmar treaty proved deeply controversial, and nearly all of the Lakes Indians considered it dead on arrival. Some Shawnees and Miamis spread the rumor beforehand that St. Clair planned to poison the conferees or murder them with infected blankets. Some of the conferees claimed afterward that the governor had compelled them to sign the treaty by withholding their rations until they complied. Even if St. Clair didn't plan to kill or starve his counterparts, he did refuse to compromise with them, rejecting Wyandot chief Shandotte's counterproposal to limit the cession to the lands east of the Muskingum River. Instead, he asserted that the terms he offered were the best a conquered people like the Lakes Indians should expect, and he made veiled threats of war if they didn't consent to the much larger cession he demanded.[15]

Small wonder, then, that most of the Lakes Indians believed the Fort Harmar treaty had created no peace at all. In the spring of 1789, Miami and Shawnee warriors resumed their offensive against the Americans, attacking flatboats on the Ohio River, farms in Kentucky, and surveyors north of the Ohio. Their attacks resumed in 1790, when Odawa and Potawatomi warriors joined the raiding parties. The state of Virginia pleaded to the United States government for aid, and one Kentucky judge estimated that his district's total casualties since 1783 had reached fifteen hundred people.[16]

The American federal government was, by now, willing and able to counterattack the southern Lakes Indians. In 1787–88, a federal convention had framed and state ratifying conventions had approved a new national constitution, which gave the US government much larger powers than it had previously enjoyed. These included the exclusive power to make treaties, as well as the authority to raise an army, mobilize the state militias, and raise or borrow sufficient money to pay for war. In the summer of 1789, as the Miami-Shawnee offensive continued, Secretary of War Henry Knox recommended that President Washington try one more time to conclude a land-cession treaty with the "Wabash" Indians. If they refused to treat, however, or broke any treaty they had signed, "the principles of justice and even humanity" would authorize use of the United States' war powers against them. In September, Congress began mobilizing those powers, authorizing Arthur St. Clair to request militia from Pennsylvania and Virginia. Six months later, St. Clair's emissary, Antoine Gamelin, went to the Indian towns on the Wabash to extend one more olive branch.[17]

Gamelin did not succeed. The Kickapoos, Miamis, and Shawnees whom he met greeted him with suspicion. One told him that "I see . . . none but the Big Knife is sending speeches to us." They indicated that their warriors' raids would stop when the American intruders moved back across the Ohio River. For the Shawnees, who still mourned the loss of Kentucky, an Ohio River boundary represented a real concession, but the US government did not accept it as such; it wanted confirmation of the Fort Harmar Treaty cession. Arthur St. Clair informed Washington that the Wabash Indians had effectively "declar[ed] that they will continue their hostilities." The time had come for the United

States to respond in kind. St. Clair and General Josiah Harmar began assembling a force to subdue the Wabash Indians: five hundred regulars and militia to attack the Kickapoo and Wea towns on the Wabash River, and fifteen hundred troops to destroy Kekionga, the complex of Miami and Shawnee towns at the Wabash-Maumee portage, which one American officer called "the residence of all the renegade Indians."[18]

The Americans' 1790 campaign came to no good end, mainly because the Indian defenders had higher morale and better leadership than their foes. The smaller division of the American force made it only a short distance out of Vincennes before the troops mutinied. The larger contingent did reach Kekionga in October, and it plundered and burned six towns, but several hundred warriors under captains Blue Jacket (Shawnee) and Little Turtle (Miami) attacked detachments of Harmar's army and killed or wounded 250 men. Harmar's defeat, or (as one should call it) the Battle of Kekionga, might have been even more decisive if the United Indians had decided to pursue the demoralized army. However, a powerful omen, namely, a full lunar eclipse, warned Odawa warriors that a pursuit would go badly for them, and they decided to go home, thus allowing the Americans to escape. Other members of the confederation, now joined by enthusiastic Delaware and Wyandot warriors, decided to build on their earlier success with a winter counteroffensive. They raided or destroyed several American settlements on the Muskingum and Great Miami Rivers. A limited punitive campaign had become, for the United States, a much larger frontier war.[19]

At least Josiah Harmar's men had demonstrated that the US Army could travel 170 miles from its operational base and land a blow on the Northwest Indians. A better-prepared campaign might succeed where Harmar's had failed. Congress and President Washington in early 1791 authorized a multipart attack on the Wabash Indians, which commenced after another half-hearted and fruitless peace mission by federal emissaries Thomas Proctor and Hendrick Aupaumut. (Neither made it much further than the Niagara River.) In the summer, mounted Kentucky militia raided the lower Wabash, destroying seven Kickapoo and Miami towns and taking about sixty prisoners. The main event, however, would be a second attack on Kekionga and occupation of the

Maumee-Wabash portage. This would lead to a glorious victory—for the United Indians.[20]

The Kekionga expedition's commander, Governor St. Clair, spent the summer marshaling his troops: two regiments of regular infantry, over a thousand volunteers and militia, and a few Chickasaw scouts. The governor devoted much of early autumn to building forts along his line of march, significantly slowing the army's advance. Illness, desertions, and expired enlistments reduced St. Clair's army to fourteen hundred men, who were encamped on St. Marys Creek (ninety miles north of Cincinnati) on the morning of November 4, 1791. On that day, one thousand Delaware, Miami, and Shawnee warriors enveloped and smashed the American army in what would become the greatest blow ever inflicted on a European or American army by Native Americans. The confederates, unburdened by heavy equipment and long supply lines, had moved rapidly against St. Clair's army, and their scouts had monitored the general's men for several days. When the warriors attacked, they displayed not only great courage (they "seemed not to fear anything we could do," recalled one eyewitness) but considerable tactical skill, using the woods for cover and deliberately targeting the army's officers and artillerists. The warriors' marksmanship and battle cries, which Winthrop Sargent recalled sounding like "an infinitude of horse bells," helped rout the Americans' militia. By the time St. Clair rallied his regulars and broke out of the Lakes Indians' encirclement, nine hundred of his men had been killed or wounded. The survivors, their morale destroyed, abandoned their equipment and artillery on the battlefield.[21]

The confederated warriors rejoiced in their victory, painting the saplings around the battlefield with red pictograms memorializing their feat of arms. Many salvaged American equipment and repurposed it: a prisoner recalled one warrior wearing two pocket watches as earrings, and Little Turtle reported that the army's "camp kettles" later served Indian women as sugaring kettles. Others buried the cannons they had forced St. Clair to abandon, hoping they might prove useful in the event of another confrontation with the Americans.[22]

News of the battle spread shock, fear, and anger through white American communities. When those initial emotions faded, white

Americans debated the best response to St. Clair's defeat. Editors and Congressmen from southern states wanted to crush the United Indian confederacy once and for all. New Englanders generally blamed the defeat on frontiersmen's land hunger and St. Clair's incompetence, and they wanted to negotiate. President Washington and Secretary Knox, in consultation with other Cabinet secretaries, decided to follow both tracks. In February 1792, Congress voted to raise taxes and to raise a much larger, professional army—five thousand men, larger than Harmar's and St. Clair's armies combined. The new Legion of the United States, under the command of Anthony Wayne, spent the next two years training and organizing. In the meantime, Knox sent a squadron of diplomats to the Great Lakes to negotiate a peace settlement. These included John Hardin and Alexander Trueman, who brought peace messages to the Wyandots and the Wabash Shawnees; territorial judge Rufus Putnam, who organized a treaty with the lower Wabash Indians and Illiniwek; and Hendrick Aupaumut and several Seneca chiefs, who attended the United Indians' council at Auglaize and invited them to a new treaty with the United States.[23]

The American diplomatic offensive proved a comprehensive failure. Some of the emissaries never made it to their destinations: Wyandot warriors killed Hardin and Trueman before they reached the upper Wabash. Some Indians met with American emissaries but refused to negotiate with them. Such was the case with the warriors attending the council at Auglaize, a large complex of towns and fields on the Maumee River to which the Wabash confederates had moved. In the fall of 1792, about two thousand Indians, including Sauks and Mesquakies from the western Lakes country and Creeks and Cherokees from the southeast, attended a confederate council there. Most of the Indian speakers at the Auglaize conference flatly rejected any cession of lands north of the Ohio River. The victory of November 1791, they argued, was not the product of good luck but a judgment by the Master of Life in favor of his Indian children, and the Senecas were mere tools of the "Town Destroyer" Washington if they believed the Lakes Indians should make any concessions. Even those who favored negotiation told Aupaumut they trusted neither the United States' intentions nor its ability to control its own settlers. Joseph Brant, who had met with

Washington and Henry Knox earlier this year, warned the confederates not to trust the "smooth" talking president.[24]

Rufus Putnam's September 1792 conference with the Illiniwek, Kickapoos, and Potawatomis saw less acrimony, though its political impact proved ambiguous. Putnam went to some trouble to conciliate the Indians who joined him in Vincennes: he met with more than thirty chiefs and matrons, distributed several tons of food and clothing to them and their seven hundred followers, and returned the prisoners of the 1791 Kentucky militia raid. The chiefs and matrons were politer than the Auglaize conferees but equally determined to keep their land. Many concurred with Kaskaskia chief Jean-Baptiste Ducoigne, who observed that the French had been charitable and "never took our lands from us" and said he "should have been glad if matters had remained as they were in the days of the French." This romanticized account of the recent past offered Putnam a model to follow: after pointing out that the Lakes Indians had in fact given land to the French for their farms, Judge Putnam negotiated a compromise proposal that let the Americans keep their existing settlements north of the Ohio River. This opened the way to a peace treaty declaring, unusually, that the Illinois and lower Wabash Indians had an unrestricted right to sell their land. This peculiar clause killed the treaty: the US Senate, believing that Putnam's accord gave too much leeway to the Indians, refused to ratify it. Judge Putnam's mission wasn't a debacle, since the Lakes Indians believed that the exchange of speeches and sentiments at a treaty council outweighed the document it produced, but it disappointed the Washington administration.[25]

In 1793, President Washington made one last attempt to negotiate with the United Indians. He sent three emissaries to Sandusky to meet leaders of the confederation, discuss with them the unfortunate recent history of US Indian relations, and offer them concessions: up to $50,000 and another $10,000 per year for validation of the Fort Harmar cession. Initially the commissioners met with a friendly reception. Joseph Brant and several Lakes Indian leaders met them at Niagara to exchange greetings and hopes for a successful negotiation. When, however, commissioners Benjamin Lincoln, Timothy Pickering, and Beverley Randolph reached the home of Indian agent Matthew Elliott (modern Amherstburg, Ontario), they received a much cooler reception. Kekewepellethe, Buckongehelas (Delaware), and other delegates from the United Indian council met the Americans and demanded, politely but firmly, that the Americans remove all of their settlements north of the Ohio River. When the dismayed officials replied that this was impossible and offered the Lakes Indians material compensation, the United Indians sent back an ultimatum. They would accept no payment for their lands because "money to us is of no value," while land brought independence and power. The United States, they suggested, should use its money to pay for the evacuation of its settlers. They also chastised the Americans for their arrogant tone. "You seem to expect that because you have at last acknowledged our independence"—by treating with all of the Lakes Indians together—"we should for a favor surrender to you our country." While they preferred peace, the confederates declared they would continue the war rather than yield an Ohio River boundary.[26]

The very different receptions that the Americans received at Niagara and at Elliott's farm corresponded to a factional split in the United Indians' confederation. Some of the confederates, in particular the Anishinaabeg and some of the Wyandots, were willing to accept American settlements north of the Ohio provided the United States accepted a western territorial boundary on the Muskingum River. A more militant, or at least more injured faction, comprising Delawares, Miamis, Shawnees, and the rest of the Wyandots, would offer no such concessions. They believed that their military victories in 1790–91 demonstrated the favor of the Master of Life, and they wanted not peace but independence, which rested on their preservation of an inviolate homeland north of the Ohio.[27]

The United Indians' triumphalist faction also believed that the king of Britain was on their side and would come to their aid if the war with the United States continued. British officials had in fact become increasingly supportive of the United Indian confederacy since the late 1780s, though they had not united behind a single policy. Lord Grenville, the British foreign secretary, endorsed a proposal made by moderate Lakes Indian confederates in 1791, which would have created a neutral Indian homeland bounded by the Great Lakes, the Muskingum River, and the

Ohio. Indian agents Matthew Elliott and Andrew McKee encouraged the confederates to take a harder line and reject any American settlements north of the Ohio River; they provided the United Indians with provisions, weapons, and black wampum (for war belts). Other British colonial officials came to support the more radical confederates during an Anglo-American war scare in 1793–94. Canadian governor Guy Carleton, Lord Dorchester, told Canadian Iroquois that the Lakes Indians might be able to recover their lands in the event of war between the United States and Britain, while in April John Simcoe, lieutenant governor of Upper Canada, built a new fort at the rapids of the Maumee River.[28]

The Americans' own warlike preparations had advanced far. In 1793 General Wayne established his headquarters near Fort Washington, cut a military road northward, and began stockpiling supplies at advanced deposit posts. Late that year he moved his headquarters to Greenville and built a new fort on the site of Saint Clair's defeat, Fort Recovery. This strongpoint became the rock that broke the United Indian confederates' military strength. Secretary Knox had meanwhile informed Wayne of the failure of the 1793 treaty commission and bid him prepare "to make those audacious savages feel our superiority in arms."[29]

The Lakes Indians had, with a few small exceptions, generally kept the peace with the United States since their victory over St. Clair. In the spring of 1794, however, with Wayne's army ready to march and Britain preparing for a possible war with the United States, the confederates decided to strike the first blow against the new American army. About eleven hundred Anishinaabe, Delaware, Miami, Shawnee, and Wyandot warriors marched south from the Maumee River to attack Wayne's army. Reaching Fort Recovery in late June, the captains decided that they could not leave such a well-defended post in their rear and resolved to destroy it or force out the garrison. The United Indians managed to kill or wound fifty Americans and barrage the stockade for two days, but the fort's defenders held out. Those who recalled the battle against Arthur St. Clair tried to locate the cannons they had buried three years earlier, but Wayne had found the guns and moved them into the fort.[30]

After two days the attackers withdrew, and their army came apart. Half of the United Indian warriors were Odawas and Ojibwas, and their nations disagreed with the southern Lakes Indians on the need for a long war. Moreover, a party of Anishinaabeg had plundered several towns on the Maumee River in early June, and in retaliation Delaware and Shawnee men fired on them during the engagement at Fort Recovery. The Anishinaabe warriors decided that they had discharged their obligation to their confederates, and most of them returned home. Other Indian participants in the battle broke into smaller parties to raid American posts and farms further south, leaving only a few hundred to return north and defend the confederacy's towns.[31]

The federal legion confronting them was the strongest force the Americans had ever fielded west of the Appalachian Mountains. Anthony Wayne commanded an army of well-trained regular troops, leavened with a few hundred mounted militia from Kentucky. The army had adequate funds and supplies, drawing provisions from the growing towns of Pittsburgh and Cincinnati and horses and cattle from American farms in Kentucky. It also had a much easier road to travel than earlier expeditions, thanks to Wayne's road building and the chain of forts he and St. Clair had built along its line of march. These comprised a new salient of American power into the Lakes country, projecting north from and anchored by the first salient (the Ohio River). When in late July the American army marched north from Greenville, it took less than two weeks to reach Auglaize, where the soldiers quickly occupied the evacuated towns of the United Indians. General Wayne sent the confederation's warriors, who had moved down the Maumee River, a final warning to surrender, but they refused, believing that the nearby British garrison would come to their aid.[32]

This proved a fatal miscalculation. On August 20, Wayne's force of fifteen hundred regulars and militia ran into the remaining five hundred United Indian warriors at Fallen Timbers, five miles from British-held Fort Miami. After a short, intense battle, American bayonets and cavalry broke the Indians' defensive line, and the warriors retreated, seeking shelter with the British. Not wanting to provoke the Americans, however, the commandant of Fort Miami closed his gates against his Native allies, forcing them to disperse. With United Indian opposition at an end and the British "compelled to remain tacit spectators," Wayne ordered his men to destroy British storehouses outside of the fort, and then to march back to Auglaize, destroying cornfields and houses "for about fifty miles on each side of the" Maumee River. Thereafter the legion advanced to Kekionga and began constructing a strongpoint, which their commander named Fort Wayne.[33]

Further resistance at this point would have been difficult and almost certainly futile. While their casualties had been light, most of the confederated warriors had dispersed or returned home, and Wayne's American troops had destroyed their food supply and occupied their towns. British military assistance was clearly not forthcoming, and in fact Britain that fall signed a new treaty with the United States, Jay's Treaty, which obliged British troops to evacuate their forts south of the Great Lakes. Some warriors wanted to continue the fight, but most realized that the time had come to sue for peace.[34]

In the summer of 1795, over one thousand Lakes Indians came to Greenville, the army's headquarters—a location to which the confederates agreed under duress—to meet with the conqueror. General Wayne behaved with civility and ceremony, smoking the calumet with Indian leaders and adorning his speeches with peaceful metaphors, but he declined to offer generous terms. He demanded that the Lakes Indians confirm the Fort Harmar cession (two-thirds of modern Ohio), cede several hundred square miles in southeastern Indiana, and give up several military reservations on their side of the boundary line. In return, the US government would pay $20,000 in gifts and a $9,500 annuity, parceled out among the thirteen signatory nations in roughly equal proportions.[35]

Few of the Lakes Indians protested the United States' terms; few found themselves in any position to refuse. The only persistent opponent of the proposed cession, Little Turtle, made limited claims and demands. Setting aside other Indian nations' interests, he denied that the Miamis had ever sold land to France, Britain, or the United States, and he proposed a nominal reduction of the cession by 1.5 million acres— five percent of what the US government demanded. Wayne refused. The other Indian nations, the general observed, stood ready to accept the Americans' deal. Those other nations' leaders saw the Greenville council less as a negotiation than as the start of a new, postconfederate political era. One prominent speaker, Tarhe (The Crane), a Wyandot war captain wounded at Fallen Timbers, used the conference as an opportunity to instruct the Americans in the arts of interethnic peace. The American government wished to act as the Lakes Indians' father, Tarhe noted, but "an impartial father equally regards all his children . . . therefore, if any of your children come to you crying, and in distress, have pity on them, and relieve their wants." The United States had proven its strength, but if it wanted to replace France and Britain, it would have to supply the Indians and resolve their disputes.[36]

Wayne agreed that his government wanted a paternal relationship with the Lakes Indians. Neither he nor his superiors, however, acknowledged that this relationship would evolve in a sociopolitical context increasingly unfavorable to Native Americans. The Treaty of Greenville and Britain's evacuation of its forts triggered a surge of white American migration across the Ohio River. By the end of 1796, American settlers had established the villages of Chillicothe, Cleveland, and Youngstown, all well north of the Ohio. Thousands more would follow, bearing axes and ploughs and cattle, determined to reshape the landscape. Clearly, the Americans had come to the Lakes Indians' homeland to stay—and most had come not to trade with or rule over Native peoples, but to replace them.[37]

+ + +

In the early post-Revolutionary years, the Great Lakes Indians saw little difference between the new American Union and the Big Knives who had harried them for the preceding twenty years. The US government's representatives made extravagant demands for land, threatened violence at treaty councils, built forts and settlements in disputed territory, and, when other forms of intimidation failed, sent their troops to destroy Native American towns. They noticed another striking similarity between the Thirteen Fires and the Big Knives: both made extravagant claims of authority and promises of protection that they could not enforce. Until the mid-1790s, the United States' actual jurisdiction extended no further than its forts on the Ohio River; Molunthy's signature on the Treaty of Fort Finney could not protect him from Kentucky militia, any more than John Hardin and Alexander Trueman's peace commission protected them from suspicious Wyandot warriors.

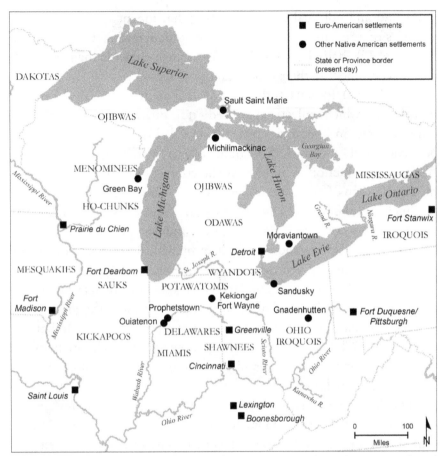

MAP 2. Native Americans and newcomers, 1810 CE. *Map by Brian Edward Balsley, GISP*

The withdrawal of Britain, the weakness of the United States, and the disruption of many Lakes Indian communities during the Revolutionary War all created a political vacuum in the southern Lakes country. Warriors and captains tried to fill it by building a confederacy, a more durable version of the alliance their predecessors had created during Pontiac's War. The new United Indian confederation had frequent conferences, a military "capital" of sorts—first Kekionga, then Auglaize—a helpful if ambivalent British ally, and sympathizers among the southeastern Indians. It also had a definite goal, namely, maintenance of its members' collective independence and the collective homeland and political unity sustaining that independence. After the victories of 1790 and 1791, some of the confederates believed that the Master of Life had blessed their enterprise, which made them less willing to accommodate their American opponents.[38]

The United Indians suffered, unfortunately, from three political weaknesses, which collectively proved fatal. First, the member nations did not agree on how much land they needed to maintain their independence, and how much they could cede to the rapacious Americans. A substantial faction believed that the confederates could safely cede the lands north of the Ohio and east of the Muskingum, and this faction included the Ojibwas and Odawas, nations whose settlements the Americans did not immediately threaten, and who also committed only halfway to the United Indians' final campaign. Second, the confederates' British allies proved unwilling to fight for the Native American allies they had armed and encouraged. Canadian officials supported the creation of an Indian buffer state, but their ultimate goal was to protect Canada from the United States, not guarantee Lakes Indian independence. When an American army forced them to choose between defending their Indian allies and protecting their own colony, British officers chose the latter.

Third, the United Indians, unlike Pontiac's confederacy or the factions who challenged the French in the 1740s, faced a more implacable foe than imperial Britain or France. The United States' empire was more compact than its European predecessors, its centers of military and political power stood much closer to the Lakes country than London or Paris, and its financial resources were secure. Between the tariffs the Treasury collected in American seaports and the interest-bearing bonds Congress introduced in 1790, the War Department was able to raise the $2.5 million needed to recruit, train, supply, and field Anthony Wayne's army. Moreover, that army, which could draw on the farms of Pennsylvania and Kentucky for support, faced fewer of the supply problems that stymied European armies. In 1784, the United States surely appeared to the Lakes Indians as the weakest imperial power that had sought dominion over the Great Lakes. Just ten years later it had built the largest colonial settlements and strongest military presence the region had yet seen—and its power was not about to decline.[39]

8

Survival and Nation Building on the Edge of Empire

SINCE THE PRE-COLUMBIAN ERA, HISTORICAL CHANGE HAD generally occurred in the Great Lakes region on two different levels, each with its own tempo. On one level, and on a time scale measured in years, warriors and soldiers fought their battles, traders and merchants sold their wares, and elites argued, negotiated, and built their monuments. On another, deeper level, at a pace measurable in decades or centuries, populations moved and grew, trading patterns shifted, and Indian peoples adopted new ways of making a living. The two levels seldom affected one another. In the late eighteenth century, the American Revolution and the United Indian War had brought upheaval and warfare to the Lakes country, but these events had only a limited impact on most Lakes Indians' lifeways. Native Americans' subsistence calendar changed little between 1775 and 1805, and for most people these decades brought little social change apart from a continuation of developments that had begun earlier: the increased use of European clothing, metal wares, and alcohol by the northern Lakes Indians, and the adoption of commercial farming by their southern neighbors.[1]

Sometimes these slow cultural changes became politically rele-
vant and affected the actions of warriors and leaders. Not all Lakes
Indians supported intensified trade and the adoption of European customs, and periodically, as for example during Pontiac's War, cultural
discontent merged with broader opposition to imperial policies. This
occurred in the first decade of the nineteenth century, when the Shawnee prophet Tenskwatawa and his charismatic brother Tecumseh organized a nativist religious revival that turned into a political movement.
The new nativists wanted to reverse the Lakes Indians' march toward
European-style "civilization" and an interdependent relationship with
the Americans and to reestablish an independent destiny for Native
Americans. Increasingly this meant that Tenskwatawa and his allies
sought to create a separate nation-state where the writ of the American
government and of accommodating chiefs did not run, a state with its
own armed force and inviolable territorial boundaries.

This necessarily put the nativist confederacy at odds with those
Lakes Indian leaders, like Black Hoof, who favored a cooperative relationship with the United States and the development of more "civilized,"
which is to say more economically diversified, Indian communities. It
also set them against American officials who had their own incom-
patible plan of nation building, one that involved restricting Indians'
independence, covering their territory with roads and forts, buying up
their lands, and assimilating them into the white population. Political
conflicts, because they are ultimately disputes about power, can lead
to violence, and when some or all of the parties to that conflict do not
consider one another legitimately self-governing nations, violence is almost inevitable. Such was the case here: enmity between the nativists
and American officials ignited another interethnic war, the fourth that
the region had seen since Pontiac's War, a conflict that augmented white
Americans' fears of Indians while demonstrating to them their growing
ability to defeat Indians on the battlefield. Long-term cultural changes,
it seemed, could have explosive short-term political consequences.

✦ ✦ ✦

At the Treaty of Greenville in 1795, Anthony Wayne had promised that
the American national government would replace France and Britain

as the Lakes Indians' "father," their provider, mediator, and regional superintendent. Actually, it would take some time before the US government could manifest itself as anything more than a weak and ineffectual political parent. The American diplomatic successes of 1794 and 1795 had, ironically, compelled the United States to expand its authority into a region, the shorelands of the upper Great Lakes, too large for it to police or govern. Jay's Treaty allowed, and American suspicion of the British required, American troops to occupy Detroit and Mackinac, just as the Greenville treaty was removing the justification for a large garrison force in the Northwest Territory. Secretary of War Pickering persuaded Congress to support a peace establishment of several thousand men, but these now had to spread themselves from Niagara to Mackinac to Illinois. Civilian officials had to cover an equally large area with even fewer resources.[2]

The weakness of the US government in the Lakes region showed itself most clearly in that government's inability to protect Indians from white settlers after the Treaty of Greenville. The white newcomers concentrated in the future state of Ohio, which twenty years of warfare had cleared of most of its Native American inhabitants. White farmers rapidly resettled this southeastern corner of the Lakes region, concentrating in the Great Miami valley, the Scioto valley, and the Western Reserve (Cleveland), which a Connecticut land company bought from the Mississaugas for a few gifts and a little whiskey. By 1800, the territory that would become Ohio had forty-five thousand white inhabitants, who effectively controlled the territory's law enforcement and thereby held considerable power over local Native Americans. In the late 1790s, territorial courts tried several whites accused of killing or assaulting Indians, and all-white juries acquitted the alleged assailants. Local American settlers, not the national government in Philadelphia, called the shots in this corner of the Lakes region.[3]

West of Ohio, white hunters poached deer, bear, and bison from the federally protected territory of the Miamis and Delawares, and squatters built claim shacks and blazed trees on Native American land. Governor St. Clair responded to these intrusions by dithering and unsuccessfully seeking help from Governor Brown of Kentucky, the intruders' home state. None of St. Clair's superiors in Philadelphia showed interest in helping him enforce the Treaty of Greenville, so he did not. Federal officials also displayed incompetence in distributing the annuities due the Lakes Indians: the annuity goods for the 1799 and 1800 distributions at Fort Wayne arrived late or not at all. This cannot have impressed the Miami and Potawatomi recipients, particularly given their continued interaction with British traders in Ontario, who surely reminded their partners that the new American father did not measure up to his predecessors.[4]

The US War Department began to address some of these problems—specifically, its inability to supply its Lakes Indian clients—during the administration of President Thomas Jefferson, when it expanded the United States' Indian factory system. This network of publicly funded trading posts bought Indians' pelts and other produce at local market rates and sold them European merchandise at below-market prices, in an effort to "secure the friendship of the Indians" and drive foreign traders out of business. The Indian factories[5] had been the brainchild of President Washington, who regarded trade as a way to ensure political loyalty. Congress had approved and funded the first experimental factories in 1796, after a political scandal had demonstrated the vast potential extent of British traders' influence. The previous year, a consortium of Detroit merchants, including John Askin, had purchased from several Odawa and Ojibwa chiefs their peoples' land claims in southern Michigan. The company then sent agents to Philadelphia to bribe members of Congress into selling them, for $500,000, the preemption right to the lower peninsula of Michigan. Congress arrested the agents, and the scheme came to naught, but the episode persuaded American leaders that the British remained dangerous and the Lakes region an actively contested borderland.[6]

American officials opened the first factories in the Northwest in 1802. One of the new posts, in Detroit, could not compete with the British and French traders who had stayed there after Jay's Treaty, and who still shipped several hundred thousand dollars' worth of furs through the town. After several years of anemic business, the secretary of war moved the trading house and such of its stock as survived an 1805 fire to Chicago. Another factory, at Fort Wayne, proved more successful. Within a few years the Miamis, Odawas, and Potawatomis were selling factor John Johnston large quantities of valuable hatters' furs, particularly raccoon skins (nearly twenty-seven thousand in one year), as well as maple sugar, moccasins, and other wares. The Fort Wayne factory also served as a depot for annuity goods and a post for spying on the misfortunes of British traders, whose business suffered during the Napoleonic Wars. Those traders found the factory sufficiently dangerous to their interests that one hired an Indian man to burn it down shortly after opening day. The War Department rebuilt the trading house, and it remained open until 1812.[7]

The War Department opened additional factories at Fort Dearborn near Chicago (1805), Sandusky, Ohio (1806), and Mackinac Island (1809). The Sandusky house purchased moderate quantities of small furs, supplying its Wyandot customers in turn with a sophisticated array of goods, like wine glasses, tin-plated stove pipes for their cabins, and ice skates. Its overall trade proved limited, owing in part to competition from British traders in northwestern Ohio, and the factory's net worth declined by 1811. Mackinac, located at one of the region's oldest trading entrepots, also proved disappointing. Native visitors were few, particularly during the long winters when ice prevented canoes from reaching the island, and the factor wound up selling goods to private traders, who then sold them on their own account to Indian communities on the western Lakes. The Mackinac factor's decision did demonstrate one weakness of the factory system: the fixed locations of the factories. In the northern Lakes country, where traders generally went to meet Indian hunters rather than vice-versa, this proved a big shortcoming.[8]

The War Department could of course move its factories closer to its customers, and apart from the Fort Wayne house, the only factory in the Lakes region that did ample business was one the Indian Trade Office had moved from another, less convenient site. This was the store at Fort Madison, Iowa, established in 1808 for Sauk and Mesquakie hunters who complained that an earlier post near Saint Louis stood too far from their towns. These complaints subsided once the new trading house opened for business. The Sauks and Foxes sold Fort Madison large quantities of peltry, along with a form of produce the other factories had not previously sold: tens of thousands of pounds of lead, from the mines in Illinois and Iowa.[9]

The US factory system was not a large enterprise, but its records help illuminate the livelihoods of Lakes Indians during what was purportedly a time of economic stress. Some historians see the late eighteenth and early nineteenth centuries as a time of resource exhaustion, economic dependence, and demoralization for the Lakes Indians, and for some communities this might have been true. In general, though, Native Americans either experienced continuity in their economic lives—as in the northern Lakes region—or strengthened their subsistence base through diversification, as did the southern Lakes Indians.[10]

In the north country, extending from the latitude of Green Bay to the shorelands of Lake Superior, the economic lives of the Ojibwas, northern Odawas, and eastern Dakotas followed a well-established seasonal round. In the spring and summer, the northern Lakes Indians lived in lakeside villages where they hunted deer and speared or netted fish, including lake sturgeon, trout, and whitefish. Lakes Indian women raised maize, beans, and other crops in ridged-bed fields, though yields often proved low owing to the region's cold climate and short growing season. In late summer (August and September), they harvested northern wild rice, a high-protein wetlands plant. Women gathered this foodstuff by canoeing into clusters of the mature plant and knocking the seeds off the stalks with wooden sticks. They later husked the rice and cooked it with grease to soften it. In October, small bands of fifty or so men, women, and children conducted the winter hunt, during which they trapped or shot bear, beaver, moose, and water fowl. The latter part of winter brought lean times, but in March Anishinaabe and Dakota women went to their sugaring camps to tap maple tree sap and boil it down to sugar, which, mixed with wild rice or corn, provided an important source of late-winter sustenance. With the onset of spring, the northern Lakes Indians returned to their villages to begin the new fishing and deer-hunting season.[11]

The arrival of French and British traders in the northern Lakes had not greatly altered this old cycle. Experienced fur traders generally sent their employees to join the Dakotas and Ojibwas in their winter hunting ranges, where the peddlers plied band leaders with gifts, treated their hosts to rum and fortified wine, and bought hunters' peltry before their competitors could do so. Indians bought in return the tools of the hunter's trade, such as knives and ammunition, as well as textiles, the staples of the eighteenth- and nineteenth-century fur trade. Increasingly, northern Lakes Indians bought and consumed alcohol, but they did so at particular times, like the end of fishing season, the wild rice harvest, or the start of the winter hunt, periods when food was plentiful and men and women were burning many calories. The Anishinaabeg and Dakotas treated liquor like a foodstuff and diplomatic good; indeed, the Ojibwas referred to it as "milk," an epitome of the kinship bond that trade created, and often refused to start trading sessions without it. The other commodities that the upper Lakes Indians purchased had similar analogues in their old material culture: one could compare firearms to bows, woven cloth to tanned pelts, metal blades to stone ones. They were efficient and convenient, but not revolutionary. Indeed, the northern Lakes Indians sometimes retained older technologies, like bows and arrows, to help preserve their economic autonomy.[12]

One should not imagine this was an idyllic life. Feasting and fellowship represented only part of the seasonal cycle; they alternated with long periods of scarcity, when provisions ran low and some died of malnutrition. According to one trader, the Ojibwas sometimes philosophically remarked, "Let's eat today . . . if there isn't anything [tomorrow] we'll do without." One could predict seasonal hunger, but disease proved more capricious and deadlier. The 1790s brought to the western Lakes country at least two epidemics, one of measles and one of an unidentified respiratory illness, which killed many Anishinaabeg. If contagious disease now proved more of a problem for the northern Lakes Indians than in past decades, this probably resulted from the expansion of the fur trade and the inundation of the region with alcohol. Midway through the Revolutionary War, several partnerships of London- and Montreal-based merchants had formed the Northwest Company (NWC), which tried to become the dominant trading outfit in the upper Great Lakes. By 1801 the company had over one thousand traders, laborers, and clerks working throughout the region, annual exports worth over £350,000 (approximately $34 million in 2015), and control of three-quarters of the Canadian fur market. Much of the NWC's success came from its emulation of French trading practices, like sending its employees deep into Indian territory to peddle their wares and providing liberal *regales,* or gifts of alcohol, to their trading partners. More traders meant more pathogens in remote Indian communities, and more alcohol meant more fights between Indian men and more health problems for imbibers.[13]

For all the rigors and complications of their lives, the Dakotas and Anishinaabeg of the northern Lakes enjoyed one advantage over their Indian neighbors to the south: the Americans were, as yet, far away. Apart from the isolated fort and factory on Mackinac Island and the new British post on Saint Joseph's Island, the Americans and British had no outposts in the northern Lakes, and apart from one or two thousand British and Francophone traders, there were no Europeans in the region. Cartographers might consider the northern districts of Michigan, Wisconsin, and Minnesota part of the United States, and British traders might consider them part of their sphere of economic influence, but from a demographic and cultural standpoint they remained Indian country. No outside power could challenge that essential fact until after the War of 1812.[14]

The southern Lakes region, by contrast, remained much more of a borderland, where the United States struggled for land and influence with a panoply of smaller Indian nations. This region, bounded by the latitudes of Green Bay and modern Indianapolis, included the Wyandot and Shawnee towns near Sandusky and Detroit, the Potawatomi settlements around Lake Michigan, the Miamis and Kickapoos of the greater Wabash valley, the diasporic Delaware communities of Indiana and Spanish Missouri, and the Sauks, Mesquakies, Menominees, and Ho-Chunks of northern Illinois and southern Wisconsin. These disparate Indian communities still relied on horticulture, more specifically on the beans, squash, fruit, and "vast fields" of maize grown by Lakes Indian women, for most of their food. Some had begun to diversify their agriculture by adding cattle, swine, and horses. Traders and missionaries had introduced domesticated animals to the Illiniwek early in the eighteenth century, to the Ohio Iroquois and Delawares by the 1760s, and to the Miamis and Shawnees by 1800, and southern Lakes Indian families began to supplement their diets with pork and dairy products and with European crops like cabbage. They also adopted the practice of fencing fields to protect crops from animal raids. Indians' unfamiliarity with livestock, however, and the great deal of care the animals required meant that Native Americans took time to adopt them.[15]

FIGURE 2. Potawatomis and other southern Lakes Indians practiced agriculture but also relied on hunting to provide meat and salable animal pelts. This illustration shows a Potawatomi family working and resting at a riverside hunting camp. George Winter, "Potawatomi Camp Scene, Crooked Creek" (1837). *Courtesy of Tippecanoe County Historical Association, Lafayette, Indiana*

The southern Lakes Indians could still rely on the woods and waterways of their homeland to provide them with wild animal and plant foods and marketable produce. The larger rivers still hosted abundant fish, which men caught with gigs or killed with arrows. The region's forests generated large quantities of oily nuts and wild berries, providing sustenance not only for humans but for many species of game animals: rabbits, deer, bear, and turkeys, among others. Most of the animal products that the southern Lakes Indians consumed came from hunting, and sufficient game still lived in the region's forests and wetlands to make hunting worthwhile. Deer supplied Indian men and women with venison and skins, muskrats and raccoons with hatters' furs, and waterfowl with meat and feathers. Hunting remained men's work, but the products of the hunt were not the only saleable goods that the Lakes Indians brought to market, and women manufactured much of their communities' other merchandise. They sewed moccasins, which they decorated with beads and porcupine quills; wove mats and baskets from rushes and other plant fibers; and made mococks (birch bark boxes), which they filled with maple sugar, a foodstuff that Lakes Indian women produced at sugaring camps in late winter. On the upper Mississippi River, Sauk, Menominee, and Ho-Chunk women mined the lead that factors and traders bought by the ton, digging pits and trenches and then hauling up earth and ore in baskets. Apart from furs, this dense metal proved the most widely saleable commodity the Lakes Indians made.[16]

Lakes Indian men and women sold their produce to private traders and federal factors, buying in exchange muskets, textiles, silver jewelry, tools, tobacco, and alcohol. The last of these often became a source of violent conduct and depressed health, but in some communities Indian women took care to disarm their male relatives before they embarked on euphoric drinking binges. In other towns, civil chiefs or nativist religious leaders denounced alcohol as a poison and dissuaded their followers from buying it. The other merchandise that southern Lakes Indians purchased was more useful or durable, and Native Americans showed a sober and discerning regard for its quality, preferring British to American-made calico, "glazed rifle powder" to cheaper gunpowder, and light silver jewelry with animal or interlocking-ring motifs to other varieties.[17]

Overall, the southern Lakes Indians had begun to develop a more diversified economy than before, one which included livestock raising, handicraft sales, mining, and consumption of new goods. Divisions of opinion did appear within and between different nations about the pace that diversification should take. Some Native Americans in the southern Lakes country preferred older clothing styles and a diet composed primarily of fish, game, corn, and beans. This was particularly true of Miami and Potawatomi communities during the first decade of the nineteenth century. Other Indians were quicker to adopt the hats and brass buttons, stovepipes and silverware, butter and beef that adorned the persons, homes, and tables of their white neighbors. The Mohawk prophetess Coocoochee, ostensibly a traditionalist, arrayed her cabin at Auglaize with kettles and pewterware and received payment for her prophecies in silver brooches. Her neighbor Blue Jacket, the Shawnee war captain, furnished his house with silverware and European-style bedsteads. A decade later, chiefs like Five Medals of the Potawatomis and Black Hoof of the Shawnees welcomed Quaker missionaries into their communities, and studied from them the use of plows and the cultivation of European crops. Some of their kinsmen regarded these innovations with suspicion, but the proponents of new consumer goods and commercial agriculture saw these as evolutionary changes, similar to those the fur trade brought to Indian communities in the eighteenth century.[18]

The division between innovators and traditionalists might not have produced serious consequences had it not dovetailed with another political division within the southern Lakes nations between those who benefited from a closer relationship with the US government and Indians who preferred their people to remain autonomous. The men who most strongly supported missionaries and most vocally favored a shift to commercial agriculture were the small group of chiefs whom the United States considered its main allies in the Northwest Territory: Black Hoof, Five Medals, Little Turtle, Tarhe, and the Delaware chief Buckongehelas. The War Department had begun trying to win these leaders' favor after the Treaty of Greenville, bringing Lakes Indian leaders to Philadelphia and Washington City for private meetings with the president, granting some of their personal requests (such as Little Turtle's application for a factory at Fort Wayne), and providing them with gifts and salaries. Such "liberalities and patronage to chiefs of influence," President Jefferson argued, offered efficient and inexpensive ways to "bribe [the Indians] into peace."[19]

The favor that these chiefs received undoubtedly rankled their political rivals. The implication of these leaders in a series of land cessions during the first decade of the new century proved even more troubling to many Lakes Indians. In 1800, Congress laid the foundation for these cessions by organizing the western two-thirds of the Northwest into Indiana Territory, and President John Adams appointed the young expansionist William Henry Harrison to govern it. In 1803, Harrison met Delaware, Piankeshaw, and Potawatomi leaders to set the boundaries of the settlement zone around Vincennes and to obtain a road easement through Indiana. The agreement netted the United States over one million acres of land at virtually no cost. A few months later, the governor signed a treaty with the Kaskaskias, who ceded the Illiniwek's claims to the southern half of modern Illinois in return for a larger annuity and a church building. The following year, Piankeshaw leaders assented to the Illinois cession, and they and Delaware chiefs also sold their land claims in southern Indiana, a region into which white squatters and hunters had been intruding for several years. Little Turtle and Five Medals protested the 1804 sales on the ground that their nations rightfully owned the ceded lands and that the Delawares had only an occupancy right, but the following year Harrison secured their consent to the cession, paying the dissenters goods and cash and increasing the annuities they had been receiving. In the interim, the governor arranged a treaty in Saint Louis with several Sauk and Mesquakie leaders, who ceded to the United States a band of territory in northern Illinois and southern Wisconsin. By all of these agreements, the US government acquired sixty million acres and possession of both banks of the Ohio River, as well as improved access to the Mississippi River, which France had just ceded to the United States through the Louisiana Purchase. The payments promised by the treaties amounted to about $6,000 in goods, livestock, and cash, plus new annuities totaling about $4,500 per annum.[20]

American officials also sought cessions of Indian territory on the eastern Great Lakes. In 1805, Anishinaabe, Delaware, Shawnee, and Wyandot chiefs signed the Treaty of Fort Industry, selling most of northern Ohio between the Cuyahoga and Sandusky Rivers. That same year Congress separated Michigan Territory from Indiana, and the new territory's governor, William Hull, followed Harrison's example of securing a large Indian land cession to attract white settlers. In November 1807, Hull concluded a treaty with leaders of the Wyandots and all three Anishinaabe nations, securing about five million acres in southeastern Michigan. The signatories received $10,000 in goods and silver, plus $2,400 worth of annuities and two blacksmiths' salaries. A separate treaty, at Brownstown (1808), granted the United States road easements from central to northern Ohio and through the Fort Industry cession, thereby ensuring that the Americans could move supplies and soldiers between all of their forts and settlements. The American salient in the eastern Lakes country now extended from the Ohio River to Lake Erie.[21]

The United States made a respectable profit from these deals, buying land from the Lakes Indians for one to two cents per acre and reselling it for $1.66 per acre. Prominent chiefs like Little Turtle and Jean-Baptiste Ducoigne also did well, acquiring wealth through direct payments from the War Department or their control of annuity payments. Most used these resources to reward their followers and allies, trading goods and money for political influence as chiefs had always done. Governor Hull reported that Odawa chiefs brought to the national annuity distributions entourages of up to eight hundred men, women, and children, and one requested a gorget (neck plate) engraved with the words "The Odawa Nation is entitled to eight hundred dollars a year forever by the Treaty of Detroit," indicating that the annuities belonged to the nation and not just its leaders. What many Lakes Indian men found objectionable about these deals was not that their chiefs were feathering their nests (they generally did not) but rather that they had sold the national birthright for a mess of pottage. Some protested that the deceitful "Bostonians" had cheated their people out of a fair price for their land, while others, like the Potawatomi captain Marpack, denounced the leaders who made the cessions as "nothing but dogs."[22]

American policy makers had offered a solution to the economic problems that land cessions might cause the Indians: the civilization policy, which would allow Native Americans to raise their own food, make their own clothing, and subsist comfortably on a reduced territory. President Jefferson found a happy connection between the two policies, as "civilized" Indians would need looms and livestock and other commodities for which they could trade their "surplus" hunting ranges. Many Lakes Indians also found a connection between land cessions and the civilization program, but they held a much less favorable view of that connection. A past generation had developed a religious ideology, nativism, that considered both land cessions and European agriculture spiritually poisonous and directed Indians to recover precontact lifeways and preserve their remaining lands. Nativism had spent its initial force by the time of Pontiac's death in 1769, but it roared back to life two decades later when warriors for the United Indian confederation attributed their military victories to the Master of Life.[23]

The United Indians and their successors also paid homage to a new generation of prophets, who offered them new paths to spiritual power. In the 1780s, a Shawnee sect known as the Powwow Brothers invoked visions of the Great Spirit, who upbraided his Indian children for their pride and abandonment of tradition. Child seers from Delaware and Seneca communities in Ontario shared the same message with their parents a decade later. The Mohawk oracle Coocoochee induced a state resembling spiritual possession to provide her neighbors, including Miami warriors, with insight into the future. In the late 1790s, a new religious association among the Ojibwas, the Wabeno Society, pursued a similar path to revelation, dancing ecstatically and handling hot coals to invite supernatural possession. In Iroquoia the Seneca prophet Handsome Lake, whom spirit guides had taken on a series of trips to heaven, taught his kinsmen to revive some of their old customs, like thanksgiving songs and the White Dog sacrifice, and to give up alcohol.[24]

The most influential new prophet, Tenskwatawa (The Open Door), began preaching in 1805–6. Formerly a Shawnee man named Lalawethika, the prophet visited the Master of Life in a series of dream visions, similar to those experienced by Neolin and Handsome Lake, and brought back to the material world a message of repentance and renewal. The Lakes Indians, announced Tenskwatawa, must give up the innovations brought to them by the whites, like alcohol and livestock, and cease marrying or trading with the dangerous Europeans. All must return to the "manner and customs of their forefathers," including the communal ownership of land. Tenskwatawa implicitly criticized Indian leaders who supported the federal civilization program, and denounced shamans who challenged his own call to spiritual purification. As he spread his teachings through the southern Lakes country, Tenskwatawa organized several witch hunts, beginning with the execution of four White River Delawares whose kinsmen accused them of causing an epidemic. Within five years the prophet's supporters had killed sixteen Indian men and women for witchcraft.[25]

Tenskwatawa had limited success recruiting Shawnees, but his message struck a chord with the Ho-Chunks, who probably viewed him as an analogue of the powerful thunderbirds who served as "open doors" between the human world and the Upper World. He also appealed to the Potawatomis, Odawas, and Ojibwas, and by 1807 hundreds of young Anishinaabe men were flocking to the prophet's settlement near Greenville. One of these followers, Le Maigouis (The Trout), preached a more radical version of the Shawnee prophet's separatist message, arguing that the Great Spirit had not actually created white Americans, who "grew from the scum of the great water when it was troubled by the Evil Spirit." To honor the Master of Life, Indians must both avoid the customs of whites and stop following other paths to spiritual renewal, such as the use of medicine bundles (which might contain fragments of dangerous underworld serpents) and participation in the rites of the Wabeno Society. Tenskwatawa supported The Trout's message, but he took care to modify it when whites visited Greenville, and he and his allies persuaded visitors that while his nativist followers were sincere, they had no violent intentions.[26]

By 1808 the Greenville settlement had grown sufficiently crowded that Tenskwatawa moved his base to a new community, Prophetstown, in northern Indiana. The prophet had become a political leader, and his six thousand or so followers, who now included a few chiefs like Blue Jacket (Shawnee) and spiritual leaders like Main Poc (a Potawatomi shaman), had become part of a movement both spiritual and nationalist. The converts sought to purify and empower themselves through rituals, such as the new dances that Tenskwatawa taught them, and through the adoption of traditional dress and diet. They also wanted the independence that their compromised national leaders could no longer guarantee, freedom from traders and whiskey peddlers and grasping American officials. In seeking that independence, the prophet's confederates, like the United Indians a couple of decades before, had assembled the elements of a national government: a capital town, an armed force of warriors, and an ad hoc diplomatic corps, headed by Tenskwatawa's charismatic brother Tecumseh, who sought to win new converts among the Ho-Chunks and Miamis. Like much of the contemporary United States, however, the independence of Tenskwatawa's nation also rested on the dependence and subordination of a large working class: Indian women, whose labor the confederates depended on for their food supply. Tenskwatawa significantly curtailed the freedom and authority of women in his city-state: councils of clan matrons could not meet, young men could beat their wives, and search parties apprehended women who ran away from Prophetstown.[27]

The Indian confederates' national autonomy also depended on stable borders, and unfortunately for Tenskwatawa the governor of neighboring Indiana Territory had no interest in recognizing those borders. William Henry Harrison suspected that the prophet and his allies were British catspaws, not realizing that Tecumseh and Tenskwatawa did not in fact trust British officials and received little aid or counsel from them prior to 1810. The presence of a potentially hostile Native American city-state in northern Indiana made the governor keen to enlarge his territory's white population and militia force. Moreover, Harrison suffered a blow to his prestige in 1808–9, when disaffected settlers in Illinois successfully petitioned Congress for separation from Indiana. A large new purchase of Indian land would salve the governor's wounded dignity and attract enough white settlers to compensate for the loss of Illinois's population.[28]

Harrison had not asked the southern Lakes Indians for land for several years, but he pressed them hard for it at Fort Wayne in 1809. The governor plied the one thousand Delaware, Miami, and Potawatomi conference-goers with alcohol, and when this did not befuddle the chiefs or move them from their initial bargaining position—no less than two dollars per acre for any further cession—he threatened to withhold their annuity payments unless they accepted his terms. In late September, under duress, Lakes Indian leaders capitulated and signed the Treaty of Fort Wayne. Harrison held several additional treaty councils later that year, at which Wea and Kickapoo chiefs signed confirming agreements; the governor deliberately separated the Indian nations from one another to prevent their uniting in opposition to him. Under the agreement, the Indians received cash, livestock, and about $3,000 per year in new annuities; the United States received three million acres of land in southeastern and western Indiana. Surveyors soon came out to blaze a quarter of a million trees in the cession zone and mark the territory as no longer Indian.[29]

The new cession infuriated many Lakes Indians, and about one thousand new Native American recruits came to Prophetstown in 1810. It also angered Tenskwatawa and Tecumseh, who saw the treaties as a direct challenge to their authority. Governor Harrison extended a thin white belt of peace to the prophet, inviting him to negotiate with the United States in Vincennes or Washington. Instead, Tenskwatawa's brother, Tecumseh, went to Vincennes that summer to declare Prophetstown's position. In a lengthy speech at Harrison's mansion, Tecumseh declared that the Americans were the cruelest of all the imperial powers the Lakes Indians had encountered, killing defenseless civilians and intimidating weakened nations into giving up their land. Henceforth the southern Lakes Indians, for whom Tecumseh professed to speak, wanted nothing to do with the United States, apart from occasional trade. Certainly they wanted no more annuities, which only ensured Native American dependence, and no more land deals. The recent land cession, Tecumseh warned in closing, was null and void. While his warriors planned no reprisals against the Americans, they would surely execute the chiefs responsible for the Fort Wayne treaties unless the United States returned the land.[30]

Harrison interpreted this pointed address as an ultimatum from a hostile power, one he had to meet with force. He believed that Tecumseh and his brother contemplated a general Indian war against the United States, and that if this occurred they would surely receive weapons and support from Britain. In 1811, two skirmishes in Illinois territory that left several Americans dead tipped Harrison over the edge: he now decided to destroy Prophetstown before it became, like Kekionga two decades earlier, the headquarters of a pan-Indian army. In the summer, the governor received the War Department's go-ahead for an attack, and he marshaled over one thousand regulars, militia, and Kentucky volunteers for his campaign. Tecumseh, he knew, would not be present to lead the defense of Prophetstown; the Shawnee captain had passed through Vincennes on his way south, where he planned to win more allies among the southeastern Indians.[31]

Governor Harrison and his troops marched up the Wabash to Tippecanoe River in late fall. Tenskwatawa had remained in Prophetstown and took charge of defending the small city, but as Harrison's army drew near the prophet decided to attack the Americans before they reached his capital. Reassuring his warriors that his spiritual medicine would protect them, he sent a war party to drive back Harrison's men, and on November 7 the two forces met at the Battle of Tippecanoe. The battle brought the Americans no glory—they took more than twice as many casualties as Tenskwatawa's warriors—and brought the Indian confederates no relief, as the American army remained strong enough after the battle to march into Prophetstown and burn it. The survivors dispersed, not returning to rebuild their community until the spring. Some, vowing vengeance on the treacherous governor, initiated a raiding campaign against American settlements in early 1812. After only a fifteen-year hiatus, war had returned to the Lakes country. This time, the consequences would prove direr than ever for Native Americans.[32]

◆ ◆ ◆

The Treaty of Greenville implied that a new era had begun for the Great Lakes Indians, but after 1795 most found that their lives remained much the same as they had been in 1775 or 1755. The seasonal round of fishing, hunting, and rice harvesting continued unchanged in the north, while in the south the Shawnees, Sauks, and Wyandots continued to diversify their economy into stock raising, mining, and intensified trade. Commerce created some disruptions, like increased susceptibility to disease and the greater availability of alcohol, but Indian men and women found they could manage some of these problems. White settlers, whose invasion of the Ohio valley had been underway for a quarter-century, created additional disruptions, especially when they killed Native American travelers or intruded on hunting preserves. They largely limited themselves to the southeastern Lakes region, within the zone created by the Greenville treaty.

The biggest upheaval in the lives of the Lakes Indians came not from economic or demographic changes but political ones, specifically the two rival plans of nation building that white Americans and Native Americans were following by the early 1800s. The United States began after 1795 to build its own influence and power in the Northwest Territory, using annuity payments and trading factories to turn Indian leaders into dependents, and negotiating treaties that transferred Indian land to the United States. American officials generally did not negotiate these transfers in response to white settlers' demands for land, which the Greenville treaty had largely satiated; instead they wanted to secure control of critical waterways and roads and to promote the growth of new frontier settlements, whose militia would augment the United States' power.[33]

If most Lakes Indians found these developments merely unsettling, a substantial minority considered them a dire threat. These were the men whom Tenskwatawa and Tecumseh began recruiting in 1805 and whom they eventually united into a new political community. The Shawnee prophet's followers wanted a religious and cultural life free of European impurities, and they also wanted political independence: leaders whom the Americans had not compromised, a land base whose borders the United States would not violate, and an armed force behind their demands. American officials, particularly those "on the ground" like William Harrison, found these demands intolerable. They were willing to accept some degree of Indian political authority, but not an armed nation-state with its own foreign policy and the power of life and death over those within its borders.

Nations can often resolve differences through diplomacy, but if one will not acknowledge the legitimacy of another, and their interests conflict, war is usually the outcome. And when one nation believes that violating another's interests is essential to its own survival, war is also likely. The United States found itself entering two interrelated military conflicts in 1811–12 as a result of such irreconcilable conflicts: one with Tecumseh and Tenskwatawa's confederation, and the other with the brothers' principal European ally, Great Britain. Only a few people bore responsibility for starting either of these wars, but the two conflicts, especially after they merged in 1812, had dismal results for tens of thousands of people innocent of their causes.

9

Reckoning with the Conquerors

BY 1812, THE GREAT LAKES REGION HAD EXPERIENCED MORE THAN a century of imperial rivalry, first between the French and British and then between Britain and the United States. Residing on a borderland between rival empires, distant from the centers of colonial settlement, the Lakes Indians had more success maintaining their autonomy than if they had faced only one imperial power. Native American nations could seek concessions from both rivals by stoking their fears of each other and making Indian alliance a negotiable asset. Political autonomy, in turn, allowed Indian communities to find different solutions to the vexing problems of environmental and economic change. Some, mostly in the southern Lakes country, selectively adapted elements of American culture, like livestock. Some adopted European goods but retained their own traditional beliefs and lifeways. Still others, motivated by the new creed of nativism, rejected commerce, acculturation, and engagement with the American empire.[1]

The problem with borderlands is that they often become battle fronts when war breaks out between the bordering empires.

Consequently, those empires view disloyalty by borderlands peoples as a security threat. The United States considered Tecumseh and Tenskwatawa's city-state of Prophetstown so grave a danger that it sent an army against the nativist defenders well before the start of the Anglo-American war, and the US force continued to harry Tecumseh's confederates until their captain died in battle two years later. When the War of 1812 ended, leaving the United States with an ambiguous peace settlement, American insecurity fastened on another group of Indians: those of the northern Great Lakes, who traded with whites but avoided adopting their culture. Before the war, their homeland had been a "native ground" where Native Americans set the rules of interaction rather than a "middle ground" where they accommodated colonial powers. After 1815, white Americans sought to change the landscape dramatically, to turn the northern Lakes country into a middle ground and, eventually, into a white man's country.[2]

In the north, after 1815, the United States augmented its political and economic power, building new forts, making the occasional show of force against nations like the Ho-Chunks, replacing British traders with the American Fur Company, and pressing the Anishinaabeg for land on which it could plant frontier settlements, future reserves of American power. In the south, American officials pressed the Miamis, Wyandots, and others for ever-larger land cessions, with the aim of either driving them across the Mississippi River or forcing them to live under the authority of settler-controlled state governments. American policy left some room for the southern Lakes Indians to maneuver, to negotiate with white officials, to find new ways of making of living, and to teach their children skills adapted to a new environment. What the region's Native American population could not forget, however, was how massively American military power had grown by the end of the 1812–15 war, and how easily that hammer could fall on them again if they tried once more to follow Tecumseh's path.

✦ ✦ ✦

The second Anglo-American war, or War of 1812, grew out of maritime disputes (trade restrictions, the impressment of American-employed sailors) between Britain and the United States. Like many imperial wars, it quickly spread to the two belligerents' continental frontiers and to the homes of indigenous peoples residing in the interimperial borderland. The conflict had little effect beyond North America, and apart from a few small naval victories and a late, lopsided win at New Orleans, American forces did not always perform well in their fight against Britain. Poorly trained American troops failed either to conquer Canada or defend the American capital from attack. However, the war proved catastrophic for Native Americans, who suffered grievous losses on the battlefield and whom the British more or less abandoned in the postwar peace settlement. If white Americans considered the war a successful one, these heavy Indian setbacks help explain their belief.[3]

Initially, the fortunes of war on the Great Lakes front favored Britain and the Lakes Indians. A Canadian and Anishinaabe war party seized Fort Mackinac just one month after the declaration of war, and five hundred Potawatomis destroyed Fort Dearborn, killing fifty Americans in the ensuing battle and capturing most of the outpost's civilians. In August, sixteen hundred British soldiers and Lakes Indian allies terrorized Governor William Hull into surrendering Detroit, the United States' regional stronghold, without firing a shot. Shawnee and Odawa warriors had already demoralized Detroit's defenders by attacking a nearby party of Americans and displaying the fallen soldiers' scalps on poles. Hull suffered a further, fatal blow to his morale when General Isaac Brock threatened to storm the town and let his warriors slaughter the inhabitants. The threat proved effective but also contributed to the Americans' perception of Indians as barbarous, "detestable," and cruel.[4]

After their initial successes, the confederated Indians ran out of momentum, and the United States' superior resources—its roads, fortifications, and large, well-armed settler population—began to tell against them. Potawatomi, Miami, and Ho-Chunk warriors besieged Fort Wayne, Fort Harrison (Indiana), and Fort Madison (Iowa) in September and attempted to burn the stockades. Effective fire control, however, allowed the garrisons to hold out until reinforcements arrived. Later that year the Americans conducted reprisal raids or preemptive attacks against Indian communities south of the Great Lakes. Territorial governor of Illinois Ninian Edwards destroyed several Kickapoo and Potawatomi towns on the Illinois River, including at least one community friendly to the Americans, while Indiana militia destroyed allegedly hostile Miami towns on the Mississinewa River, taking forty captives in the process. American militia then built Fort Meigs on the Maumee River and occupied Frenchtown, on the Raisin River. British troops and Lakes Indian warriors attacked this second post in January 1813, killing nearly four hundred Americans in the battle and executing fifty prisoners. The United States lost the battle, but American recruiters gained a rallying cry, "Remember the Raisin."[5]

The year 1813 proved the decisive one for Tecumseh's confederacy and for the southern Lakes Indians. In April and May an army of British regulars and Lakes Indian warriors besieged Fort Meigs. The attackers brought ample manpower and half a dozen field guns to the battle, and they killed, wounded, or captured about one thousand Americans who sallied out to silence the British cannons. The attackers took abundant plunder and other trophies from the bodies of the slain, though when disaffected warriors tried to kill and scalp American prisoners, Tecumseh rode into their camp and ordered them to desist. Despite their gains, neither the British nor their Indian allies could breach the Americans' fortifications, which had been designed by West Point graduate Eleazar Wood, and the arrival of fourteen hundred American reinforcements forced the redcoats and warriors to withdraw. Two months later, in July 1813, Tecumseh persuaded General Henry Proctor to support another attempt on Fort Meigs, to which the Shawnee captain brought twenty-five hundred warriors, but after a desultory fusillade and a futile assault on nearby Fort Stephenson, the attackers withdrew. It was the last Indian offensive in the region and carried with it an implicit lesson for anyone who cared to contemplate it: an American military force that could survive a loss as great as Arthur St. Clair's 1791 debacle, shrug off an assault by a massive Native American army, and still hold its ground was probably too powerful for the Lakes Indians to defeat without greater British assistance.[6]

Some of Tecumseh's and Tenskwatawa's confederates probably understood this, but they had little alternative to fighting after William Henry Harrison invaded Upper Canada. Harrison's expedition followed one of the few decisive naval engagements of the war, the Battle of Lake Erie (September 10, 1813), in which a flotilla of American warships under the direction of Commodore Oliver Hazard Perry ran into a smaller British squadron. In an intense close-range battle, Perry's ships heavily damaged four of the six British war vessels and forced their adversaries to surrender. Thereafter the Americans held control of Lake Erie and the forts and settlements around it. A few weeks later Harrison, Isaac Shelby, and fifty-five hundred troops crossed the lake by boat or marched up its western shore. British troops and their Indian allies withdrew from Detroit. Harrison then crossed the Detroit River to pursue Tecumseh and his confederates into Ontario.[7]

The nativist confederacy's final act soon followed. On October 5, 1813, about 1,300 weary British regulars and Indian warriors stood to fight the Americans near the Delaware community of Moravian-town. Their attackers, who outnumbered them nearly three-to-one, included 260 Delaware, Shawnee, and Wyandot warriors, allied with the United States because they considered Tecumseh a greater danger than the Americans. The battle proved short and decisive: American infantry broke the British battle line, and mounted gunmen subdued the warriors defending the British flank, killing Tecumseh in the process. About 100 of the Indian defenders were killed or wounded, with Kentucky militiamen taking their scalps or cutting pieces of flesh to make razor strops. Six hundred British soldiers surrendered.[8]

The Battle of Moraviantown destroyed Tenskwatawa's confederacy, whose warriors never fought again as a unified force. The Americans sought to press their strategic advantage in 1814, building a fort near Prairie du Chien, Wisconsin, and organizing a naval expedition to retake Mackinac Island. Sauk warriors prevented the Americans from reinforcing their new fort. British troops took the town of Prairie du Chien. And the Mackinac expedition ran afoul of Menominee warriors who repelled the American landing party. The American retreat left the upper Great Lakes in the hands of the British and their Indian allies.[9]

By the end of 1814, the Americans and British had agreed on a peace treaty, which both governments ratified—without consulting Native Americans—a few months later. The Treaty of Ghent left the nations' borders as they had been before the war, their disputes unresolved. The war had, however, drastically altered the political situation in the Lakes

Indians' homeland. Tecumseh was dead, his brother in exile, their confederacy broken, and their allies' lands now open to an American invasion. Even in the northern Lakes region, the Anishinaabeg and their neighbors faced an ominous future. The Americans had tried to push into the region in 1814, and they would try again, with much greater success, when the war ended and Britain found other occupations.

+ + +

While the 1814 peace treaty restored the status quo ante bellum, the British government altered its North American policy soon thereafter. The British government made one feeble gesture toward protecting its Indian allies and cobelligerents: Lord Bathurst, the head of Britain's War Department, protested a twenty-two-million-acre land cession that Andrew Jackson had extorted from the southeastern Creek nation, calling it a violation of the Treaty of Ghent. (Jackson took the land as reparations for a bloody war he had fought against a Creek faction, the Red Sticks, who had joined Tecumseh's confederacy.) Britain's other cabinet secretaries and officials refused to second Bathurst's objection. They had come to the conclusion that Britain had nothing more to gain from Indian alliances. As one officer wrote in 1815, "the western Indians are [now] completely hemmed in, thoroughly in the power of the Americans, & their assistance in any future war, hopeless." The Colonial Office, assuming it could no longer rely on Native allies to defend Canada, decided it now had to promote increased European settlement, just as the Americans had done south of the Great Lakes. During the first five years after the war, about thirty thousand British immigrants moved to Canada, and to provide farmland for them, Canadian officials negotiated seven land cession treaties with the Ojibwas and Mississaugas of eastern Ontario. The Mississaugas had already lost much of their prime hunting and fishing grounds to Loyalist refugees in the 1790s; now, the British Indian department persuaded them to surrender their remaining lands in exchange for agricultural training. British and American Indian policies were becoming interchangeable.[10]

Concurrently, British garrison commanders on the upper Great Lakes began reducing the amount of presents and provisions they gave

to Indian visitors. Ho-Chunk and Sauk leaders attending one conference blasted British officials for abandoning their Native American
allies, while at an 1818 council, Odawa leaders reminded the Indian
superintendent of his obligations by giving him a wampum belt their
ancestors had received from Sir William Johnson. The protests did not
fall on deaf ears, and officials at Fort Malden and Drummond Island
continued to give gifts to the Anishinaabeg, Sauks, and others into the
1830s. Otherwise Britain took little interest in Native peoples on the
American side of the Lakes.[11]

As the British pulled back, the United States expanded into the
power vacuum that the collapse of Tecumseh's confederacy left behind.
Five groups of Americans advanced their nation's sphere of influence
into the upper and western Lakes country during the decade after the
War of 1812. These were the diplomats whom the president commissioned to negotiate land-cession treaties with Britain's former Indian
allies; the soldiers whom the War Department sent to garrison strategic posts on the frontier; private American traders seeking to displace
their British rivals; missionaries who wanted to turn the Lakes Indians
into settled Christian farmers (even if many already answered to that
description); and white settlers who wanted to occupy and transform
Indians' homelands.

Members of the first group, the treaty commissioners, began their
work soon after ratification of the Treaty of Ghent. In the spring of
1815, commissioners Ninian Edwards and William Clark invited several
dozen Indian communities in the western Lakes region to a multitribal
conference. That summer, Edwards and Clark signed peace treaties at
Portage des Sioux, Missouri, with the Potawatomis, Sauks, Sioux, and
others. A separate conference later that year gave the dubious privilege of the United States' friendship to the Anishinaabeg and to those
southern Lakes Indians (Delawares, Shawnees, Wyandots) who had
fought for both sides during the war. At this conference, held at Spring
Wells, a chastened Tenskwatawa announced that the nations formerly
allied with Britain would accept the Americans' peace offer, and that
he would now call President James Madison his father. William Henry
Harrison then warned the southern Lakes nations to reunify under
their American-allied chiefs, if they wanted American protection. The

Dakotas and Ho-Chunks, absent from Spring Wells, formally ended hostilities with the Americans in 1816.[12]

After these preliminaries, federal commissioners resumed the quest for Indian land that had formerly occupied so much of the War Department's attention. Local officials wanted Indians' land base drastically reduced so that they could encourage white immigration, and President James Monroe agreed with them, arguing that a growing white population would improve military security and increase the value of federally owned lands. The Americans had in their treaty with Great Britain promised to respect Native Americans' prewar "possessions, rights, and privileges," but they placed no restrictions on postwar cessions or sales. Scarcely eighteen months elapsed after the end of the war before American officials signed the first of the new land cession treaties, which surrendered Anishinaabe land claims in northern Illinois. One year later, at the Treaty of Maumee Rapids (September 29, 1817), commissioners persuaded Delaware, Shawnee, and Wyandot chiefs to cede all remaining Indian lands in Ohio, except for eighty square miles designated as family and town reservations. At another multitribal conference at Saint Mary's, Ohio, the following autumn (October 1818), the Miamis and Potawatomis sold most of their remaining lands in central Indiana, the Weas gave up all of their land claims outside of small reservations, and the Delawares agreed to move across the Mississippi River. Subsequent treaty councils in July and September 1819 exchanged the Kickapoos' land claims in Indiana for a reservation in Missouri (to which the United States encouraged them to move) and ceded several million acres of Anishinaabe land in central Michigan. The signatories of the 1817–19 treaties collectively received $97,500 in cash and goods and annuities totaling $30,500 per year, about half of which went to the Miamis. The one hundred Anishinaabe chiefs who signed the September 1819 Treaty of Saginaw also secured sixteen individual land grants and sixteen town reservations. Slowly but steadily, the remaining Indian lands in Ohio, Indiana, and Illinois turned into American property.[13]

The new treaties bore some resemblance to those that William Henry Harrison and other officials had negotiated earlier in the century. In exchange for land cessions, these agreements promised the Indian

signatories annuities—which would help keep the Lakes Indians economically dependent on the Americans—and offered many of them
agricultural tools and other technical assistance. What was new in
these treaties was the provision in two of them (with the Delawares
and Kickapoos) for removal across the Mississippi River, a policy that
the US government had begun to adopt after the war, and the reduction
of Native American resistance through the creation of multiple reservations. Town reserves allowed southern Lakes Indian towns to stand
while white settlers engrossed the lands around them, and individual
land grants gave the US government a way to bribe influential chiefs
and traders. Both kinds of reservation helped commissioners overcome
the resistance of nations like the Wyandots whose leaders knew how
valuable their lands were to the federal Land Office.[14]

The United States employed similar tactics during a second round of
treaty making in the 1820s. Two treaties negotiated with the Potawatomis
in 1821 and 1826 ceded nearly all of that nation's land claims in southern Michigan and northern Indiana for $130,000, payable in cash and
goods, and salaries for smiths and teachers. Perhaps more importantly,
the American commissioners set aside reservations for Potawatomi
towns and several dozen land grants for biracial Potawatomi children,
including the offspring of influential white traders. Meanwhile, agreements with the Sauks and Mesquakies (1824) and the western Shawnees
(1825) liquidated all of those nations' land claims in Missouri except a
small reserve for Sauk and Fox "half-breeds," paid the ceding nations
$22,000 and some agricultural aid, and gave the Shawnees a new res-
ervation in the future state of Kansas. The US government was already
beginning to consider this last region a suitable transfer site for eastern
Indians it could persuade to remove. The rest it would encapsulate in
town reservations, tie down with annuities and economic dependence,
and control with federal agents and troops.[15]

The Lakes Indians did not necessarily see these treaties as acts of
submission. Many continued to view diplomacy and annuity distributions as a way to protect community assets, assert their collective identity, and build reciprocal ties with the Americans. Inserting individual
land grants into treaties, for example, gave the Indian signatories continued access to the waterways, fisheries, and other resources those

grants adjoined. In 1817–18 the Miamis, Shawnees, and Wyandots had used family reservations to ensure their continued access to navigable rivers like the Wabash, and the Anishinaabeg and Sauks followed the same strategy in the 1820s. Awarding land grants also allowed Native Americans to name the recipients as part of the nation and to hospitably provide for their sustenance. The Potawatomis, in the Treaty of the Wabash (1826), included a schedule of individual grants identifying the eighty-four recipients by their blood or marital relations: "of Indian descent," "Indians by birth," "married to an Indian woman," "grandchild of" a chief's sister. This language identified relationships as the basis of tribal connections and asserted a Native right to define national identity. In the northern Lakes region, Ojibwa *ogimaa*, or town chiefs, used diplomatic speeches to identify the bands they represented, reminding American commissioners that they dealt not with individual leaders but with entire communities. In the 1830s, the Ho-Chunks used annuity distributions as opportunities for all households in the nation to gather, receive their share of the tribal annuity, and purchase supplies from traders, while in the 1840s Ojibwa men and women danced on annuity days for local white families, who reciprocated by treating them to food and drink, thus turning these events into festivals of exchange and national pride. White Americans themselves increasingly considered diplomatic events festive occasions, and when Lakes Indians visited Washington and other eastern cities, they rarely lacked for visitors, eager to see "wild Indians." One Ho-Chunk woman, known as "The Washington Woman," decided to turn a profit from these spectators' attentions by charging them ten cents per visit, the same admission price as a museum or theater. She desisted when officials politely asked her to do so.[16]

◆ ◆ ◆

The second group of American agents who expanded the United States' power and authority were the soldiers and engineers sent to fortify the American frontier with British Canada. In hindsight, one can see that Britain posed no threat to American territory after 1815 and that the war had severely damaged the Lakes Indians' military power, but in the immediate postwar years, US officials like Lewis Cass still distrusted the British and worried about the possibility of a revived Indian alliance. The War Department, mirroring such concerns, sent soldiers to reoccupy Detroit and Mackinac in 1815. Over the next seven years it rebuilt Fort Dearborn and authorized new forts and garrisons at Green Bay and Sault Sainte Marie. The army also resumed its push up the Mississippi River, stationing troops in Prairie du Chien and on Rock Island and building a large new stone fort at the confluence of the Minnesota and Mississippi Rivers.[17]

Fort Snelling, as the Americans named the Minnesota establishment upon its completion (1824), stood near an Ojibwa sacred site and a multiethnic trading rendezvous on land that explorer Zebulon Pike had purchased. It soon became a major military base and diplomatic center. While construction of the fort was underway, Lawrence Taliaferro established there the United States' principal agency to the Dakotas, and he invited them and the other principal nations of the upper Mississippi valley (the Sauks, Mesquakies, Menominees, and Ho-Chunks) to exchange their old British flags for American ones and send delegates to Washington, DC. These served as preliminaries to a multinational peace conference that federal commissioners held in Prairie du Chien in 1825, which committed the upper Mississippi nations and the Anishinaabeg to make peace with one another and establish boundary lines between themselves. Federal officials believed this would create a more manageable frontier and allow the continued growth of American influence and trade.[18]

The third group of American expansionists to enter the Lakes country were bearers of American economic power: public and private fur traders. Federal officials had long seen Canadian traders as an unwelcome extension of British influence into the United States, and this view persisted after the war; as late as 1820, Lewis Cass and Henry Schoolcraft expressed alarm that the Ojibwa chiefs they met at Sault Sainte Marie wore British clothing and bore guns "from the manufactories of Birmingham." To shore up the United States' influence in the Lakes region, Congress in 1816 prohibited foreign traders from working in the United States, and the War Department began reestablishing the public trading factories it had operated before the war. The trading house at Fort Dearborn reopened in 1816, joined by new factories at Green Bay,

Prairie du Chien, and a branch factory for the Sauks and Mesquakies at Fort Edwards in Illinois. Only one of these posts did more than incidental business. During his first four years of operations, the factor at Prairie du Chien trading house bought, among other produce, 45,000 muskrat pelts and about 135 tons of lead from his upper Mississippi valley trading partners. By 1819, private competitors from the town and from the new American Fur Company had cut deeply into factor John Johnson's purchases. The Fort Edwards subfactory saw only anemic trade, as many of its intended trading partners, from the Sauk and Mesquakie communities of the Des Moines River, had moved to the Rock River or Missouri. Green Bay's receipts came mainly in the form of maple sugar and cash, the latter paid by private traders who, like their counterparts at Mackinac Island several years earlier, undertook winter trading missions to Ho-Chunk and Menominee communities. As for the rebuilt Chicago factory, its factor had little to do but "fight mosquitos" before his post closed in 1822.[19]

Congress voted to close the factories in the spring of 1822, in part because of pressure from a new fur-trading corporation, the American Fur Company, that had established a larger set of trading outfits in the North American interior. Chartered in 1808 by the merchant John Jacob Astor, the AFC revived after the War of 1812, becoming a Great Lakes–based company with over one hundred employees. Its brigades of traders fanned out from Detroit and Mackinac to the shorelands of Lakes Superior, Michigan, and Erie, and into the Wabash and upper Mississippi River valleys. Astor's political power also grew, as he provided financial assistance to prominent men in Washington and cultivated relationships with officials like Missouri senator Thomas Hart Benton. Benton, with assistance from some of Astor's lieutenants, led the drive in Congress to shutter the trading factories, but by that time American leaders had already concluded that the American Fur Company could fulfill the same political functions as the factory system.[20]

Native American hunters sold Astor's agents tens of thousands of beaver, muskrat, and raccoon pelts, and Indian men and women sold them provisions: whitefish, tallow, and maple sugar. This last commodity the American Fur Company turned into a cash good, selling it to the growing white settler population in Detroit and Cleveland. While at least one prominent American officer, Zachary Taylor, called the AFC's employees "the greatest scoundrels the world ever knew," they knew how to play the trading game according to Lakes Indian rules. They provided their trading partners with that important symbol of hospitality, whiskey, which the AFC procured by the kiloliter; with liberal presents of clothing, silver, sugar, and other goods; and with credit for their winter hunting, albeit at usurious interest rates of up to 100 percent.[21]

Many AFC traders married Lakes Indian or biracial wives, either informally (*à la façon du pays*) or in sacramental marriages, and had biracial children with them. Métis, or mixed-race, families had lived in Lakes Indian communities since the seventeenth century. By the early 1800s, several thousand Métis lived in the region, many of them enjoying extensive business and kinship networks and considerable local influence. Biracial families celebrated Christmas together in Green Bay, "genteel . . . mixed-blood businesswomen" like Madame Le Framboise dominated the social scene at Mackinac, and several Potawatomi and Miami leaders, like Madeleine Bertrand and Jean-Baptiste Richardville, hailed from Métis families. Métis generally spoke multiple languages and combined the lifeways of their parent cultures. Many wore European clothing but adorned it with animal quills or trade beads, a practice they shared with non-Métis. Ojibwa Métis often lived in log lodges like their Anishinaabe kinfolk, but they adorned their homes with European-style bedsteads and other furniture. In Green Bay and Prairie du Chien, Métis families employed indigenous maple sugar in European rituals, like Easter feasts and the giving of billets-doux to sweethearts. By the nineteenth century, however, many biracial parents recognized that the economic future of the region lay with the Americans and those who spoke their language. To help their children acquire skills that would let them thrive in this world, they turned to another group of American invaders: Protestant missionaries.[22]

This fourth group of American expansionists hoped to serve as agents of a cultural revolution. European missionaries had been sojourning in the Great Lakes region and building churches for Native American communities there since the 1630s. By the early nineteenth century, most of the Illiniwek, many Wyandots, and some Delawares had become at least nominal Christian converts, generally of the Roman

Catholic faith. Most Protestant missionaries stayed out of the Lakes region until the early nineteenth century, when a national religious revival known as the Second Great Awakening (1800–1840) increased American Protestant churches' membership, zeal, and willingness to travel. The American Board of Commissioners for Foreign Missions (ABCFM), a coalition of northeastern Congregationalists and Presbyterians, helped lead the evangelical migration. In the 1820s and early 1830s, it established mission stations at Mackinac Island, Green Bay, and La Pointe (Chequamegon Bay). La Pointe served as a base for board missionaries who took up residence with Ojibwas in Wisconsin and Minnesota, while on Mackinac missionaries William and Amanda Ferry established a school for Ojibwa and Métis children, teaching arithmetic and English to 175 pupils between 1823 and 1836.[23]

Other Protestant denominations established smaller, but not necessarily less influential, missions and schools in the southern Lakes country. A Moravian mission to the Delawares in Goshen, Ohio, remained open until 1821–22, when an epidemic killed many of its converts and the survivors moved to Sandusky. The Quakers' agricultural station in Wapakoneta, Ohio, established in 1807 at the invitation of Shawnee chief Black Hoof, remained open for two decades. On the Wyandot reserve at Upper Sandusky, Ohio, Methodist missionaries James Finley and John Stewart received permission to open a church and school. By 1823 they had over fifty Indian students, and by 1828 over three hundred Wyandot men and women had joined the missionaries' church. Methodist and Presbyterian missionaries a few years later opened stations for Peoria and Wea communities in Illinois, and Methodists and American Board missionaries moved into Dakota communities later in the 1830s, though most of the missions to the eastern Sioux attracted only a few people and closed within a few years. Perhaps the most energetic single missionary in the region, the Baptist Isaac McCoy, worked among four different Indian nations in the space of a decade (1818–26): the Weas, the Miamis, the Saint Joseph's Potawatomis, and the Odawas of Grand Rapids.[24]

Some of the Lakes Indians found these missionaries appealing, though mainly for pragmatic reasons. Parents wanted their children to learn English and reading, and some approved of curricula that taught farming, spinning, and weaving to their sons and daughters. Missionaries could occasionally serve as intermediaries with the US government, a role the Quakers (for instance) played for the Shawnees at Wapakoneta. A few also found Protestant conversion appealing or useful. The Wyandots believed it an effective way to form a community front against the dangers of alcohol, and leaders of that nation thought that becoming Protestants would improve their relationship with the United States, making it easier to resist land cessions. Moreover, converts found they could combine the new faith with their older religious convictions. One Wyandot woman, for example, persuaded others to become Methodists by combining the Christian message of salvation with her kinsmen's belief in prophetic dreams: she recounted a dream vision of a white house filled with beautiful music, whose door a white man armed with a blazing sword barred to nonconverts. Another Wyandot convert, Between-the-Logs, compared conversion to self-torture—cutting "the limbs of sin from the body"—an experience both painful and empowering.[25]

Missionaries did, however, meet considerable resistance. An Episcopalian mission near Green Bay attracted few students, probably because local Oneida and Menominee parents opposed the missionaries' use of corporal punishment and their failure properly to feed their students. (Oneidas provided far better hospitality to whites, serving one group of visiting missionaries "pork & beans . . . chicken pies, squashes, potatoes, peas, and rice pudding.") Wyandot nativists opposed missionaries' evangelism, arguing that different creator-gods had prescribed different religious practices for each race they created, while Ohio Senecas who followed the *Gaiwaio*, the creed of Handsome Lake, said their prophet would protect them from evil. Ojibwa traditionalists regarded as dangerous the domestic animals that missionaries brought with them, fearing they might spread disease or facilitate witchcraft, and Ojibwa Catholics objected to Presbyterians trying to woo their children away from the Roman church. Protestant missionaries may have imagined they were moving into a landscape of poverty and ignorance, but in fact they were preaching to Native communities with ample resources and a rich history of religious observances.[26]

Missionaries also lived and preached in a region where, as nativists would have been happy to remind them, Indians had come under increased pressure from other whites who wanted them not to change but to leave. The peace of 1815 had opened up white American migration into the southern Lakes region, where the non-Native American population had already reached 300,000 in Ohio and 70,000 in Indiana. Central and western Illinois's non-Indian population rose to somewhere between 40,000 and 50,000 in 1818, the year Congress admitted it to statehood, and a booming hemp and provisions market in Missouri drew thousands of migrants to that territory as well. The Indian population of the three southern Lakes states had meanwhile fallen below 15,000, a few percent of the regional total.[27]

The rapid growth of the southern Lakes' white settler population presented some Native Americans with new economic opportunities. American towns became markets for Indian women's maple sugar, which white settlers found an acceptable substitute for cane sugar, particularly after Lakes Indian women began straining maple sap and adding egg whites to their sugar to lighten it. White farmers, meanwhile, purchased goods and hired services, like cattle retrieval, from the residents of nearby Indian communities. However, the newcomers also competed with Indians for resources, particularly game animals. Less than a year after the end of the War of 1812, chief Pacane of the Miamis reported that white hunters were intruding on the southern Lakes Indians' territory and that game was running short. In the Lake Michigan shorelands, the Potawatomis and other Native groups, as well as the factor at Fort Dearborn (on his own hunting trips), found that whites had bagged most of the animals nearby, and by the late 1810s Indian men in the region sometimes could not catch enough meat for their families. This was far from a universal problem; Anishinaabeg in the northern Lakes still found abundant wildlife and little competition from white hunters, Miamis could still prosper as commercial hunters in central and northern Indiana, and Wyandot men continued to catch bears and raccoons in the wetlands and oak barrens of northwestern Ohio. But white competitors were becoming a much more serious problem now that much of the southern Lakes Indians' territory belonged not to them but to the US government, or white landowners.[28]

The southern Lakes Indians' communities increasingly became small islands in states dominated by white American settlers. As this occurred, the new state and territorial governments imposed restrictions on Native Americans' legal status and autonomy. Ohio, Indiana, and Illinois all prohibited Indians from voting in their elections, and the latter two states barred them from testifying in court cases to which "whites were parties" until the 1860s. In 1821, Michigan Territory made it clear that Indians, though not under its protection, remained under its legal jurisdiction: a territorial court convicted and executed Ketaukah, an Ojibwa man, for killing a white doctor on Ho-Chunk land. Only on rare occasions did white American institutions protect the rights of Native American people. In 1825, Indiana courts surprised many regional residents by convicting a party of white men who had killed nine Seneca and Shawnee travelers—the so-called Fall Creek Massacre—the previous year. Four of the murderers went to the gallows for the crime. The episode became famous for its rarity: white juries almost never sided with Indians in interracial criminal cases.[29]

Much more common among the white settler population was fear of and contempt for Indians, products of the imperial wars that had divided the peoples of the Lakes country for six decades and of the anti-Indian rhetoric spread by white American propagandists. That such fears lay very close to the surface became evident when fighting broke out between white miners and Ho-Chunk men in the upper Mississippi valley. White Americans had begun moving into the Illinois and Iowa lead-mining district in 1822, seeking quick profits from this growing extractive industry, and within ten years over four thousand newcomers had entered the region. Initially, relations between the American miners and their Indian competitors were peaceful, with the Ho-Chunks and Sauks and others selling provisions to the Americans and the latter minding their business. Within a few years, however, the American miners, chiefly young men, began sexually harassing and abusing the women who worked the Lakes Indians' lead mines. In 1827, Ho-Chunk men began robbing American miners in the region, and that June Ho-Chunk warriors killed or wounded nine American settlers and boatmen in western Wisconsin. The attacks ignited a panic within the American mining community, and federal and state officials mobilized a 750-man army to punish the Ho-Chunks, who, overmatched, chose to surrender. The leaders associated with the killings, Red Bird and We-Kau, came into Prairie du Chien with a white flag and calumet. Red Bird died in prison soon thereafter, and President John Quincy Adams pardoned the other warriors convicted of the June killings.[30]

"Red Bird's War" ended quickly, but the insecurity and fear that it revealed lingered on. The Fall Creek Massacre had already demonstrated the murderous distrust between whites and Indians, and so too, in a less dramatic way, had the debate between commissioners and chiefs at the 1826 Wabash treaty council. Michigan governor Lewis Cass asked the assembled chiefs and captains to cede all of their lands east of the Mississippi River and move to Indian Territory, predicting that otherwise horse stealing and whiskey peddling would unsettle both white and Indian communities and lead to violence. "You must all see," Cass asserted, "you cannot live in the neighborhood of the white people." In reply, Potawatomi leader Aubenaubee charged Cass and the other commissioners with "speak[ing] to us with deceitful lips, and not from your hearts." Whites, he said, were the ones responsible for selling the Lakes Indians liquor and driving off their game. The Miami leader Legro adopted a more confrontational tone, declaring that "it appears you have come to procure our land and bring on our destruction." Neither he nor other Miami chiefs remained at the treaty, and in the end the Potawatomis agreed only to a land cession. Cass and his colleagues maintained their equanimity. Most likely they understood that it was only a matter of time before they could get what they wanted, and what they believed the local white population wanted, from the Miamis and the Potawatomis: a removal treaty.[31]

◆ ◆ ◆

By 1812 the southern Lakes country had become a borderland between two rival empires, the United States and Britain, a region in which Indians pursued two different strategies to retain their autonomy. Some negotiated with the United States and selectively adopted elements of the Americans' culture, while others renounced Anglo-American civilization and attempted to form a fully independent Indian state. The Americans would not long tolerate the second movement, and during the war of 1812–14 the United States devoted much of its resources to destroying Tecumseh and Tenskwatawa's confederacy. The Americans built new forts, burned Indians' towns and fields, and ultimately used both land and naval forces to cut off and defeat the confederates.

Thereafter the Americans began turning the upper Great Lakes, formerly an autonomous Indian homeland, into a new borderland and the southern Lakes country into an exclusive white settlement zone, where Indians survived only in isolated enclaves. In the northern Lakes and upper Mississippi valley, large new army bases and trading posts, the latter operated primarily by the American Fur Company, extended American military and commercial influence into the homelands of the Menominees, Ho-Chunks, Dakotas, and Anishinaabeg. In the southern Lakes country, new land-cession treaties converted Indian nations from large landholders into annuity recipients living on small reserves, while state governments excluded Native Americans from the privileges of citizenship. The Wyandots, Potawatomis, Miamis, and other southern Lakes Indians resumed the process of managed cultural change and accommodation that many had embraced before the war, trading with their white neighbors, intermarrying with fur traders, and inviting missionaries to teach their children to plow and sew and read. What they could not do was persuade the battle-scarred white majority that they could peacefully coexist with Indians. Nor could they persuade white lawmakers that Native Americans did not threaten their plans for economic development and for a republic based on white supremacy and exclusivity. By the end of the 1820s, the only choice left to the southern Lakes Indians was not whether to engage with their white neighbors, but when and where they would have to move.

10

Trails of Death and Paths of Renewal

ON TWO OCCASIONS IN THE SEVENTEENTH AND EIGHTEENTH centuries, outsiders had turned the Great Lakes region into a "shatter zone," where hundreds died, communities collapsed, and many surviving Native Americans abandoned their homelands. One of these episodes occurred in the mid-1600s, when European epidemics and Iroquois warriors swept away the peoples of the eastern Lakes country. A second took place during the American Revolutionary era, when rebel armies and settler militias drove Native Americans out of modern Ohio and the lower Wabash valley. A third shattering struck the region in the 1830s and '40s, when the US War Department implemented the Indian Removal Act. This mass ethnic-cleansing operation had precursors earlier in the century, when federal officials persuaded several thousand lakes Indians to move voluntarily. The more concentrated and coercive program of Andrew Jackson and his successors, however, swept nearly all of the remaining Indians in the southern Lakes states and confined to enclaves the more populous nations of the northern Lakes. What the gun and the microbe could not do, the "pen and ink work" of federal treaty commissioners accomplished in just two decades.[1]

One should not view removal as a collision between an implacable, all-powerful American empire and a weak, victimized indigenous population. The United States certainly had more people and economic assets than the Lakes Indians, but it did not enjoy unlimited resources, and the Jackson, Van Buren, and Harrison/Tyler administrations could ill afford to remove all the Lakes Indians by force given their concurrent effort to remove the more populous Indian nations of the southeast. American officials responsible for removal in the Northwest thus preferred to follow the less expensive paths of negotiation, economic pressure, and fraud to induce Indians there to emigrate "voluntarily." These tactics gave shrewd Native leaders room to maneuver, to delay, to seek more compensation for their peoples' lands, or to look for white allies who would help them persuade the federal government to suspend its removal plans.[2]

The coerced emigration of fifteen or twenty thousand Lakes Indians often proved disastrous for the emigrants. Adults and children sickened and died during their long trek to their new reservations. Illness and hunger claimed the lives of three score Wyandots newly arrived in Kansas, and of four hundred Ojibwas tricked into coming to central Minnesota, and they drove a thousand Sauks and Mesquakies back to Illinois, starting a bloody war that killed more than five hundred people. Many so dreaded removal that they fled federal troops and officials and hid out, as many Miamis and Ho-Chunks did, or escaped to Canada, like many Potawatomis. Yet most of the emigrants survived, and while they did not forget their losses and trauma, they did not allow their tragedies to overwhelm them. The Shawnees and Delawares invested their energy in creating a prosperous new homeland, making a living as commercial farmers and traders, and building communities that reminded one New Englander of a "New England village among the mountains of New Hampshire or the Vermont woods." Meanwhile, in the northern Lakes country, the Odawas and Menominees used negotiation and local white allies to delay and then neutralize official demands for their expulsion. Removal left the landscape of the

Great Lakes region crisscrossed with trails of death and sorrow, but between and beyond those trails there remained room for new growth.[3]

✦ ✦ ✦

"Indian Removal" was the antiseptic name that American historians gave to the relocation, usually forced, of ninety thousand Native Americans from the eastern United States to reservations in Oklahoma, Kansas, Nebraska, and Iowa. Most of the relocations took place over two decades, from 1830, when Congress and President Jackson initiated their intensive program of Indian expulsion with the Indian Removal Act, to the early 1850s. Most of the Indian expellees came from the southeastern United States, but a substantial number hailed from the Great Lakes region. Indeed, Indian removal swept away the remaining Indian land claims and most of the actual Native American inhabitants of the three southern Lakes states.[4]

Removal proved expensive, costing the United States nearly $70 million during Andrew Jackson's presidency (1829–37). The motives driving the United States to organize an ethnic-cleansing operation of such magnitude, rather than simply leave the eastern Indians on their enclaves, ranged from the material to the visceral. Sweeping up the remaining Indian land in the eastern United States was certainly an important motive, and the seventy million acres that the Land Office acquired in the first set of removal treaties offset much of the cost of the relocations while enriching land speculators and Native Americans' creditors. Officials' broader political-economic motive for removing the eastern Indians was their belief that Native Americans impeded economic development. Small as they were, Indian enclaves often stood in the way of future canals and railroads, and their inhabitants paid no taxes and did not count toward each state's census population and political weight. Moreover, while this particular prejudice had never accurately reflected reality, most white Americans assumed that Indians primarily lived by hunting and gathering, and that whites could make better use of their land by converting it from woodland to commercial agriculture. "The rough appearances of nature must be overcome," insisted Indiana governor James Ray in the 1820s, "and made to yield to human enterprize."[5]

Finally, one must not discount racism as a crucial cause of Indian removal, particularly since it grew more virulent in the 1820s and '30s. Where previous white policy makers had proposed "civilizing" Native Americans and assimilating them into the mainstream population, official advocates of removal now described Indians as congenitally incapable of hard work and settled life, and prone to violence or wasting away from disease and alcohol when living near white settlements. Those Indians who had successfully adopted the practices of white civilization their critics branded as "half-breeds," guilty of a corruption of blood that made them untrustworthy. Absent relocation to the trans-Mississippi West, the eastern Indians endangered themselves and their white neighbors.[6]

Having assured themselves, or at least a majority of voters and Congressmen, of the necessity of Indian removal, policy makers also persuaded themselves that they could accomplish this mass ethnic cleansing with a minimum of force and expense. They based their reasoning on American officials' observation that eastern Indians had been voluntarily moving westward for several decades. In the 1790s and early 1800s, the Stockbridge Mohican sachem Hendrick Aupaumut had urged his kinsmen to move from western New York to the southern Lakes country. In the early 1820s the Stockbridges and their larger neighbors, the Oneida nation of Iroquois, purchased reserves in Wisconsin from the Ho-Chunks and Menominees. Pressured to relocate by the land-hungry New York state government, and inspired to move by the Kahnewake missionary Eleazar Williams, a few hundred Stockbridges and seven hundred Oneidas emigrated to Green Bay in the 1820s and '30s. While preserving customs (like commercial hunting and dispersed settlement) that they would have found hard to maintain in their settler-engulfed New York enclave, the Oneidas quickly built new homes and a prosperous agricultural economy on a new land base far from the white settlement frontier.[7]

Concurrently, some Indians emigrated from the southern Lakes region. Delaware, Kickapoo, and Shawnee families had begun moving to Spanish Missouri in the 1780s, and by the 1810s they had established there nearly a dozen settlements with a total population of two thousand. While the westerners sought to distance themselves from avaricious American settlers, their departure from the Ohio valley also insulated them from that region's Native American political conflicts and kept them favorably inclined toward the US government. During the War of 1812, Shawnee warriors, including Pappiqua, who had helped capture Daniel Boone in 1778, served alongside Missouri Territory's American militia. Voluntary emigration struck some American officials as the only way to isolate Indians from vicious frontiersmen and traders who might alienate them from the United States. This idea lay behind the War Department's temporary relocation of Sauk and Mesquakie neutralists to Missouri in 1813.[8]

The US government had begun encouraging voluntary removal earlier in the century, when President Jefferson advocated using the new Louisiana Purchase as a reservation for the eastern Indian nations and persuaded several hundred Cherokees to move to Arkansas. After the War of 1812, President James Monroe's Indian commissioners pressured select groups, such as the eastern Delawares and Kickapoos, to emigrate. At the end of his presidency, Monroe supported a bill setting aside the territory of future Oklahoma, Kansas, and Nebraska as a reserve for Indian emigrants. Under Monroe's successor, John Quincy Adams, federal commissioners stepped up the pressure on nations like the Potawatomis, offering them western land and travel expenses if they moved. Removal did not, however, become the core of US Indian policy until after the election of Andrew Jackson, who made Indian expulsion one of the highest priorities of his presidency.[9]

Jackson had made his political reputation fighting the Creeks and Seminoles and denouncing his foes as "barbarians," "savages," and "fiends." He tended to see all Native Americans as threats to white Americans, and by the start of his presidency he had persuaded himself that removal also served the best interest of Indians, perhaps the only way to save them from "annihilation." Jackson whipped his supporters in Congress into passing the Indian Removal Act of 1830, which authorized him to negotiate removal treaties with the eastern Indians and offer them reservations in Indian Territory if they gave up their lands in the east. Federal commissioners began negotiating the first treaty under the new law later that year, with the Choctaws, and the first northern removal treaty in 1831.[10]

The Shawnees numbered among the first Lakes Indian nations to sign removal agreements. Indeed, some did so even before passage of the removal act. In the early 1810s, white settlers in Missouri had plundered the western Shawnees' livestock and harried them out of their homes, and most of the emigrants relocated to new settlements in the Ozark Mountains. After fighting a war with the Osages, the western Shawnees and their Indian allies tried to form a western Indian state, which one of the movement's leaders, Colonel Lewis (Quatewepea), advertised to the US government as a partner in its voluntary Indian-removal program. The War Department rejected the proposal, and in 1825 federal commissioners persuaded the western Shawnees to leave Missouri for a reservation in modern Kansas. The aging Shawnee prophet Tenskwatawa, now working with Lewis Cass, was concurrently persuading several hundred eastern Shawnees to accompany him to Kansas, an arduous though not generally fatal overland journey. Some Shawnees rejected the Kansas option and moved instead to the Mexican province of Texas. In 1831, the Shawnees at Wapakoneta in Ohio agreed to cede their last few square miles of land and join their western kinsmen.[11]

American officials began pressing the Wyandots to leave Ohio at roughly the same time, though thanks to delaying tactics the Wyandots managed to avoid moving for a decade. In 1831, Wyandot chiefs declined to consider removal until they sent a reconnaissance party to their prospective reservation in Kansas. Once the party returned, its members urged their kinsmen to continue holding out against removal. Several years later Wyandot leaders flatly rejected another proposed removal treaty and prohibited private discussion of land sales, though they did allow the nation's principal chief, the biracial trader William Walker, to swap a thirty-eight-thousand-acre tract for famine-relief funds. Federal officials, now under pressure from the anxious Ohio legislature, resumed removal negotiations in 1837 and began employing a divide-and-conquer strategy. Treaty commissioners drove a wedge between the Christian Wyandots and the traditionalists of the so-called Pagan Party, plying the second group with alcohol and inviting its leading men to Washington to negotiate removal. Facing the prospect of internal secession, Walker and the Christian Party finagled authorization for two more reconnaissance parties, thereby managing another couple of years of delay. In 1841, however, the murder of antiremoval chief Summondewat and several of his relatives fatally demoralized those Wyandots who hoped to remain in Ohio, and Walker and other chiefs signed a final removal agreement. The Treaty of Upper Sandusky (1842) traded the Wyandots' 110,000-acre tract in Ohio and a smaller tract in Michigan for a 168,000-acre reserve in Kansas, plus thirty-five individual land grants to chiefs and to Anglo-Americans married to Wyandot spouses. It also paid compensation for lost houses and farms and $27,500 in emigration funds. In the summer of 1843 Wyandot families shuttered their homes and headed for their new reserve in Kansas, where illness and exposure would kill one in twelve of the emigrants over the course of the next year.[12]

Coerced and pressed as they had been, the Shawnees and Wyandots avoided confrontation with American troops and experienced few casualties during their semivoluntary migration. Their western neighbors, the Miamis and Potawatomis, were not so lucky. The 1834 Wabash Forks treaty liquidated most of the Miamis' remaining landholdings in Indiana, whose legislature wanted to clear the way for the Wabash and Erie Canal. Indiana settlers, meanwhile, continued to view the Miamis as a security threat, a view sharpened by the Black Hawk War a few hundred miles west. President Jackson concurred with the Hoosiers and forced the War Department to renegotiate the 1834 treaty to ensure Miami removal. In 1836–37 commissioner Jonathan Keller submitted to the president and Senate an unsigned draft treaty and an "agreement-in-principle" memorandum approved by a few Miami chiefs. The Senate approved the unsigned treaty, and President Martin Van Buren sent it back to the Miamis' agent, who used the unlawful fait accompli to procure signatures from thirty chiefs. This extortionate agreement took most of the Miamis' remaining lands in the east in exchange for a reservation in Kansas and $335,000, of which about 45 percent ($150,000) would go to pay debts owed to local traders. (One agent estimated that 70 percent of the white families in northeastern Indiana made their living selling overpriced goods and alcohol to the Miamis, in expectation of just such a payoff.) The nation would not have to move until they "may be disposed to emigrate," but a subsequent 1840 treaty ordered the Miamis, apart from those living on small individual farms, to leave Indiana. For their remaining tribal lands the Miamis would receive $250,000, and their traders another $300,000.[13]

It took the US government several more years to recruit supply and transportation contractors for the Miamis' removal. When at last the War Department began rounding up Miami families in 1846, some refused to cooperate, taking refuge in Michigan or trying to hide in the woods and marshlands near their homes. Armed white officials apprehended most of these fugitives and shipped them to Kansas. Several hundred Miamis with individual land grants remained in Indiana, where their ancestors still lived a century later.[14]

Some of the Miami fugitives took refuge in Michigan with a community of Potawatomis, part of a nation that had faced similar removal pressures and whose people had split into factions as they responded to the crisis. In order to wear down the Potawatomis' resistance and mop up their lands in Indiana, Illinois, and Michigan, federal commissioners negotiated twenty separate treaties with Potawatomi leaders between 1827 and 1837. The most important were three treaties negotiated in 1832, which reduced the Potawatomis' eastern land holdings to 120 tracts and paid them $1.3 million, and an 1833 treaty at Chicago, attended by about a thousand Potawatomi families and a motley gathering of whiskey peddlers, fur traders, and property claimants. At the 1833 conference Potawatomi leaders exchanged their nation's remaining lands in the Great Lakes region for a five-million-acre reserve west of the Mississippi River, and $1 million in cash and emigration funds. Twelve percent ($285,000) of the Potawatomis' compensation from the 1832–33 treaties went to pay trading debts. In 1835, after the Senate moved the Potawatomi reservation to Iowa and chiefs and commissioners signed a confirming agreement, the War Department began organizing the first emigration parties.[15]

More than one-third of the Potawatomis refused to comply with the removal agreements, which some believed fraudulent. They evaded or confronted officials who came to take them from their homes. Some found refuge near modern Saint Joseph, Michigan, where chief Leopold Pokagon had purchased a tract of land for his and other Potawatomi families and held it with the aid of a sympathetic state judge, Epaphroditus Random. Some departed for Iowa and Kansas with their removal parties but slipped away while on the trail and headed back east. In Wisconsin the army rounded up and deported several hundred Potawatomi returnees in 1848 and six hundred more in 1851. Still others fled to Canada, where about three thousand Potawatomis lived on the eastern shore of Lake Huron by the 1840s.[16]

Ironically, the Canadian region that the Potawatomis viewed as a refuge was one that some Britons wanted to use as a reservation for all Canadian Indians. Lieutenant Governor Sir Francis Bond Head proposed in 1836 moving all the Native peoples (Mississaugas, Mohawks, and others) from eastern Canada to Manitoulin Island, arguing that this would preserve Indians from the "corruption"—alcohol and disease—of white settlements. However, Sir Francis's proposal proved short-lived. Canadian Indians and missionaries objected to it, and provincial legislatures balked at paying removal's expense. The government of Upper Canada preferred instead to "civilize" Native Americans in situ, using a £20,000 annual fund established by the Crown (1829) to subsidize Protestant missions and schools, and prohibiting whites from buying Indian lands or selling them alcohol. Not all whites in North America, not even in the Great Lakes region, wanted Indians expelled from their homelands.[17]

Removal proved difficult and deadly for many Potawatomis. Those forcibly evicted from their homes suffered the greatest casualties. In 1838 Indiana militia arrested a Potawatomi band headed by chief Menominee, who had refused orders to move and burned a squatter's cabin. The stress of eviction, combined with poor rations and typhoid, caused 300 of the 850 involuntary migrants to sicken and 43 to die on what the nation later called "the Trail of Death." During one thirty-four-day period of the expedition, William Polke in his journal made nineteen separate references to the death of one or more children. As the survivors marched or rode through the towns of central Illinois, white settlers turned out to watch them, regarding the Potawatomis as exotic specimens of a dying race.[18]

This represented a significant change from white Illinoisans' attitude toward another group of Native Americans, who had resisted removal from their state just six years earlier. The Sauk and Mesquakie Indians had since the eighteenth century resided on both sides of the Mississippi River, but in the 1820s American officials began pressuring the nations' leaders to leave their lands in Illinois, which the Sauk and Fox had allegedly ceded to the United States in 1804. In 1829, the Sauk and Mesquakie agent convened a treaty council and secured the chiefs' and captains' confirmation that they would stay in Iowa. A substantial faction, led by the charismatic war captain Black Hawk, refused to abandon their homes and the graves of their ancestors at Saukenuk.[19]

In 1830–31, Black Hawk led several hundred of his followers back to Illinois, where they planted their crops and warned off American settlers. In the summer of 1831, after the Sauks and Mesquakies destroyed the homes of several white intruders, the local US Army commandant made a show of force, bringing thirty-four hundred regular troops and militia to Saukenuk to disperse the insurgents. While the Indian returnees reluctantly agreed to withdraw, the winter months in Iowa brought sickness, hunger, and death to many of them. These more powerful forces pushed Black Hawk's band back into Illinois the following spring, touching off what the Americans called Black Hawk's War.[20]

Black Hawk believed he could either mollify the Americans or intimidate them into letting his people stay in the east. His twelve hundred followers included disaffected Potawatomis and several hundred Kickapoos and Ho-Chunks who did not wish to leave Illinois, and he hoped for additional aid from other Indians in the region and from British agents. Moreover, the Sauk leader had a close relationship with a Ho-Chunk prophet, Wabokieshiek, who had established a multi-tribal town on the Rock River, and he hoped to use the prophet's settlement as a refuge. These hopes dissolved shortly after Black Hawk's return to Illinois, and by May 1832 he had decided to surrender to the Americans, if they allowed him to do so. Unfortunately, the first American troops to encounter Black Hawk's band were trigger-happy Illinois militia, who opened fire on Sauk men approaching them under flag of truce (May 14, 1832). The warriors counterattacked, killing twelve militiamen and routing the rest. Some of the insurgents subsequently attacked white travelers and raided American settlements in northern Illinois, satisfying their desire for vengeance but also strengthening the Americans' determination to crush them.[21]

The rest of the grim story swiftly unfolded. Black Hawk and his companions retreated to Lake Koshkonong in southern Wisconsin, where they paused for several weeks to resupply before heading for the Mississippi River. The Americans raised an overwhelming force to destroy the insurgents: seven thousand federal soldiers and state militia, some brought in by steamboat from the eastern Great Lakes, and several hundred Dakota, Ho-Chunk, and Menominee warriors. American troops caught up with Black Hawk's band at Wisconsin Heights, where they fought an indecisive battle on July 21. The final act came at Bad Axe on the Mississippi River (August 2, 1832), where the Americans pinned Black Hawk's followers between white soldiers on land and a gunboat, the *Warrior*, on the river. The American forces opened fire on the Sauk leader when he tried to surrender, and they killed at least three hundred Indians in the ensuing battle, some of them women and children shot as they tried to flee across the river. While the smoke cleared several American soldiers took skin from Sauk and Mesquakie warriors' bodies to make into razor strops. Black Hawk, who managed to escape the battle alive, became a different kind of trophy: Ho-Chunk warriors arrested him, and the War Department sent him eastward to display in American cities.[22]

The Black Hawk War left a heavy mark on the Great Lakes Indians. Fear of Native American insurgency led white settlers in Indiana to demand removal of the Miamis and probably lay behind the Ohio legislature's insistence on Wyandot removal. The Sauks and Mesquakies had to sign a new treaty ceding seventeen thousand square miles of land, much of it prime lead-mining country, on the west bank of the Mississippi River. The United States took the land "as indemnity for the expense incurred" in the war and as a buffer zone for Illinois, thereby "secur[ing] the future safety . . . of the invaded frontier." (This essentially constituted a Sauk and Mesquakie war-guilt clause.) Having withdrawn from the Mississippi valley, the two nations came under renewed pressure from their creditors, from bad harvests that left them short of food, and from American officials and settlers who wanted their remaining land.

Tribal leaders signed four new treaties in 1836–37, selling 1.5 million more acres of land in Missouri and Iowa for $700,000 in debt payment, goods, and bank stock. Federal commissioners in 1841 began negotiating a final removal treaty, which the Sauks and Mesquakies signed in the fall of 1842, liquidating their remaining territory—about one-third of the present state of Iowa—in exchange for another $1.05 million in bank stock and debt payment, and a reservation on the Osage River. The Sauks began moving to Kansas the next year, with small bands continuing the migration into 1845. Most of the Mesquakies managed to elude removal agents and remain in Iowa, where they cultivated a nonthreatening public image and fit themselves peacefully into the local economy. In 1856, responding to petitions from white Iowans who wanted the Mesquakie nation to remain in the state, the Iowa legislature created a permanent reservation for them.[23]

While their government pushed and bullied the Sauks and Mesquakies, federal officials also pressed those nations' former neighbors, the Indians of Wisconsin, to leave that territory permanently. Army officers in the region feared that a new Black Hawk might form another alliance against the United States, and the immigration of white settlers into eastern Wisconsin supposedly made it impossible for the Native Americans to subsist there. This seemed true of the Ho-Chunks, Black Hawk's former allies, most of whom the United States obliged to withdraw north of the Wisconsin River in an 1832 treaty. By 1836 army officers reported that the small nation was in a wretched state, wracked by hunger, dressed in rags, and beset by whiskey peddlers and traders' duns. Hard winters and temporary privation were nothing new to the northern Lakes nations, however, and the Ho-Chunks had not become so demoralized that they accepted exploitation and removal without resistance. Their leaders rejected many traders' claims as fraudulent and opposed officials' demands for their removal.[24]

In 1837 the War Department resorted to underhanded tactics. Commissioners invited two dozen Ho-Chunk men, including the prominent war captain Waukonhaucau, to Washington City, then kept them there until the delegates signed a removal treaty. The translator asserted that the agreement would give the delegates' people eight years to remove, but the actual document said eight months. Not surprisingly, Ho-Chunk leaders determined to stay in Wisconsin and refused to inspect their reservation until 1839. General Henry Atkinson began organizing mandatory emigration parties that same year, but many Ho-Chunk families refused to join them and stayed in their homes, where federal officials eventually arrested them and deported them to Iowa. The Ho-Chunk reservation in Iowa did not last long: lead miners and land speculators coveted the region, and traders further up the Mississippi River coveted Indian annuities, which they hoped to tap by moving potential customers closer to themselves. In 1846 trader Henry Rice and federal commissioners persuaded the Ho-Chunks to exchange their lands in Iowa for an eight-hundred-thousand-acre reserve in central Minnesota. Along with some of their kinsmen from Wisconsin, the Iowa Ho-Chunks boarded a steamboat for Minnesota in 1847.[25]

The new Ho-Chunk reservation in the northern woods adjoined a six-hundred-thousand-acre tract set aside for the Menominees, whom Wisconsin settlers and Minnesota traders wanted to move. By 1847 the twenty-three-hundred-strong Menominee nation had been fighting to keep its old homeland for more than a decade, and their leaders would expend more effort fighting to remain in Wisconsin, a fight they ultimately managed to win. In an 1831 treaty Menominee delegates had agreed to cede three million acres of land to the United States and to emigrant Indians from New York. The treaty also obliged the Menominees to make additional cessions whenever "the President . . . shall deem it expedient to extinguish their title." When in 1836 Wisconsin Territorial Governor Henry Dodge reminded Menominee chiefs of this obligation, Ayamataw, who had attended the earlier treaty, declared that no one had told him or the other signatories anything about the mandatory-sale clause. Under pressure from Dodge, Oshkosh and other chiefs agreed to cede another four million acres of land for $650,000 in annuities, provisions, smiths' salaries, and traders' claims. As with other Lakes Indians, these claims had become quite large, since private traders bought furs cheaply, sold expensive merchandise on credit, and then claimed the Menominees' land-sale proceeds and annuities in payment; one traveler described the Menominees' traders as so many "vampires . . . [and] leeches," eager to drain the nation's economic lifeblood.[26]

FIGURE 3. This 1842 lithograph shows a Menominee (Folles Avoines) summer settlement in present-day Wisconsin. Francis de Castelnau, "Village of Folles Avoines." *Courtesy of the Wisconsin Historical Society, Image WHi-6049*

The Menominees now confined themselves to the region north of Green Bay, but whites' demand for their land and resources persisted. The territorial legislature petitioned Congress to liquidate the nation's land claims on the Fox River, while loggers trespassed on Menominee territory and territorial governors made Menominee removal one of their priorities. In 1848, the year Wisconsin became a state, commissioner William Medill negotiated the Treaty of Lake Powawhaykonnay, committing the Menominees to move to their new reserve in Minnesota, and offering them $350,000 in return. Like the Menominees' earlier treaties with the United States, the 1848 agreement rested on coercion and fraud. Medill understated the amount of land the Menominees were ceding (somewhere between 5 and 7.5 million acres) in order to lowball their compensation. The federal secretary of the interior, whose department assumed responsibility for Indian affairs in 1849, admitted the fraud a few years later. Federal commissioners told

Menominee chiefs that if they didn't sign the treaty the army would march their people out of the state without compensation. At least one leader, Shoneon, refused to sign even under such a threat, asking of Medill, "Why don't he go there [Minnesota] himself and live in such a fine country?" A Menominee reconnaissance party sent to Minnesota affirmed Shoneon's skepticism, reporting that the land was "bleak [and] barren," and this helped persuade national leaders to petition for reversal of the removal treaty. President Zachary Taylor did not restore the Menominees' ceded lands but did allow them to move to a temporary reservation on the Wolf River. By now even white settlers had come to sympathize with the Menominees, seeing them as a small and unthreatening remnant confined to an isolated corner of the state; some petitioned Taylor's successor, Millard Fillmore, to let the tribe remain in Wisconsin. In 1854 the US government agreed to make the Menominee reservation permanent and paid the nation $240,000 for the lands taken from them without compensation six years earlier.[27]

In contrast to the southern Lakes region, where a swelling white settler population and ambitious state legislatures pushed federal officials to remove the Indians, removal pressures in the upper Lakes country proved easier for Native Americans to resist. Michigan, Wisconsin, and Minnesota attained statehood and the political leverage accompanying it between 1837 and 1858, up to half a century later than the lower Lakes states. Their white population grew more slowly, and the lower population density in the region made it easier for officials to create reserves for nations like the Menominees and (eventually) the Ho-Chunks. In some areas, like Minnesota, local economies still depended on Indian labor and capital, in the form of the fur trade and annuity payments, while northern Lakes states with a large Métis or "civilized" Indian population wanted to incorporate bicultural Native Americans into their tax base and census count.[28]

Thus, while the Jackson administration wanted to remove Odawa Indians from Michigan and liquidated most of that nation's remaining land in the territory, Odawa leaders managed to put off removal until both state and federal governments accepted their continued residence in Michigan. An 1836 treaty with Odawa and Ojibwa chiefs ceded the two nations' lands throughout the state, except for seventeen small tracts or islands that the Anishinaabeg could occupy for five more years while awaiting removal. Shortly thereafter Odawa leaders declared their new homeland in Kansas unsuitable for their kinfolk—it lacked sufficient maple groves for Odawa women, among other deficiencies—and demanded a northern woodland reserve, which the Jackson and Van Buren administrations could not easily provide. While grounding their opposition on their traditional economy, the Odawas concurrently pursued, in the words of one historian, "their own 'civilization policy.'" They bought previously ceded land from the United States' land offices and set up agricultural villages on the Grand River, at Arbre Croche, and at Traverse Bay, where they raised livestock, grain, and potatoes. This won them the support of local missionaries, while men's continued hunting and drawing of annuities ensured that Michigan traders would stay interested in keeping them nearby. Moreover, the Odawas had cross border ties to British Indian agents and to Anishinaabeg living on Manitoulin Island. In the early 1840s small parties of Michigan Odawas and Ojibwas had joined Potawatomis moving to Upper Canada, and the administration of John Tyler, whose relationship with Britain had soured, had no wish to turn more Indians into British subjects. In the 1840s the US War and Interior Departments did not press the issue of Odawa removal, and the Michigan legislature petitioned Congress to let the Odawas remain in their state, even offering (in 1850) state citizenship to those who gave up their separate tribal identity. In 1855 the Senate ratified a new treaty with the Odawas and Michigan Ojibwas, allowing them to remain in Michigan if they accepted the division of their remaining lands into family allotments.[29]

The Ojibwas pursued a similar accommodative strategy, and in the long term they managed to remain in their upper Great Lakes homeland, though in the shorter term American greed and party politics forced several thousand of them into a deadly exile. The Ojibwas had strengthened their ties to the Americans throughout the 1830s, accepting missionaries into their communities to strengthen their tie to the US government, and trading with the American Fur Company (and piling up ever-larger debts with them). In 1837 they sold the United States ten million acres of timberland for $870,000 in cash, provisions, and claims payments, plus their retention of hunting and fishing rights in the cession. In the 1840s, Ojibwa leaders ceded several million more acres of copper-rich territory in Michigan's Upper Peninsula in return for increased annuities, which they received at La Pointe, the Ojibwas' ceremonial "capital."[30]

Despite, or more likely because of, the Ojibwas' determination to keep the peace, white Americans increased their efforts to appropriate the nation's remaining resources. Throughout the 1840s whites squatted on the Ojibwas' remaining lands and illegally cut their timber. At the end of that decade an ambitious federal official, Governor Alexander Ramsey of Minnesota Territory, attempted to gain control of the annuity payments and teachers' salaries that the Ojibwas were receiving for their land cessions. Like Henry Rice and other northern fur traders, Ramsey believed that bringing annuity-drawing Indians to Minnesota would strengthen the new territory's economy. The governor also had political motives for seeking the Ojibwas' relocation: he belonged to the American Whig Party, the national rival to the Jacksonian Democratic Party. While the Democrats controlled the state government of Wisconsin, the Whigs, through their president Zachary Taylor, controlled the territory of Minnesota, and moving the Wisconsin Ojibwas would transfer their resources from the Democrats' control to the Whigs'. In 1850, Ramsey moved the Ojibwas' agency and annuity distribution site to Sandy Lake in Minnesota, and President Taylor used the false pretext of Ojibwa "depredations" to command their removal from Wisconsin.[31]

There followed the deadliest episode (aside from the Black Hawk War) of northern Indian removal. Over five thousand Ojibwas gathered at Sandy Lake in the fall of 1850, only to find a near-total lack of food: the local rice harvest had failed and the US government's rations had spoiled. The emigrants from Wisconsin and Michigan's Upper Peninsula left the reserve a few months later, trudging back home through the snows. Hunger, illness, and exposure killed over four hundred people by winter's end. The survivors did not allow the Americans to forget the crime their government had committed, though they took care to hang the blame on Governor Ramsey and on their agent, John Watrous. Ojibwa chiefs testified to the Sandy Lake disaster in speeches and written memorials, and in 1852 a party led by the elderly *ogema* or chief Bizhiki (Buffalo) went to Washington to seek restoration of the Ojibwas' eastern reservations. As with the Michigan Odawas, local whites supported the Ojibwas' campaign against removal; many of them were copper miners who depended on Anishinaabe women for food and clothing. White miners, settlers, and newspaper editors in northern Wisconsin and Michigan signed antiremoval petitions, which Bizhiki and his companions brought to Washington. President Millard Fillmore lifted his predecessor's removal order, and a few years later an antiremoval commissioner of Indian Affairs, George Manypenny, took office. Manypenny negotiated or organized new treaties in 1854–55 that granted permanent reservations in Michigan and Wisconsin to the Lake Superior Ojibwas and larger reserves, including Leech Lake and White Earth, to the Anishinaabeg of northern Minnesota. With a few exceptions during the American Civil War, the removal era had effectively ended in the Old Northwest.[32]

◆ ◆ ◆

Removal hardly marked the end of history for those Indians, chiefly from the southern Lakes region, whom the United States persuaded or forced to emigrate. To be sure, removal proved deadly for some. Several hundred Potawatomis sickened or died on the trail to Kansas, sixty Wyandots died within a year of their arrival in the West, part of a group of Odawa migrants died in an 1845 flood of the Kansas River, and upwards of three hundred Sauk emigrants died of cholera and smallpox between 1849 and 1851. But the great majority of the fifteen to twenty thousand Lakes Indian migrants rebuilt their homes in Minnesota, Kansas, Oklahoma, and Texas and resumed the everyday tasks of making a living, educating their children, and governing themselves. The Potawatomi chief Pepishkay declared that his people "had been taken from homes affording them plenty, and brought to a desert . . . to be scattered and left as the husbandman scatters his seed." He intended the simile to illustrate the United States' neglect of its Indian subjects, but it also pointed to a hidden truth: even in a desert, seeds can germinate and new life grow.[33]

One immediate change that most of the emigrants had to make was the acceleration of their shift from a mixed subsistence economy to commercial agriculture. The Lakes Indians found themselves in a new environment, a flat tallgrass prairie with patchy tree cover and violent weather. Their new reserves lacked the freshwater fisheries, maple groves, and wild rice marshes that had previously provided much of their food. Moreover, locally well-established Indian nations, like the Comanches and Otos, already claimed the principal trans-Mississippi hunting ranges, and on some of those ranges stocks of game had steeply declined; by the 1840s the prime hunting frontier had moved north to the Dakotas and Minnesota. Commercial hunting remained viable for newcomers willing to take risks, like the Delawares, who hunted for furs and bison hides well beyond their settlements in eastern Kansas. Within a few years of removal, however, most of the southern Lakes Indians were raising horses, hogs, cattle, grain, and potatoes, and they were selling their surpluses to the army or to nearby white settlers. More prosperous emigrants, like the Shawnee chief Joseph Parks, had large commercial farms worked by African-American slaves, technically a violation of a federal ban on slavery in the northern Louisiana Purchase, but a ban that Indian agents declined to enforce. To the north, in Minnesota Territory, the Ho-Chunks who voluntarily emigrated from Iowa found themselves excluded from commercial hunting by their Dakota and Ojibwa neighbors. They spent several lean years in their reserve on Saint Peters River before swapping the land, in 1855, for a tract of prairie in southwestern Minnesota. There the Ho-Chunks established productive farms and enjoyed a fair standard of living for seven years.[34]

The Lakes Indian migrants did not base their economies solely on agriculture. They worked as wage laborers for the army and for white farmers in Missouri. The Wyandots, Potawatomis, and Delawares operated ferries for white migrants heading for Oregon and California; by 1848 these generated enough revenue that the Wyandot government made the position of ferryman an official and elected one. In Texas, Delaware and Shawnee migrants whom the Texas Republic had expelled in 1839 returned a few years later by invitation of President Samuel Houston, who encouraged them to settle on the republic's northwestern frontier. Prior to their permanent removal from Texas in 1853, the emigrants worked as intermediary traders, buying furs and pelts from the Comanches and selling them to the Texas republic's frontier trading houses. Some Shawnee and Delaware men continued to follow the traditional male profession of warrior: over one hundred Shawnees went to Florida to fight alongside American soldiers in the Second Seminole War, while other Lakes Indians scouted for the US Army in Texas.[35]

The emigrants also continued, despite some missionaries' fears that they would lose interest after removal, to seek vocational and grammar-school education for at least some of their children. Christianity it-self still held little attraction for most Lakes Indians, but men like the Shawnee Blackhoof had a pragmatic appreciation for the other subjects missionaries could teach, like English literacy and blacksmithing. Ac-cording to one white observe, Blackhoof told other chiefs that Indian children needed to "learn the cunning of the white faces, and thus be able to compete successfully." The Kansas Shawnees took this to heart, allowing Protestant missionaries to establish missions and schools on their reservation. The Methodists built the massive Shawnee Manual Labor School (1839), a twelve-building complex on a two-thousand-acre site adjoining the Santa Fe Trail, where several hundred Shawnee and other Indian students enrolled in the 1840s and '50s. Isaac McCoy and his Baptist associates opened a day school and sought to promote adult literacy by developing an orthography of the Shawnee language and publishing a Shawnee newspaper, the *Shuwaunowe Kesauthwau* (or *Shawnee Sun*). Several of the other southern Lakes nations permitted missionaries to open churches and schools on their land, as did the Ho-Chunks once they moved to southwestern Minnesota.[36]

The removed Indians viewed education as important adaptive training for their children. Schools also helped Native Americans assert their national sovereignty, insofar as the money for construction and salaries came from tribal funds under control of Indian leaders. Chiefs used the allocation of school funds to favor particular denominations or particular approaches to schooling, like boarding schools—which helped Indian parents feed some of their children in lean years—instead of day schools. The nations' political leaders concurrently struggled to maintain control of other tribal resources, along with some kind of autonomous decision-making capability. The Shawnees repeatedly protested an 1847 federal statute requiring the payment of annuities to heads of household (rather than chiefs), arguing that this would undermine their authority. To bolster their local authority, they and the Wyandots created elective tribal assemblies in the early 1850s. The Shawnees and the Kansas band of Odawas drafted written law codes that outlawed alcohol sales and property crimes and, in the Odawas' code, levied taxes for support of the poor. These laws did not benefit all Indians equally; a few, like a Shawnee ordinance requiring that all women who drank excessively have their heads shaved, clearly discriminated against a large group. Some of the new Indian governments, however, maintained a greater degree of equity. The Wyandot constitution permitted women to vote, and the nation held its elections during the Green Corn ceremony, an affirmation of fertility and (matrilineal) clan membership.[37]

The American federal government tolerated the emigrants' political autonomy as long as they resided in an unorganized part of the Louisiana Purchase, on the borderland between white settlements and Plains Indians (like the Osages) whom the United States had not subdued. Federal agents did not even object when the Lakes Indian governments created a diplomatic league, reminiscent of the confederations of the eighteenth century, to ensure intertribal amity and discuss military defense. This tolerance ended in 1854, when the US Congress decided to open the Kansas and Nebraska Territories to white settlement. White farmers had wanted these territories opened for some time, and the Wyandot government supported territorial status because they believed it would increase local demand for their people's goods and services. In addition, the California Gold Rush persuaded Congress that the United States should build a railroad that could securely transport gold from the Pacific coast to the eastern states. Senator Stephen Douglas of Illinois wanted to run that railroad through the central rather than the southern Plains, and he convinced Congress to organize Kansas and Nebraska Territories in order to facilitate railroad land grants and construction. As part of the "opening" of Kansas, the Interior Department negotiated a new set of treaties with the Indian nations in Kansas, including the emigrants. These imposed on the Miamis, Shawnees, and Wyandots allotment provisions similar to those in concurrent treaties with the northern Lakes Anishinaabeg. The emigrants received land allotments of two hundred acres per person, plus payments of cash and stock—totaling about $1.85 million—for their remaining lands and as liquidation payments for their annuities, which Commissioner George Manypenny considered sources of pernicious dependency. The Delawares and Kickapoos, meanwhile, retained reservations but sold most of their remaining lands, either outright or with the proviso that the US government would market them and invest the proceeds for their "civilization, education, and religious culture." Through these and other treaties with Kansas's Native American nations, the federal government obtained about two-thirds of all the Indian land in the territory, or twenty-seven million acres.[38]

Shortly thereafter, the emigrants witnessed a preview of the war that would soon spread through half the continent. The Kansas-Nebraska Act permitted white settlers in the new territories to choose whether or not to outlaw slavery. A faction from the neighboring slave state of Missouri, determined not to allow another free state and refuge for runaways on their own state's borders, moved into Kansas to establish a proslavery territorial government and militia. Another "free-soil" group from the northeastern United States moved to Kansas to prevent slaveholders from turning it into another slave state. (Free-soil militia captain John Brown and his sons moved to the territory from Ohio, for instance.) They organized their own territorial government and militia and by the end of 1855 had entered a shooting war with proslavery settlers, which by the time it ended in 1860 had killed about fifty people. The Lakes Indians in Kansas endeavored to stay out of this internecine war, and the federal commissioner of Indian Affairs said their behavior compared "favorably with the disorderly and lawless conduct of many of their white brethren." They did give their names to some of the combatants' towns, battle sites, and even their nicknames, like "Osawatomie" John Brown, who killed five proslavery settlers in 1856; Pottawatomie Creek, the site of Brown's attack; and Wyandotte, the town where free-soil legislators drafted Kansas's final constitution shortly before statehood and the outbreak of the Civil War.[39]

✦ ✦ ✦

Indian removal had no one single architect, and no single motive drove its supporters. Andrew Jackson bore more responsibility for the mass expulsion of the eastern Indians than any other individual, but his presidential predecessors certainly favored Indian emigration, and his successors, right up to the 1850s, continued to implement removal. So did a host of officials and government employees: the commissioners who negotiated removal treaties, the army officers who rounded up and escorted emigrant parties, the contractors who provided (or failed to provide) transport, and the agents who urged their Native American clients to move. And private citizens by the thousands supported removal. They feared Indian warriors' attacks, or desired Indians' land and resources, or believed that Native Americans impeded economic and social progress. Indian removal was both a mass movement of people and a mass political movement.

Viewed in this light, removal seemed a nearly irresistible force, pitting the will and resources of thirty million Americans against only thirty thousand or so Lakes Indians. On the ground, though, appearances changed. Federal officials like Henry Dodge argued that Indians could not resist the flood tide of white settlement and American power, but not all Indians found such threats compelling. In practice the War and Interior Departments needed not only substantial outlays of money but also manipulation, fraud, and force to move the southern Lakes Indians. The Ohio Shawnees departed voluntarily, mainly because many of their kinsmen had already moved west of the Mississippi River. The Wyandots held out for a decade before federal commissioners split them into factions and threatened to procure a removal treaty from one or the other. The Ho-Chunks learned they had signed a treaty with deceptive and mistranslated terms. Commissioners beat down Potawatomi resistance with twenty separate treaties and obtained the Miamis' consent to removal with a "preapproved" treaty that chiefs then felt compelled to sign. Each of the latter three nations had communities whose inhabitants evaded removal or suffered arrest and deportation by federal troops. The Sauks and Mesquakies suffered still worse fates, losing between 450 and 600 people when one band resisted their removal orders and federal troops intervened.[40]

Black Hawk and his companions might disagree, but American power had not become utterly irresistible by the 1830s. The US government's resort to irregular treaty negotiations and outright fraud demonstrated not its strength but the ongoing limits on its financial and military resources, particularly in a part of the country that the Jackson administration saw as less valuable than the southeast. Lakes Indians took advantage of these limits, and of the negotiating power they derived from the treaty-making process, by delaying removal and in many cases avoiding it altogether. True, most of the southern Lakes Indians ultimately left for Kansas, sometimes at gunpoint, but several hundred Miamis and several thousand Potawatomis remained in Indiana and Michigan or crossed over to Canada. In the northern Lakes states, where Indians were more numerous and more important to whites' extractive economy, most Native Americans were able to remain in their homelands. The Menominees, most of the Michigan Odawas, and the Lake Superior Ojibwas agreed, as the southern Lakes Indians had done several decades earlier, to confine themselves to an archipelago of residential enclaves. All of these nations lost millions of acres of land, and the Ojibwas lost four hundred people to an abortive attempt to move them. However, thanks to their remoteness from the white-settlement frontier and their chiefs' bargaining skill, they could postpone removal until the American federal government no longer wanted to pursue it.[41]

Between 40 and 50 percent of the Lakes Indians thus remained in the Great Lakes region, either in the United States or Canada, after removal. Those who did move generally survived the ordeal, and they soon began to confound the US government's expectations of them. Andrew Jackson and his supporters had pushed removal in part because they assumed Native Americans were incapable of change and needed a refuge where they could roam and hunt, far from white settlements. Instead, the removed Lakes Indians resumed their shift to a predominantly agricultural and commercial economy. Far from separating themselves from whites, the emigrants sold them their produce, worked for them as ferrymen, and invited missionaries to educate their children. Far from becoming unsophisticated nomads, the Ho-Chunks, Shawnees, Wyandots, and others established new farming communities and, in many cases, drafted law codes and national constitutions. It would be a stretch to say that Indian removal was a positive good; too many people had died and too many more had suffered the trauma of losing beloved kinsmen and homes. Yet the southern Lakes Indians generally survived and sometimes prospered in their new homeland.

One might well describe this homeland using a label that formerly applied to the Great Lakes region: a borderland. This new borderland occupied the geographical space between white American settlements and the domain of those Plains Indians whom the United States had not subjected to its authority. As the Lakes Indians knew well, borderlands could easily turn violent, especially when they became contested zones between empires—like the new "empire" that Southern white separatists launched following the election of a free-soil Republican to the presidency. Thereafter the emigrants would experience another convulsive wave of violence, a result of what would prove the last imperial war in North America.

Conclusion

The Last Imperial War and the Last Removals

IF ONE DEFINES AN EMPIRE AS AN EXPANDING NATION WITH ONE or more subordinate subject peoples, then the United States certainly qualified for the name, even if Americans might have objected to it. From its creation in the late 1700s, the US government and its citizens sought to obtain new land and resources in North America, and it actively pursued the conquest and exploitation of subject peoples, namely, Native Americans and Mexican citizens. The nation-state that tried to secede from the United States in 1861, the Confederate States of America, also displayed imperial characteristics, which grew naturally from the political vision and interests of its founders. Southern white slaveholders depended for their wealth on AfricanAmerican slavery, and by the 1820s many believed that this institution would turn unprofitable and unstable if it could not expand into new territories, such as Missouri, Texas, and Kansas. When Northern whites elected a president, Abraham Lincoln, determined to prevent the admission of new slave states, Southern slave owners rebelled. They removed their states from the Union, raised an army, and even tried to conquer new territories for their Confederate empire, notably New Mexico, during their war for independence in the early 1860s.[1]

The victors ultimately labeled this conflict the "Civil War," but Native Americans could just as easily have viewed it as an international, indeed an interimperial conflict. Certainly, both belligerents wound up mobilizing far more men and resources than in any previous North American war, and both the Union's and Confederacy's demand for manpower and the enormous geographical reach of the conflict drew thousands of Native Americans into it. Some held influential or high-ranking military positions: Ely Parker (Seneca), future commissioner of Indian Affairs, served as an aide-de-camp to Ulysses S. Grant, while Stand Watie (Cherokee) became the last Confederate general to surrender. The participants also included many Great Lakes Indians. News of the fighting quickly spread through the United States by newspaper and telegraph, and by late 1861 the Indian agent at Mackinac could observe that "I find the Indians everywhere interested in the momentous struggle in which the nation is now engaged." Many, he continued, "have desired to enlist in the military service."[2]

Enlistment appealed to Native American men as a way to demonstrate their valor, earn military bounties, and strengthen their ties to a government that could protect their lands from grasping white settlers. The War Department made little effort to recruit Indians during the first two years of the war, but by 1863, with white recruitment flagging and opposition building to a military draft, the states of Michigan and Wisconsin changed course and began recruiting Lakes Indians into the Union Army. About 120 Menominee men enlisted in Union regiments during the war (one-third of them died before its end), while Company K of the First Michigan Sharpshooters consisted entirely of Native Americans, mostly Ojibwas and Odawas. More than half of the 150 riflemen of Company K died or were wounded during Ulysses Grant's 1864 plunge into Confederate Virginia, in the bloody battles of the Wilderness and Spotsylvania Courthouse. After the war, the surviving Native servicemen remained in touch with one another by joining the Union veterans' association, the Grand Army of the Republic.[3]

In the postwar years much of the northern Lakes Indians' homelands continued changing into white man's country, thanks to another influx of white settlers and to Anglo-American officials' efforts to tighten administrative control. These efforts became particularly pronounced on the Canadian side of the international border: the government of Upper Canada reinforced border controls in the 1850s and erected very high barriers to Native citizenship in the Gradual Civilization Act (1857), while the Canadian parliament acquired effective plenary power over Indians through the imperial Dominion Act of 1867. Indian resources became scarcer owing to the twin pressures of white settlement and colonialism. Overhunting and livestock raising wiped out the elk and caribou populations of the Lakes country by the end of the 1840s, Canadian border-crossing restrictions barred the Anishinaabeg from some of their fisheries, and the Grand River Iroquois, whom Upper Canada had consolidated on a small reserve in 1847, lost some of their timber to white thieves.[4]

Nonetheless, the northern Lakes Indians continued the dual work of survival and survivance. Menominees and Odawas continued to make maple sugar, one of their principal sources of revenue in the 1860s, and to raise livestock. Odawas and Michigan-based Métis continued to tap the Great Lakes' immense fisheries, buying their own boats or working for whites as wage laborers. The growing involvement of whites in the fishing industry raised the specter of species depletion—between the 1830s and 1868 Indians and whites took twenty-eight million pounds of fish from the Lakes—but with one exception this remained only a potential threat. (The exception was the Lake Ontario salmon population, whose spawning rivers white settlers had contaminated with sawdust from their mills and alkali runoff from their potash works.) North of the Lakes, Anishinaabeg hunters could still ply their old trade, as viable deer and beaver populations remained north of Lakes Erie and Huron until the end of the century. Some found new ways to make a living: Oneidas in New York sold handicrafts and musical performances, and Menominees in Wisconsin gained permission from the Interior Department (1871) directly to sell pine to timber companies. Most Lakes Indians worked to retain not only older economic practices but older sociopolitical traditions. Menominee chiefs preserved the legitimacy of their old tribal government by uniting against land cessions and in favor of direct timber sales, while the Grand River Iroquois continued to maintain the Six Nations' venerable political culture (including condolence ceremonies and matrons' appointment of chiefs) and the *Gaiwaio* faith of Handsome Lake.[5]

The pressures that the northern Lakes Indians faced, while significant and challenging, were not overtly military ones. Several hundred Menominee and Anishinaabe men did fight in the American Civil War, but their families and kinsmen remained distant from the actual fighting and suffered few of the usual hazards of war. The southern Lakes Indians who had moved to Kansas and Oklahoma had a very different experience, as these territories became a contested borderland between the Union and the Confederacy. In 1861, Confederate commissioners visited the slave-owning nations of Indian Territory (Oklahoma) and recruited political allies and volunteer riflemen for their new empire. Native Americans in the territory who wanted to support the Union or avoid reprisals from pro-Confederate kinsmen began relocating to Kansas, where seven thousand found refuge. These included Delawares, Kickapoos, and Shawnees whom Texas had removed in the 1830s and '50s, and who now had to leave their homes and property in Oklahoma. Joining them were the members of the Black Bob Shawnee band, which had retained its own communal lands when the other Kansas Shawnees accepted allotment. The band had acquired a reputation for holding Unionist loyalties after the war began. In 1862, Confederate raiders under William Quantrill attacked the Black Bob Shawnees' settlement, robbing houses and raping Shawnee women, and persuading the victims to move to the more protected site of Belmont.[6]

Some of the western Shawnees, and many of the Kansas Delawares, took an active part in the fighting. More than 170 Delaware men enlisted in the Union Army early in the war and participated in the Union's 1863 capture of Fort Gibson in Oklahoma and its invasion and occupation of the western Cherokee Nation. Moreover, in the fall of 1862 a party of two hundred Delaware, Kickapoo, and Shawnee volunteers raided the Wichita Agency in Oklahoma, killing a Confederate Indian agent and five other people. The raiders then tracked down a large encampment of Tonkawa Indians, who were Confederate allies, and attacked them, killing nearly 140 men, women, and children. A later historian argued that responsibility for the attack largely rested with officer Ben Simon and the other Delaware volunteers. Most likely they recognized that borderlands were dangerous and a fearsome reputation their people's best hope for security.[7]

Military service did not shield the emigrants from the animosity of the Kansas government, which wanted the remaining Indians in eastern Kansas brought under state law or removed. From 1859 to 1865, the state's commissioners imposed property taxes on the Shawnees, claiming that the dissolution of that nation's communal lands ended their immunity from taxation. The United States Supreme Court disagreed, reversing an 1865 state supreme court ruling, *Blue-Jacket vs. Commissioners of Johnson County,* on the grounds that the Shawnee people retained federal protection despite lacking a collective land base. By then, however, the Shawnees had agreed to sell their lands to the US government to pay back taxes, and they had moved to Indian Territory. By that time, too, the US government, under pressure from Kansas settlers, had negotiated the removal of most of the Delawares to Oklahoma. White settlers' desire to create a "white man's country," free of independent Indian nations and other artifacts of the past, remained strong as ever, as the Delawares, driven from Pennsylvania, Ohio, Texas, and now Kansas, could attest.[8]

Kansas and Oklahoma were not the only interimperial borderlands to witness significant fighting during the Civil War, and not the only regions where Lakes Indians took a part in that fighting. Minnesota, a new white-settlement frontier bordering British Canada, became in 1862 the scene of a major interethnic war, which some Americans blamed on Confederate agents, and for which the Indian participants hoped to acquire British assistance. In its causes, namely, resentment toward grasping American officials and traders and growing concern over encroaching white settlers, the Dakota War resembled earlier conflicts between Lakes Indians and whites. The Dakotas had for several decades grown reliant on credit from their traders, as the bison and elk population of western Minnesota declined, and when those traders tightened credit in the 1830s, many had to turn to the US government for aid. The principal eastern Dakota division, the Mdewakantons, sold most of their lands in 1837 for claims settlements and an annuity, which kept them fed but made them dependent on their agents.

Fourteen years later the Mdewakantons and the western Dakotas (such as the Wahpetons and Sissetons) sold nearly all of their remaining lands, including the confluence of the Minnesota and Mississippi Rivers, a sacred gathering place where the Dakotas' water deity dwelled. The United States promised the Dakotas $3 million in cash, claims settlements, and interest-bearing bonds as payment. However, the Dakotas' traders tricked or bribed chiefs into signing a supplementary agreement that assigned much of their compensation to their creditors, which undermined the confidence the Dakotas felt in their erstwhile "kinsmen."[9]

The treaties exacerbated a growing split within Dakota communities between traditionalists and proponents of cultural change. Some Dakotas had supported the land-cession agreements because they had begun to adopt some of white Americans' lifeways: cutting their hair, wearing European-style clothing, and raising grain and livestock. They supported the 1851 treaty, and a subsequent 1858 land cession, because these provided funds for gristmills, teachers' salaries, and other elements of the federal "civilization" program. The acculturated Dakotas had not completely split from their traditionalist kinsmen—many continued to attend religious feasts and dances and to consult medicine men when they were sick—but they no longer shared their economic interests. Traditionalists derided them as "cut-hairs" and "breeches men" for their American-style short hair and long trousers, or they called them "Dutchmen" after newly arrived German farmers, whom they did not trust.[10]

Meanwhile the traditionalists watched with alarm as thousands of white settlers occupied their former homes and hunting territories. Many of the newcomers were German immigrants, who had begun immigrating to the United States by the tens of thousands a decade earlier, driven by poor harvests and political upheaval in their central-European homeland. Few of the Germans spoke a language the Dakotas could understand, and most regarded Indians with contempt. Some Dakotas began to discuss the possibility of military action against the hostile *iásica* ("bad-talkers") and to organize secret soldier societies as a display of solidarity and strength. Civil chiefs might in peacetime have managed the tension between whites and traditionalist Dakotas, but the Civil War delayed the annuities on which many had come to depend, and in 1862 the Dakotas came out of a "starving winter" of poor hunting with no way to feed themselves, other than begging corn and potatoes from a few sympathetic farmers. In the spring and summer, Dakota leaders tried to obtain more credit from their traders, but according to Muza Katemane the Dakotas' former trading partners refused and told them to "go eat grass like the oxen . . . [as] they were a lazy set and would have to starve if they did not." This appears to have ignited the war that erupted in August and that, before it ended, had killed over five hundred white soldiers and civilians and forced the evacuation of twenty-three Minnesota counties.[11]

♦ ♦ ♦

The Dakotas' experiences resembled those of tens of thousands of other Lakes Indians during the centuries after European contact. Since the 1600s Lakes Indian history had been dominated by two struggles: one against submission to European empires, and one to survive in a world reshaped by European diseases, technologies, and institutions. The first struggle had become more difficult with time, though Native Americans held the upper hand for more than a century. Indians had been cocreators of the French "empire," which they regarded as an equal partnership sustained by familial metaphors and trade. When Britain tried to create a more hierarchical dominion over the Lakes country in the 1760s, the Lakes Indians dealt its army a sharp blow in Pontiac's War, only later becoming King George's allies in his wars against his rebellious colonists. This alliance included the Dakotas, who had sent war parties to aid the British in the Revolutionary War and the War of 1812. In their protracted conflict with the aggressive new American empire, the United States, the Lakes Indians had adopted a harder-edged policy of military resistance tempered with diplomatic negotiation. They formed pan-Indian alliances, sought British military aid, and fought bloody battles with American soldiers, while also negotiating, agreeing to partial cessions of territory, and eventually accepting American traders and missionaries into their communities. Such was Dakota leaders' policy in the nineteenth century, with an emphasis on diplomacy and trade rather than conflict.

The struggle to survive and maintain cultural integrity proved equally challenging, and the Lakes nations undertook it with similar resourcefulness and flexibility. The population losses that Indians suffered from disease and warfare were not merely challenging but traumatic, and individuals do not readily "adapt" to trauma. In the longer term, Lakes Indian nations defended themselves by forming multitribal town complexes and acquiring European weapons, and they halted their population decline by intermarrying with other ethnic groups, including French and British traders. The new European goods sold by those traders offered the benefit of an increased living standard at the price of reliance on white trading companies, along with the depletion of the game animals whose pelts traders wanted. To keep their economic options open, Lakes Indians retained older handicraft skills where they could, developed other means to buy European goods (like selling food or obtaining merchandise as annuities), and periodically embraced nativist movements that eschewed European technology and customs.

As American settlers encroached on and engulfed Native American settlements, some Lakes Indians, like the Shawnees in the eighteenth century and traditionalist Dakotas in the nineteenth, resisted with force. Most chose a more peaceful strategy of adaptation. They traded with the newcomers, learned their language, adopted their practice of commercial agriculture, established new homes in distant borderlands, or did all of these things at once. Unfortunately, most white Americans didn't want peaceful, acculturated Indians living near them; they wanted the Lakes Indians' land, and they viewed Indians through a racial lens that distorted them into irredeemable and dangerous barbarians. In the 1820s and '30s, the US government, which shared western settlers' motives, placed massive pressure on the Lakes Indians to leave their homelands and move to the western prairies. Some successfully used diplomacy or evasion to stay in the Lakes country, but many could not. When a minority of resisters, like Black Hawk's band or traditionalist Dakota insurgents, resorted to force or the threat of it to recover their lands, the United States used overwhelming counterforce to deny them that option and drive them from their homeland forever.

Such was the outcome of the Dakota War. In mid-August 1862, traditionalist warriors began their offensive, destroying trading posts, capturing the Lower Dakota Agency, killing the inhabitants of Milford, raiding the German town of New Ulm, and skirmishing with militia at Fort Ridgely and Birch Coulee. As in previous wars between Native American traditionalists and white settlers, the insurgents sought to purify and strengthen themselves by rejecting white culture; Little Crow and his colleagues forbade the Dakotas to wear European-style clothing or live in frame houses. Little Crow's principal goal was also spiritually charged: he wanted to recapture the sacred confluence of the Minnesota and Mississippi Rivers and clear Saint Paul of whites. Like Black Hawk a generation earlier, Little Crow hoped to secure the support of other Indian nations in Minnesota, particularly the Ojibwas and Ho-Chunks, and possibly obtain aid from British officials in Canada. Unlike Black Hawk, Little Crow and his associates probably recognized from the beginning that these were merely hopes. Their Dakota kinsmen repeatedly upbraided them for thinking they could win the war; one, Paul Mazakutemani, said the insurgents "might as well try to bail out the waters of the Mississippi as to whip" the Americans.[12]

Little Crow and the seven hundred warriors and captains allied with him stopped bailing on September 19, when Colonel Henry Sibley, at the head of sixteen hundred Minnesota troops, met and defeated Dakota warriors at the Battle of Wood Lake. Sibley then advanced into the Dakotas' reservation and compelled the surrender of the remaining insurgents. As Minnesota's governor demanded the "extermination" of the Dakotas, and local newspapers accused insurgent warriors of lurid atrocities—including the mass rape of female captives and the impalement of white babies—newly arrived Union general John Pope subjected four hundred Dakota prisoners to summary trials by military commission. His use of this new, hybrid military-civilian court indicated that he saw the Dakota warriors not as legitimate belligerents but as rebels subject to American criminal jurisdiction. By November 1862 the commissioners had condemned over three hundred Dakota men to death. The sentences required presidential approval to carry, and President Abraham Lincoln ultimately decided to let stand thirty-nine death sentences and commute the remainder. Thirty-eight warriors died on Christmas Day, in the largest mass hanging in American history. (Lincoln's commutation was also the largest of its kind.) Another one hundred warriors and civilian prisoners died in confinement before their release.[13]

The following year President Lincoln ordered the War Department to deport the remaining Dakotas to Crow Creek, a barren site in Dakota Territory, where they spent three difficult years before receiving a more inhabitable reservation in Nebraska. The president and War Department also deported the Ho-Chunks, whom many Minnesotans considered Dakota sympathizers, to Crow Creek, where several hundred Ho-Chunks and Dakotas died over the next two years. Ho-Chunk families eventually left Crow Creek of their own accord, many heading back to Wisconsin, where they joined several hundred "roving" kinsmen who had returned to the state illegally over the previous decade. During the 1860s and '70s, some used a law intended for white American settlers, the Homestead Act (1862), to claim fee-simple farmsteads for themselves in their old homeland—a tactic that Potawatomis and Odawas had previously used to remain in Michigan. In 1875, Congress formally extended the homesteading privilege to all Indians who had given up their legal membership in a tribe; later, the Wisconsin Ho-Chunks recovered their official identity and became a recognized Indian nation.[14]

The Ho-Chunks, and the ancestral Ho-Chunk culture that had covered pre-Columbian Wisconsin with effigy mounds, had lived in the Lakes country for more than thirteen hundred years. They had suffered grievous losses to disease and war in the seventeenth century and recovered; they had supported Tecumseh and Tenskwatawa's nativist movement in the early nineteenth century and survived its defeat; they had been accused by whites of supporting Black Hawk's and Little Crow's insurgencies and harried from their homeland to Iowa and Minnesota and Dakota Territory. They had retained their creation stories, medicinal rituals, and language, even while some adopted plow agriculture and American-style schooling. Now, hundreds were finding ways to return to their old homeland and, using a policy designed to aid the same kind of white settlers who had displaced them, to remain.[15]

FIGURE 4. Emma Holt (Waukonchazeewinkah), a Ho-Chunk woman born during that nation's gradual return to Wisconsin, appears in this ca. 1895 photograph in semitraditional attire. Charles Van Schaick, "Studio Portrait of Emma Blackhawk Holt." *Courtesy of the Wisconsin Historical Society, Image WHi-60604*

A wronged people can avenge themselves by surviving and maintaining their cultural distinctiveness in the teeth of those who wish them harm. They can even use the institutions and technologies of their adversaries to aid their own survival, grow their families, and keep their homes. There is little enough justice in history, but there is continuity and irony, and sometimes these can suffice.

Acknowledgments

I have learned that acknowledging one's intellectual debts is one of the more pleasant parts of writing a book. For their helpful comments, questions, and suggestions, I wish to thank Dawn Bakken, Dave Beck, Daniel Clark, John Craig Hammond, Eric Jurgens, Jacob Lee, Roger Laybourn, Scott Shoemaker, and Cary Miller. Susan Wade shared with me her master's thesis on the culture of sugar making, and Michelle Cassidy and Casey Keeler discussed their research-in-progress on the nineteenth-century Dakotas and Ojibwas. My colleagues in Indiana State University's History Department created a supportive and stimulating environment for research and writing. The faculty and staff of Cunningham Memorial Library, Tippecanoe County Historical Association, the Wisconsin Historical Society, and the Yale Center for British Art supplied images and sources. Brian Balsley prepared the volume's excellent maps. Diane Barnes, Paul Finkelman, and Gillian Berchowitz kindly invited me to undertake this project and provided encouragement, enthusiastic support, and keen editorial insight. My anonymous readers dramatically improved the book with their recommendations, urging me to push beyond the restrictions I had initially placed on my inquiry. Nancy Basmajian, Beth Pratt, and Samara Rafert masterfully edited, produced, and publicized the book's final version.

Special thanks are due Susan Livingston, who persuaded me that this book was within my abilities and, through many writing dates on two continents, ensured I would see it through to completion. And as with my previous books, my siblings' support and good humor proved some of my most valuable resources in writing this one. I dedicate this book to my younger brother, Patrick, whose own creativity and willingness to seek new challenges always inspire me.

Notes

ABBREVIATIONS

ASPIA Walter Lowrie and Matthew St. Clair Clarke, eds., *American State Papers, Class Two: Indian Affairs*, 2 vols. (Washington, DC: Gales and Seaton, 1832)

CSHSW State Historical Society of Wisconsin, *Collections of the State Historical Society of Wisconsin*, 40 vols. (Madison: State Historical Society of Wisconsin, 1888–1931)

MPHC Michigan Pioneer and Historical Society, *Michigan Pioneer and Historical Collections*, 40 vols. (Lansing: Michigan Pioneer and Historical Society and Michigan Historical Commission, 1876–1929)

TPUS Clarence E. Carter et al., eds., *Territorial Papers of the United States*, 28 vols. (Washington, DC: US Government Printing Office, 1934–75)

INTRODUCTION

1. Dennis, *Living Great Lakes*, 26–28.

2. Ibid., 153–55, 159–61; Bogue, *Fishing the Great Lakes*, 6–7.

3. Axtell, "Ethnohistory: An Historian's Viewpoint"; Trigger, "Ethnohistory: Problems and Prospects"; Galloway, *Practicing Ethnohistory*.

4. Clifton, *Prairie People*; Edmunds, *The Potawatomis*; Trigger, *Children of Aataentsic*; Howard, *Shawnee!*; McConnell, *Country Between*; Kugel, *Main Leaders of Our People*; Richard White, *Middle Ground*, second quote, page x; Sleeper-Smith et al., "Forum: The Middle Ground Revisited"; Cayton, *Frontier Indiana*; David Nichols, *Red Gentlemen and White Savages*; Cary Miller, *Ogimaag*; McDonnell, *Masters of Empire*; DuVal, *Native Ground*.

5. Vizenor, *Native Liberty*, 85–103; Merrell, *Indians' New World*; Horsman, *Expansion and American Indian Policy*; Dowd, *Spirited Resistance*, esp. 90–122; and see the DuVal, Miller, and McDonnell sources cited above. In general, this book defines the "southern" Lakes region as the territory between the Ohio River and the shores of Lakes Erie and Michigan.

6. In 1775 the Old Regime livre was equal to about 1/23 of a British pound. In modern purchasing-power terms, it equaled (roughly) £5 (2016, pre-Brexit) or $6.

7. One should not confuse this with the later American anti-immigrant movement.

8. A handful of colonial officials did understand the relationship between French trade, Indian alliance, and French power; see Shannon, *Crossroads of Empire*, 73–75, 110.

9. On American underperformance in the War of 1812, see Hickey, *Don't Give Up the Ship!*, 299–305.

10. My spelling of Sauk conforms to the usage in Helen Tanner's indispensable *Atlas of Great Lakes Indian History*.

11. Veracini, *Settler Colonialism*, 35–50.

CHAPTER 1: ONCE AND FUTURE CIVILIZATIONS

1. See "Relation of 1636," in Thwaites, *Jesuit Relations*, 10:125–37; Klinck and Talman, *Journal of John Norton*, 88–90; "Anishinaabe" and "Winnebago," in Leeming, *Creation Myths of the World*, 1:40–41 and 274–75; Dowd, *War under Heaven*, 12–14; Radin, *Crashing Thunder*, 33–36 (quotes 34–35). The Shawnees' creation story resembled the Anishinaabeg's; see Cave, *Prophets of the Great Spirit*, 71–72.

2. Flannery, *Eternal Frontier*, 178–79; Curry, "Ancient Migration: Coming to America." Vine Deloria Jr. has expressed skepticism about the Beringian migration hypothesis, arguing that high mountains on both sides of the Strait would have blocked west-east migration and that late-Pleistocene Siberia was a far more appealing environment for hunters than Alaska or Canada. See Deloria, *Red Earth, White Lies*, 67–92.

3. Flannery, *Eternal Frontier*, 149–50; Snow, "Differentiation of Hunter-Gatherer Cultures," 145; Christopher Morris, *Big Muddy*, 2; Sunderman, "Fort Wayne," 328–31; Gwen Schultz, *Wisconsin's Foundations*, 160, 166–69; Riley, *Great Lakes Country*, 12.

4. Flannery, *Eternal Frontier*, 199; Fitting, De Visscher, and Wahla, *Paleo-Indian Occupation*; Birmingham and Eisenberg, *Indian Mounds of Wisconsin*, 71.

5. Snow, "Differentiation of Hunter-Gatherer Cultures," 154–56; Styles and McMillan, "Archaic Faunal Exploitation"; Abrams and Nowacki, "Active and Passive Promoters," 1128; Wiant, Farnsworth, and Hajic, "Lower Illinois River Basin"; Birmingham and Eisenberg, *Indian Mounds of Wisconsin*, 88; Benn, "Woodland People," 109–10.

6. Pleger and Stoltman, "Archaic Tradition in Wisconsin"; Wyman, *Wisconsin Frontier*, 26.

7. Cordell and Smith, "Indigenous Farmers," 234–35; Abrams and Nowacki, "Active and Passive Promoters," 1124–27; Black, Ruffner, and Abrams, "Native American Influences," esp. 1272–73.

8. This assumes a North American Indian population of about three million in 1600, and a Great Lakes Indian population in the same year of 150,000. The

author has compiled the 1600 Lakes Indian population estimate from the sources employed in chapter 2, below.

9. Flannery, *Eternal Frontier*, 243; Silverberg, *Mound Builders*, 176–79.

10. Lepper, "Ceremonial Landscape"; Pacheco, "Why Move?"; Birmingham and Eisenberg, *Indian Mounds of Wisconsin*, 92–95.

11. Cordell and Smith, "Indigenous Farmers," 243. On prestige goods, see Galloway, "Choctaws at the Border."

12. Coon, "Ohio Hopewell Political Economies."

13. Buikstra, Konigsburg, and Bullington, "Fertility in the Prehistoric Midwest."

14. Birmingham and Eisenberg, *Indian Mounds of Wisconsin*, 100–41; George Nelson, *My First Years*, 174–75.

15. Pauketat, *Cahokia*; Bruce Smith, "Agricultural Chiefdoms," 300–306.

16. Snyder, *Slavery in Indian Country*, 14–16. "Social death" is from Patterson, "Slavery," 90.

17. Pauketat, *Cahokia*, 108–9; Pauketat, "Making of a Mississippian Polity," 44, 52–53, 56–58. My thanks to Jacob Lee for the latter source.

18. Benson, Pauketat, and Cook, "Cahokia's Boom and Bust"; Trubitt, "Mound Building and Prestige Goods Exchange."

19. Birmingham and Eisenberg, *Indian Mounds of Wisconsin*, 152–62; Richter, *Before the Revolution*, 32–33; Cordell and Smith, "Indigenous Farmers," 251–53. Chunky was played with polished round stones and javelins. Two players rolled the stones across a field, then flung their javelins in turn toward the stones' stopping places. Whichever player's javelin landed nearer the mark won the round.

20. Warren, *Worlds the Shawnees Made*, 38–41; Pollack, *Caborn-Welborn*; Byers, "'Heartland' Woodland Settlement System"; Birmingham and Eisenberg, *Indian Mounds of Wisconsin*, 163–72; Shackelford, "Illinois Indians in the Confluence Region," 19–21.

21. Silverberg, *Mound Builders*, 50–73, 130–67; Conn, *History's Shadow*, 127–33.

22. For "Western World," see Caleb Wallace, "To James Madison from Caleb Wallace, 12 July 1785," *Founders Online*, http://founders.archives.gov/documents/Madison/01-08-02-0171.

CHAPTER 2: THE EUROPEAN DISRUPTION

1. On Lakes Indian creation stories, see Willig, *Restoring the Chain of Friendship*, 25–26, and chapter 1, above.

2. Fagan, *People of the Earth*, 150–51, 184–87; Goldsworthy, *How Rome Fell*, 33, 375–76; Fagan, *Great Warming*, 28–30; Braudel, *Structures of Everyday Life*, 114–18, 134–36, 192–96, 345, 355–56; Huppert, *After the Black Death*, 41–53, 56–66.

3. Kurlansky, *Cod*, 32–35, 51–60; Kupperman, *Atlantic in World History*, 72–73.

4. Turgeon, "French Fishers, Fur Traders, and Amerindians"; Eccles, *Canadian Frontier*, 18–20.

5. Eccles, *Canadian Frontier*, 20–23; Fischer, *Champlain's Dream*, 235–45.

6. Axtell, *Invasion Within*, 46–47; Snow, "Migrations in Prehistory"; Richard White, *Middle Ground*, 17–18; Heidenreich, "Huron," 373–79.

7. Heidenreich, *Huronia*, 162–66; Trigger, *Children of Aataentsic*, 1:350–62, 424–25.

8. "Huron Relation of 1636," in Thwaites, *Jesuit Relations*, 10:175–80, 210–25, 278–304; Labelle, "'Faire la Chaudière,'" 3–4.

9. Crosby, "Virgin Soil Epidemics"; Diamond, *Guns, Germs, and Steel*, 195–214; Snow, "Disease and Population Decline," 178–79; Calloway, *New Worlds for All*, 27–33, 35–36; "Relation of 1637," in Thwaites, *Jesuit Relations*, 13:85–173 and 14:5–55.

10. Greer and Mills, "Catholic Atlantic." The nineteenth-century Hurons mentioned here were Wyandots, descendants of Hurons who fled their homeland after the Iroquois wars. See Buss, "Politics of Indian Removal," 189n18.

11. "Relation of 1637," in Thwaites, *Jesuit Relations*, 13:127; Trigger, *Children of Aataentsic*, 2:699–724.

12. Richter, *Ordeal of the Longhouse*, 14–21, 31–37; Bogaert and O'Connor, *Journey to Mohawk Country*, 43–45, 52; Riley, *Great Lakes Country*, 25; Shannon, *Iroquois Diplomacy*, 15–19; Fenton, *Great Law and the Longhouse*, 135–62.

13. Richter, *Ordeal of the Longhouse*, 55–62; Brandão, "Your Fyre Shall Burn No More," 36–44, 73, 78–79.

14. Eccles, *Canadian Frontier*, 55; Tooker, "Wyandot," 399; Bellfy, *Three Fires Unity*, 73–74; Quaife, *Alexander Henry's Travels*, 37, 60–61.

15. The Odawas were among the first Anishinaabeg contacted by Europeans. Samuel Champlain, who met Odawas on Lake Huron in 1615–16, called them *cheveux relevés*, or "high hair," for their piled-up hairstyles.

16. Bohaker, "*Nindoodemag*"; Charles Garrad, "Champlain and the Odawa"; Quaife, *Alexander Henry's Travels*, 36; Schmalz, *Ojibwa of Southern Ontario*, 17–20; Edmunds, *The Potawatomis*, 15–16.

17. Bohaker, "*Nindoodemag*," 38–39; McDonnell, *Masters of Empire*, 25; Fletcher, *Eagle Returns*, 7–9; Schoolcraft, *Narrative Journal*, 68–69, 86; Hickerson, *Chippewa and Their Neighbors*; Cary Miller, *Ogimaag*, 33–35, 43–44, 148–52; Witgen, *Infinity of Nations*, 63; "The Mission of the Holy Ghost among the Algonquins (1642)," in Thwaites, *Jesuit Relations*, 23:204–33. The last document describes a Feast of the Dead among the Nipissings. Miller notes that all Anishinaabeg who had dreamed the proper dreams could join the *midewiwin*.

18. Nicolas Perrot, *Memoir on the Customs, Dress, and Religion of the North American Savages*, in State Historical Society of Wisconsin, *Collections of the State Historical Society of Wisconsin* (hereafter *CSHSW*), 16:16–17; Tanner, *Atlas of Great Lakes Indian History*, 32; Wyman, *Wisconsin Frontier*, 15, 32–37; "Voyages of Jacques Marquette," in Thwaites, *Jesuit Relations*, 59:93–113; Edmunds and Peyser, *Fox Wars*, 31–37; Lucy Murphy, "Autonomy and Economic Roles," 78–79; Child, *Holding Our World Together*, 20, 24–26.

19. Bacqueville de La Potherie, *History of North America*, in *CSHSW*, 16:4–7; Perrot, *Memoir*, in *CSHSW*, 16:12–13; Wyman, *Wisconsin Frontier*, 75; Gary Anderson, *Kinsmen of Another Kind*, 6–9, 19, 29–39.

20. Perrot, *Memoir,* in *CSHSW,* 16:12–13, 16–21, 28–30; "Of the Mission of Saint Esprit," in Thwaites, *Jesuit Relations,* 55:171; Witgen, *Infinity of Nations,* 65, 122; Gary Anderson, *Kinsmen of Another Kind,* 23–27; Tanner, *Atlas of Great Lakes Indian History,* 32. The Sioux migration onto the Plains began after 1717–18, when an epizootic killed many of the deer and elk in northern Wisconsin.

21. Wyman, *Wisconsin Frontier,* 13–14; Tanner, *Atlas of Great Lakes Indian History,* 36–37; Potherie, *History of North America,* in *CSHSW,* 16:33, 38–41.

22. "Of the Peoples Connected with the Mission of Saint Esprit," in Thwaites, *Jesuit Relations,* 54:165–67; Morrissey, "Power of the Ecotone," 679–80.

23. "Voyages of Jacques Marquette," in Thwaites, *Jesuit Relations,* 59:117–29 (quote from page 129); Morrissey, "Power of the Ecotone," 668–69; Belue, *Long Hunt,* 39–41; Hinderaker, *Elusive Empires,* 10–11; Thornton, *American Indian Holocaust and Survival,* 87–88.

24. "Voyages of Jacques Marquette," in Thwaites, *Jesuit Relations,* 59:125–27; Rushforth, *Bonds of Alliance,* 11, 36–37, 44–51, 58–59, 67–69.

25. Birmingham and Eisenberg, *Indian Mounds of Wisconsin,* 171–72; "Voyages of Jacques Marquette," in Thwaites, *Jesuit Relations,* 59:129–37; Perrot, *Memoir,* in *CSHSW,* 16:27; "Allouez's Account of Various Tribes," in ibid., 16:57; Rushforth, *Bonds of Alliance,* 30–35.

26. Francis Jennings, *Ambiguous Iroquois Empire,* 131–32, 145–50.

27. Brandão, *"Your Fyre Shall Burn No More,"* table D-1; Morrissey, "Power of the Ecotone," 685; Thornton, *American Indian Holocaust and Survival,* 87.

28. Emrick, "Monyton Diaspora"; Warren, *Worlds the Shawnees Made,* 31–32; Clark, *The Shawnee,* 7–25.

29. Part of the reason for the Lakes Indians' high agricultural yields rests with the greater productivity of maize versus European wheat; Indian corn produces 75 percent more calories per hectare than the Old World staple. See Crosby, *The Columbian Exchange,* 174–75.

30. Riley, *Great Lakes Country,* 159–68; Charles Mann, *1493,* 30–33; Richard White, *Middle Ground,* 41–48.

CHAPTER 3: FRANCE'S UNEASY IMPERIUM

1. "Vincennes Conference Journal, 25 Sept. 1792," in Buell, *Memoirs of Rufus Putnam,* 347–48; Parkman, *Jesuits in North America,* 131 (quotes). On the distinction between colonialism and imperialism, see Vinovetsky, *Russian America,* 10.

2. Eccles, "Fur Trade and Eighteenth-Century Imperialism"; Rushforth, *Bonds of Alliance,* 155–56.

3. Pagden, *Lords of All the World,* 88–89, 108.

4. Francis Jennings, *Ambiguous Iroquois Empire,* 180, 184, 190–91; Eccles, *Canadian Frontier,* 115–19.

5. Potherie, *History of North America,* in *CSHSW,* 16:134–41; Skinner, *Upper Country,* 73–78.

6. Skinner, *Upper Country*, 83–87; "Letter of Claude Chauchetière, 14 Oct. 1682," in Thwaites, *Jesuit Relations,* 62:166–85; Shoemaker, "Kateri Tekakwitha's Tortuous Path"; Greer, *Mohawk Saint,* 90–110.

7. Richter, *Ordeal of the Longhouse,* 173–74, 185–88; Brandão, *"Your Fyre Shall Burn No More,"* 126–27; McDonnell, *Masters of Empire,* 65–66; Donald Smith, *Sacred Feathers,* 7–8, 19–20.

8. Shannon, *Iroquois Diplomacy,* 56, 59–61; Bohaker, "Nindoodemag," 23–26. Cf. Witgen, *Infinity of Nations,* 277.

9. François Vaillant to Cadillac, 23 Sept. 1701, in *CSHSW,* 16:206; C.B. Avereau to Cadillac, 4 June 1702, in ibid., 16:213; Cadillac's addendum to letter from Joseph Manent, 12 May 1703, in ibid., 16:213; Weyhing, "'Gascon Exaggerations,'" 95; Sturtevant, "'Inseparable Companions' and Irreconcilable Enemies," 229.

10. Speech of Miscouaky, Chief of the Odawas, to Marquis de Vaudreuil, 26 Sept. 1706, in Michigan Pioneer and Historical Society, *Michigan Pioneer and Historical Collections* (hereafter *MPHC*), 33:288–94; Vaudreuil to Pontchartrain, 4 Nov. 1706 and 24 July 1707, in *CSHSW,* 16:240–42 and 249–50 (quote); Richard White, *Middle Ground,* 82–90.

11. Richard White, *Middle Ground,* 77–82, 90–93; Witgen, *Infinity of Nations,* 200–207.

12. Richard White, *Middle Ground,* 110–19; Eccles, *Canadian Frontier,* 137; Beauharnois and Mssr. Hocquart to the Minister of Marine, 15 Oct. 1730, quoted in Havard, "'Protection' and 'Unequal Alliance,'" 122; Quaife, *Alexander Henry's Travels,* 49–50. Henry wrote about events in 1761 but described behavior that predated the end of French imperial rule.

13. Galloway, "'Chief Who Is Your Father'"; Faragher, *Sugar Creek,* 21; Richard White, *Middle Ground,* 143–49, 170–75. On matrilocality and authority, see chapter 2.

14. Jean Mermet to Cadillac, 19 April 1702, in *CSHSW,* 16:211–13; Jacques-Charles Sabrevois de Bleury, "Memoir on the Savages of Canada" (1718), in ibid., 16:371–74; M. de Champigny to unknown, 13 Oct. 1697, in *MPHC,* 33:72–77; Pontchartrain to Cadillac, 14 June 1704, in ibid., 33:187–89; Richard White, *Middle Ground,* 119–21, 133–36.

15. Richard White, *Middle Ground,* 121–22, 136–38; Skinner, *Upper Country,* 100–101; Shannon, *Iroquois Diplomacy,* 65; Nassaney, Cremin, and Malischke, "Native American-French Interactions," esp. 67–68.

16. Skinner, *Upper Country,* 36–40; "Memoir on Detroit (1714)," in *CSHSW,* 16:308; Sabrevois, "Memoir," in ibid., 16:363–64; Sleeper-Smith, "Women, Kin, and Catholicism," 433; Wyman, *Wisconsin Frontier,* 112.

17. Richard White, *Middle Ground,* 64–66; Calloway, *New Worlds for All,* 174; Sophie White, *Wild Frenchmen and Frenchified Indians,* 89; Sleeper-Smith, "Women, Kin, and Catholicism," 430.

18. David Smith, *Folklore of the Winnebago Tribe,* 155–57; McBride, *Women's Wisconsin,* 4.

19. Pagden, *Lords of All the World*, 149; Richard White, *Middle Ground*, 66–67; Axtell, *Invasion Within*, 126–27; Morrissey, "Terms of Encounter," esp. 46–49, 51 (quote), 60; Parsons, "Natives, Newcomers, and Nicotiana," esp. 32.

20. Sleeper-Smith, "Women, Kin, and Catholicism," 427–32, 436; Sleeper-Smith, *Indian Women and French Men*, 23–37; "Father Jacques Gravier Describes Indian Conversions at the Illinois Mission," in Kathleen DuVal and John DuVal, *Interpreting a Continent*, 206–11; Sophie White, *Wild Frenchmen*, 5, 88, 117–18. There was Biblical precedent for believing Christian wives would convert or reform apostate husbands; see, for example, 1 Pet. 3:1–2.

21. Sophie White, *Wild Frenchmen*, 25, 39; Stearns, "Joseph Kellogg's Observations," 354; Sleeper-Smith, "Women, Kin, and Catholicism," 430–35.

22. Hinderaker, *Elusive Empires*, 89–90, 93–99; Skinner, *Upper Country*, 116–24; Sophie White, *Wild Frenchmen*, 28–30, 136.

23. Rushforth, "Slavery, the Fox Wars," 57–59; Skinner, *Upper Country*, 93, 97–99; Edmunds and Peyser, *Fox Wars*, 62–65, 72–75; Dubuisson to the Governor General, 1712, in *CSHSW*, 16:268–74, 284.

24. Skinner, *Upper Country*, 102–5 (quote 104); Vaudreuil to the Council of Marine, 14 Oct. 1716, in *CSHSW*, 16:343; Louis de Louvigny to Louis Alexandre de Bourbon, 1 Oct. 1717, in ibid., 16:348–49.

25. Vaudreuil to Minister of the Colonies, 2 Oct. 1723, in *CSHSW*, 16:428–31; Richard White, *Middle Ground*, 163–64; Resume of French Relations with the Foxes, 1715–26, in *CSHSW*, 17:2–6; Lignery to Beauharnois, 30 Aug. 1728, in ibid., 17:32–34; Skinner, *Upper Country*, 105–8; Edmunds and Peyser, *Fox Wars*, 105–6, 109–15; Rushforth, *Bonds of Alliance*, 206–16; Rushforth, "Slavery, the Fox Wars," 71–72.

26. "Victory over the Foxes," De Villiers and Anonymous to Beauharnois, Sept. 1730, in *CSHSW*, 17:110–12; Skinner, *Upper Country*, 108–10; Edmunds and Peyser, *Fox Wars*, 134–56; Rushforth, "Slavery, the Fox Wars," 76.

27. Rushforth, "Slavery, the Fox Wars," 79; Rushforth, *Bonds of Alliance*, 253–98.

28. Lee, "'At War with All Nations'"; Bienville to Jean-Frédéric Phélypeaux, Comte De Maurepas, 26 July 1733, in Rowland et al., *Mississippi Provincial Archives*, 1:211 (quote); Skinner, *Upper Country*, 115, 123, 127.

29. Account of Bienville, 25 May 1736, in Dunn and Dunn, *Indiana's First War*, 95, 99–101; Bienville et al. to the Ministry of the Colonies, 1 June 1740, in Rowland et al., *Mississippi Provincial Archives*, 1:428–30; DuVal, "Interconnectedness and Diversity," 148–51; Skinner, *Upper Country*, 123–34; Dumont de Montigny, *Memoir of Lieutenant Dumont*, 273–74; Atkinson, *Splendid Land, Splendid People*, 74–87.

30. Shoemaker, *Strange Likeness*, quote 44; Rushforth, *Bonds of Alliance*, 229–34.

CHAPTER 4: THE HAZARDS OF WAR

1. Colley, *Captives*; Mapp, *Elusive West*, 429–33.

2. Darwin, *After Tamerlane*, 167–171. The Seven Years' War takes its name from its European phase (1756–63).

3. Goldsworthy, *How Rome Fell,* 337–40; Morgan, *Oxford History of Britain,* 118–21, 137–41, 150–51, 213–15, 233–36, 288–90, 327–29, 365–67, 399–401; Taylor, *Colonial America,* 42, 51–52, 92–94; Andrews, *Colonial Background of the American Revolution,* 3–66; Richter, *Before the Revolution,* 174–75. On the English government's experiments with colonial intervention, see Pulsipher, *Subjects unto the Same King,* 54–69, 252–55; Bradburn, "Visible Fist"; Richter, *Before the Revolution,* 254–55, 290–91, 327–29.

4. Anderson and Cayton, *Dominion of War,* 31–32, 39–40; Shannon, *Iroquois Diplomacy,* 63–64; Gallay, *Indian Slave Trade,* 171, 294–99; Richard White, *Middle Ground,* 120–21; Skinner, *Upper Country,* 91–92; Rushforth, *Bonds of Alliance,* 163–64.

5. Anderson and Cayton, *Dominion of War,* 65–68, 72–73.

6. Landsman, *Crossroads of Empire,* 103, 197; Fur, *Nation of Women,* 21, 29, 44–49, 137, 180–83.

7. Francis Jennings, *Benjamin Franklin,* 49–58; Philadelphia Treaty Journal, 10 July 1742, in Kalter, *Benjamin Franklin, Pennsylvania, and the First Nations,* 80; Merritt, "Metaphor, Meaning, and Misunderstanding," 77–80; Lambing, "Céloron's Journal," 347; David Nichols, *Red Gentlemen and White Savages,* 102.

8. McConnell, *Country Between,* 21–46; Jay Miller, "Old Religion among the Delawares"; Clark, *The Shawnee,* 23–24, 43–45; James Smith, "Prisoner of the Caughnawagas," 31–32, 35–41, 43, 51–52, 54; Jacques-Charles Sabrevois, "Memoir on the Savages of Canada," in *CSHSW,* 16:364 (quote).

9. Dowd, *War under Heaven,* 41–42, 62, 91–92; David Nichols, *Red Gentlemen and White Savages,* 33; McConnell, *Country Between,* 47–48.

10. Fred Anderson, *War That Made America,* 19–22; Kalter, *Benjamin Franklin, Pennsylvania, and the First Nations,* 142–59.

11. See chapter 3.

12. Sabrevois, "Memoir on the Savages of Canada," in *CSHSW,* 16:375–76; Hinderaker, *Elusive Empires,* 17–18, 35–36; Warren, *Worlds the Shawnees Made,* 32; Shackelford, "Illinois Indians in the Confluence Region," 25–26; McConnell, *Country Between,* 66, 72. Population figures are based on Sabrevois's estimate of sixteen hundred Miami and Ouiatenon (a Miami division) warriors, multiplied by five to include women and children.

13. McConnell, *Country Between,* 62–63; Sturtevant, "'Inseparable Companions' and Irreconcilable Enemies," 225–30; Tanner, *Atlas of Great Lakes Indian History,* 40–41, 44; Diary of the Governor and Intendant, 14 Nov. 1747, in *CSHSW,* 17:479–85.

14. Mapp, *Elusive West,* 283–311.

15. McConnell, *Country Between,* 83–88; Fowler, *Empires at War,* 13–14; Lambing, "Céloron's Journal," 339–47, 348 (second quote), 350–54, 357, 364–66 (first quote 365), 369, 374–75. "Beautiful River" was the Delawares' name for the Ohio.

16. Fred Anderson, *War That Made America,* 32–36; Wyman, *Frontier Wisconsin,* 83–84; Francis Jennings, *Empire of Fortune,* 49–53.

17. McDonnell, *Masters of Empire*, 153–62.

18. Anderson and Cayton, *Dominion of war*, 108–10; Titus, *Old Dominion of War*, 10, 76; Hofstra, "Extension of His Majesties Dominions." From 1700 to 1790, Virginia's slave population grew by 2,000 percent.

19. Francis Jennings, *Ambiguous Iroquois Empire*, 360–62; Mulkearn, *George Mercer Papers*, 2–8; Titus, *Old Dominion of War*, 9, 12–13, 26–28.

20. Titus, *Old Dominion*, 52–53; Fowler, *Empires at War*, 34–47; Fred Anderson, *War That Made America*, 37–52, 57–61. For a description of Fort Duquesne, see Bond, "Captivity of Charles Stuart," 67.

21. Fred Anderson, *War That Made America*, 64–71; Fowler, *Empires at War*, 55–57, 61–63, 68.

22. Fred Anderson, *War That Made America*, 88–91; Titus, *Old Dominion*, 74 (quote), 94; Louis Billouart de Kerlerec to the Minister, 1 June 1756, in *CSHSW*, 18:106.

23. Marie Le Roy and Barbara Leininger, "Two Captives from Penn's Creek," in Shannon, *Seven Years' War*, 92–93; Bond, "Captivity of Charles Stuart," 60–62, 74–78; Seaver, *Life of Mary Jemison*, 75–78; James Smith, "Prisoner of the Caughnawagas," 35, 44, 53, 60; Ward, *Breaking the Backcountry*, 48, 50–58, 72.

24. Ward, *Breaking the Backcountry*, 48, 72; Fred Anderson, *War That Made America*, 159; Silver, *Our Savage Neighbors*, 39–94; Titus, *Old Dominion*, 76.

25. Ward, *Breaking the Backcountry*, 47–48; McDonnell, *Masters of Empire*, 178; Fletcher, *Empires at War*, 101–3, 121–29; Pierre Roubaud, "A French View of the Fort William Henry Massacre," in Shannon, *Seven Years' War*, 128–30.

26. Fletcher, *Empires at War*, 137–39; MacLeod, "Microbes and Muskets," 48–49; Edmunds, *The Potawatomis*, 55–56.

27. Fred Anderson, *War That Made America*, 122–25, 130–31.

28. Francis Jennings, *Empire of Fortune*, 364–68, 396–401; Kalter, *Benjamin Franklin, Pennsylvania, and the First Nations*, 296, 301–3, 317–19; Ward, *Breaking the Backcountry*, 183.

29. Fred Anderson, *Crucible of War*, 330–39, 344–68, 381–84, 397–409.

30. Richter, *Facing East*, 187–88; Richard White, *Middle Ground*, 256–59; Fred Anderson, *War That Made America*, 233–35.

31. MacLeod, "Microbes and Muskets," 51; Calloway, *World Turned Upside Down*, 136–37 (quote); Bruce White, "'Give Us a Little Milk'"; James Smith, "Prisoner of the Caughnawagas," 52–53.

32. Louis-Joseph Montcalm to François-Charles de Bourlemaque, 15 March 1759, in *CSHSW*, 18:209; MacLeod, "Microbes and Muskets," 52–53 (quote).

CHAPTER 5: NATIVISTS AND NEWCOMERS

1. "Master of Life" may have originated as an Ojibwa term for *gichi-manitou*, the Supreme Spirit. See Witgen, *Infinity of Nations*, 78.

2. "The Royal Proclamation—October 7, 1763: By the King. A Proclamation," *The Avalon Project*, http://avalon.law.yale.edu/18th_century/proc1763.asp; Barr, *Colony Sprung from Hell*, 109–11. On population doubling, see Benjamin

Franklin, "Observations Concerning the Increase of Mankind," in Labaree, *Papers of Benjamin Franklin*, 4:225–34.

3. Dowd, "French King Wakes Up."

4. Quaife, *Alexander Henry's Travels*, 43–44.

5. Ibid., 44–45.

6. Webster, *Journal of Jeffery Amherst*, 306–11, 315; Dowd, *War under Heaven*, 118–31; Calloway, *Scratch of a Pen*, 70–73; McConnell, *Country Between*, 190; Tanner, *Atlas of Great Lakes Indian History*, 40–41.

7. Skinner, *Upper Country*, 111; Dowd, *War under Heaven*, 131–32; Tanner, *Atlas of Great Lakes Indian History*, 6–7.

8. Webster, *Journal of Jeffery Amherst*, 315; Thomas Morris, *Journal of Captain Thomas Morris*; Francis Jennings, *Empire of Fortune*, 444–47; Dowd, "French King Wakes Up," 258–59, 265–66; Calloway, *Scratch of a Pen*, 74.

9. Parmenter, "Pontiac's War," 621–25; William Johnson, "A British Diplomat Extends the Covenant Chain," in Shannon, *Seven Years' War*, 120–25; Francis Jennings, *Ambiguous Iroquois Empire*, 170–71, 177, 297–98, 368–74; Francis Jennings, *Empire of Fortune*, 75–79, 163–64; David Nichols, *Engines of Diplomacy*, 19; McConnell, *Country Between*, 171–73.

10. Parmenter, "Pontiac's War," 626; McConnell, *Country Between*, 175–78; Sosin, *Revolutionary Frontier*, 57; Barr, *Colony Sprung from Hell*, 99, 101.

11. Dowd, *Spirited Resistance*, 29–33; Dowd, *War under Heaven*, 101; Richter, *Facing East*, 180–82.

12. Pontiac's Speech to an Ottawa, Potawatomi, and Huron Audience, 1763, in DuVal and DuVal, *Interpreting a Continent*, 79–82 (first quote 82); Quaife, *Alexander Henry's Travels*, 43–44 (second quote); Dowd, *Spirited Resistance*, 33–35.

13. Journal of Christian Post, 19 May 1760, in Grumet, *Journey on the Forbidden Path*, 48; Pontiac's Speech, 1763, in DuVal and DuVal, *Interpreting a Continent*, 81–82 (quotes); Jordan, "Journal of James Kenny," 165–66, 188; Dowd, *War under Heaven*, 95–97, 101–5.

14. Dowd, *War under Heaven*, 37–41; McConnell, *Country Between*, 186–87; Blair, *Indian Tribes of the Upper Mississippi*, 1:270 (quote); McDonnell, *Masters of Empire*, 94; Sleeper-Smith, *Indian Women and French Men*, 49; Seaver, *Life of Mary Jemison*, 81–82, 95. On intermarriage and language acquisition see Calloway, *New Worlds for All*, 174.

15. Jordan, "Journal of James Kenny," 158–59, 187, 196; Thomas Morris, *Journal of Thomas Morris*, 13, 23; Timothy Smith, "Wampum as Primitive Valuables"; Calloway, *Pen and Ink Witchcraft*, 25–32.

16. Webster, *Journal of Jeffery Amherst*, 315; Quaife, *Alexander Henry's Travels*, 76–77; Thomas Morris, *Journal of Thomas Morris*, 17; Richard White, *Middle Ground*, 287, 328; Ward, "'Indians Our Real Friends,'" 71–72; Vennum, *American Indian Lacrosse*, 93–94; Dowd, *War under Heaven*, 118–21; also Ingram, *Indians and British Outposts*, 89–90.

17. Nester, *"Haughty Conquerors,"* 114 (quote); Calloway, *Scratch of a Pen*, 73; Fenn, "Biological Warfare in Eighteenth-Century America," 1553–58.

18. Calloway, *Scratch of a Pen*, 74; Calloway, *Shawnees and the War for America*, 35; Webster, *Journal of Jeffery Amherst*, 316–20.

19. Thomas Morris, *Journal of Thomas Morris*, 1, 4, 6, 10–11, 19–22, 24; Richard White, *Middle Ground*, 292–96. On southern Indians and "coups," see Matthew Jennings, *New Worlds of Violence*, 94–95.

20. "Croghan's Journal, 1765," in Thwaites, *Early Western Travels*, 1:126–70, esp. 146–48, 155–58; Calloway, *Shawnees and the War for America*, 37–39 (quotes); Calloway, *Pen and Ink Witchcraft*, 47–48. For captives as "flesh" or "meat," see also Speech of Captain Pipe, Nov. 1781, in Calloway, *World Turned Upside Down*, 162.

21. Richter, "Plan of 1764," 192–96; Sosin, *Revolutionary Frontier*, 11–12, 30–31; Horsman, *Matthew Elliott*, 1–6.

22. Richter, "Plan of 1764." 198–99; Sosin, *Revolutionary Frontier*, 12 (quote); Paul Phillips, "Fur Trade in the Maumee-Wabash Country," 93–94; Alan Taylor, *Divided Ground*, 397–99.

23. Mancall, *Deadly Medicine*, 161–64; Dowd, "Indigenous Catholicism and Resistance," 158; Thomas Gage to William Johnson, March 31, 1773, in Sullivan et al., *Papers of William Johnson*, 8:749 (first quote); Johnson to Gage, 13 April 1773, in ibid., 8:764 (second quote); Speech of Ishwabama and Minitowabe, 9 May 1773, in ibid., 8:788–89. Mancall estimates that British traders annually imported at least eighty thousand gallons of rum in the 1770s.

24. Richter, "Plan of 1764," 199; Sosin, *Revolutionary Frontier*, 13–15; Dowd, *War under Heaven*, 235, 237.

25. Anderson and Cayton, *Dominion of War*, 149; Alexander McKee's Journal of the Scioto Conference, 6 April 1773, in Sullivan et al., *Papers of William Johnson*, 8:756 (quote); Dowd, *War under Heaven*, 238; Clark, *The Shawnee*, 31; Aron, "Pigs and Hunters," 187–88; McConnell, *Country Between*, 259.

26. Calloway, *Pen and Ink Witchcraft*, 49–79.

27. Sosin, *Revolutionary Frontier*, 20–38; Sosin, *Whitehall and the Wilderness*, 240–49; Dowd, *War under Heaven*, 242–45; Blake Watson, *Buying America from the Indians*, 61–62, 66–73, 77, 90–93. The Piankeshaws, who resided in the lower Wabash valley, were affiliates of the Miami confederation. The Quebec Act, which extended that province's boundaries to the Ohio River, stipulated that the new boundary would not interfere with the claims of other colonies. For the text of the act, see "Great Britain: Parliament—The Quebec Act: October 7, 1774," *The Avalon Project*, http://avalon.law.yale.edu/18th_century/quebec_act_1774.asp.

28. Calloway, *Shawnees and the War for America*, 41; Johnson to Thomas Wharton, 24 Dec. 1772, in Sullivan et al., *Papers of William Johnson*, 8:674–75; Johnson to Gage, 1 Jan. 1773, in ibid., 8:688–89; McConnell, *Country Between*, 241–42, 265–67; Larry Nelson, *Man of Distinction*, 59–61.

29. Cayton and Anderson, *Dominion of War*, 153–54; David, *Dunmore's New World*, chapter 3.

30. Hinderaker, *Elusive Empires*, 190–91; McConnell, *Country Between*, 274–76; Hammon and Taylor, *Virginia's Western War*, xxix–xxx; Richard Butler,

"Account of the Rise of the Indian War," 23 Aug. 1774, in *Pennsylvania Archives,* First Series, 4:568–70.

31. Lakomäki, *Gathering Together,* 89; Calloway, *Shawnees and the War for America,* 13–15.

32. Dunmore to Lord Dartmouth, 24 Dec. 1774, in Thwaites and Kellogg, *Documentary History of Dunmore's War,* 368–95; Sosin, *Revolutionary Frontier,* 60, 85; Hammon and Taylor, *Virginia's Western War,* xxx–xxxiii; Hinderaker, *Elusive Empires,* 193–94; Sugden, *Blue Jacket,* 40–45.

33. Calloway, *Shawnees and the War for America,* 53–56; Friend, *Kentucke's Frontiers,* 41–62.

34. Holton, *Forced Founders,* 144.

35. J. H. Elliott, *Empires of the Atlantic World,* 298–302, 305–6.

36. Maier, *American Scripture,* 3–28; Breen, *American Insurgents, American Patriots,* 185–206.

CHAPTER 6: REVOLUTIONARY STALEMATE

1. Shy, *Toward Lexington,* 322–25; Francis Jennings, *Creation of America,* 145–48; Kevin Phillips, *1775,* 88–90, 136–38.

2. McDonald, introduction to *Empire and Nation,* xii–xiv; Calloway, *Pen and Ink Witchcraft,* 75–77, 87, 89–90.

3. Knouff, "Soldiers and Violence." For "anti-Indian sublime" and "nativist," see chapters 4 and 5, respectively.

4. Anderson and Cayton, *Dominion of War,* 168–69; Shannon, *Iroquois Diplomacy,* 27–28, 42–43, 86; Proceedings of the Treaty of Fort Pitt, 7 Oct., 10 Oct., and 11 Oct. 1775, in Thwaites and Kellogg, *Revolution on the Upper Ohio,* 81–82, 95 (second quote), 98, 108, 110–11 (first quote).

5. Instructions for Silas Deane, 2 March 1776, in Peter Smith et al., *Letters of Delegates to Congress,* 3:162; Frazier, *Mohicans of Stockbridge,* 198–99; Hatch, *Thrust for Canada,* 38–40.

6. Journal of James Wood, 1 Aug. 1775, in Thwaites and Kellogg, *Revolution on the Upper Ohio,* 61; Proceedings of 10 and 14 Oct. 1775, in ibid., 99, 118; Calloway, *Shawnees and the War for America,* 59–60; Deposition of Jarret Williams, July 1776, reprinted in Ramsey, *Annals of Tennessee,* 148–49.

7. John Cook to Andrew Hamilton, 2 Oct. 1776, in Thwaites and Kellogg, *Revolution on the Upper Ohio,* 205, 205n–206n; William Crawford to the President of Congress, 22 April 1777, in ibid., 250–51; Reminiscence of Joseph Doddridge, in Thwaites and Kellogg, *Frontier Defense,* 54–55; Hammon and Taylor, *Virginia's Western War,* 47–48, 51–52, 56–57, 59, 63–64.

8. Hinderaker, *Elusive Empires,* 217–20; George Morgan to President of Congress, 31 March 1778, in Thwaites and Kellogg, *Frontier Defense,* 256; Friend, *Kentucke's Frontiers,* 79–80; Randolph Downes, *Council Fires on the Upper Ohio,* 206–7, 215; Paul Wallace, *Travels of John Heckewelder,* 43.

9. Henry Hamilton to Guy Carleton, 5 April 1778, in *MPHC,* 9:435; Friend, *Kentucke's Frontiers,* 80–81, 83–84; Hammon and Taylor, *Virginia's Western War,*

71–72, 82–87; Arthur Campbell to Charles Cummings, 10 June 1778, in Kellogg, *Frontier Advance on the Ohio River*, 86–87; William McKee to Edward Hand, 21 June 1778, in ibid., 98.

10. Hammon and Taylor, *Virginia's Western War*, 76–78, 92; Cayton, *Frontier Indiana*, 83–84; Treaty of Fort Pitt, in Kappler, *Indian Affairs, Laws, and Treaties*, 2:3–5; Downes, *Council Fires*, 216–21.

11. Calloway, *World Turned Upside Down*, 156; Calloway, *American Revolution*, 37; Downes, *Council Fires*, 222–27; Richard White, *Middle Ground*, 382, 385; Lachlan McIntosh to Washington, 12 March 1779, in Kellogg, *Frontier Advance*, 241; Henry Bird to Richard Lernoult, 12 March 1779, in ibid., 252.

12. Patrick Henry to Virginia Delegates in Congress, 16 Nov. 1778, in James, *George Rogers Clark Papers*, 1:72–73; Instructions to Clark from Virginia Council, 12 Dec. 1778, in ibid., 1:79–80; Clark to George Mason, 19 Nov. 1779, in ibid., 1:120–29; Clark's Memoir, 1773–1779, in ibid., 3:224, 242–46 (quotes 244, 245, 246); Richard White, *Middle Ground*, 369–70.

13. Richard White, *Middle Ground*, 372–77; Larry Nelson, *Man of Distinction*, 96–99, 109–11.

14. Clark to George Mason, 19 Nov. 1779, in James, *George Rogers Clark Papers*, 144–48, quotes 146, 148.

15. Cayton, *Frontier Indiana*, 84–85; Hammon and Taylor, *Virginia's Western War*, 105–7; Larry Nelson, *Man of Distinction*, 111; Aron, *How the West Was Lost*. On Kentucky's 1780 population, see Greene and Harrington, *American Population before 1790*, 192.

16. Seaver, *Life of Mary Jemison*, 98–100; Joseph Fischer, *Well-Executed Failure*, 25–30, 36, 42–45; Graymont, *Iroquois in the American Revolution*; Shy, *People Numerous and Armed*, 229–31.

17. Abler, *Chainbreaker*, 110; 114–15; Seaver, *Life of Mary Jemison*, 101–2, 104; Calloway, *American Revolution*, 136–41; Joseph Fischer, *Well-Executed Failure*, 43–52, 59, 146–148, 192–94.

18. Kerr, "'Why Should You Be So Furious?'" 883–87; Griffin, "Destroying and Reforming Canaan," 43–44, 46.

19. Hammon and Taylor, *Virginia's Western War*, 127; Arent De Peyster to Mason Bolton, 10 March and 4 Aug. 1780, in *MPHC*, 19:501–2 and 553–54; Quaife, "When Detroit Invaded Kentucky"; Cleary, *World, Flesh, and Devil*, 222–35; Delavillebreuve to Bernardo de Galvez, 24 June 1780, in Kinnaird, *Spain in the Mississippi Valley*, 1:378–79.

20. Hammon and Taylor, *Virginia's Western War*, 127–30, 138; Standage, *Edible History of Humanity*, 149–51; Cleary, *World, Flesh, and Devil*, 200; Memorial of the Inhabitants of Vincennes to Minister Luzerne, 22 Aug. 1780, in James, *George Rogers Clark Papers*, 3:444–45. See also Thomas Jefferson to Bernardo de Galvez, 8 Nov. 1779, in Kinnaird, *Spain in the Mississippi Valley*, 1:362–63.

21. Birzer, "French Imperial Remnants," 146; Dodge to Franco Cruzat, 11 Nov. 1780, in Kinnaird, *Spain in the Mississippi Valley*, 1:393; Cruzat to Bernardo

Galvez, 12 Nov. 1780, 21 Nov. 1780, and 10 Jan. 1781, in ibid., 1:395–96, 400, and 415, respectively; People of Vincennes to Cruzat, in ibid., 1:406–7.

22. Cruzat to Galvez, 10 Jan. 1781, in Kinnaird, *Spain in the Mississippi Valley,* 1:415–16; Cruzat to Esteban Miro, 6 Aug. 1781, in ibid., 1:431–33; Gitlin, *Bourgeois Frontier,* 200n52.

23. Daniel Brodhead to Joseph Reed, 22 Jan. 1781, in *Pennsylvania Archives,* First Series, 8:708 (first quote); Speech of the Shawnees to Captain Lernoult, 26 Sept. 1779, in *MPHC,* 19:469; Petition of the Merchants of Detroit, 5 Jan. 1780, in ibid., 19:493–94; Richard White, *Middle Ground,* 405; Speech of Captain Pipe to De Peyster, Nov. 1781, in Calloway, *World Turned Upside Down,* 162 (second quote). My currency conversion is based on the assumption that £1 New York currency equaled $2.50 Continental.

24. Downes, *Council Fires,* 263–66; Simon Girty to De Peyster, 9 May 1781, in *MPHC,* 10:478–79; Daniel Brodhead to Joseph Reed, 22 May 1781, in *Pennsylvania Archives,* First Series, 9:161–62; Calloway, *American Revolution,* 37–38.

25. Tanner, *Atlas of Great Lakes Indian History,* 79–80; McConnell, *Country Between* 226–32; Journal of James Wood, Aug. 1775, in Thwaites and Kellogg, *Revolution on the Upper Ohio,* 64; Simon Girty to De Peyster, 9 May 1781, in *MPHC,* 10:479; Dowd, *Spirited Resistance,* 64, 83–84; Richard White, *Middle Ground,* 389–90; Paul Wallace, *Travels of John Heckewelder,* 189–95; Sadosky, "Rethinking the Gnadenhutten Massacre."

26. William Croghan to William Davies, 6 July 1782, in James, *George Rogers Clark Papers,* 2:71–73; David Nichols, *Red Gentlemen and White Savages,* 2–3; Spero, *Frontier Country,* 223–46, quotes 240; Knouff, "Soldiers and Violence," 183–84.

27. Hammon and Taylor, *Virginia's Western War,* 151, 153, 155–63; Sugden, *Blue Jacket,* 63–64; Larry Nelson, *Man of Distinction,* 123–28; Account of Levi Todd, 19 Aug. 1782, in James, *George Rogers Clark Papers,* 2:90–93; Andrew Steele to Benjamin Harrison, 26 Aug. 1782, in ibid., 2:96–97.

28. Benjamin Harrison to George Clark, 17 Oct. 1782, in James, *George Rogers Clark Papers,* 2:134; Clark to Harrison, 18 Oct., 22 Oct., and 27 Nov. 1782, in ibid., 2:136, 140 (quote), and 157–58, respectively; Irvine to Clark, 7 Nov. 1782, in ibid., 2:149; Hammon and Taylor, *Virginia's Western War,* 169–70.

29. Calloway, *American Revolution,* 40, 42; Speech of Captain Pipe, Nov. 1781, in Calloway, *World Turned Upside Down,* 161; Anderson and Cayton, *Dominion of War,* 175–76; Andrew Steele to Benjamin Harrison, 12 Sept. 1782, in James, *George Rogers Clark Papers,* 2:115; Tanner, *Atlas of Great Lakes Indian History,* 80–83.

CHAPTER 7: THE UNITED INDIANS VERSUS THE UNITED STATES

1. Richter, "Onas, the Long Knife," in Richter, *Trade, Land, Power,* 202–26, esp. 203–5; Fernando Leyba to Bernard Galvez, 21 July 1778, in Kinnaird, *Spain in the Mississippi Valley,* 1:298.

2. Aron and Adelman, "From Borderlands to Borders"; Calloway, *Victory with No Name,* 94–96.

3. For fiscal-military states, see Edling, *Revolution in Favor of Government.*

4. David Nichols, *Red Gentlemen and White Savages,* 21–22, 28, 29–33 (first three quotes), 40–41 (last quote); Calloway, *Pen and Ink Witchcraft,* 100–103. For the treaties of 1784–86, see Kappler, *Indian Affairs, Laws, and Treaties,* 2:5–8, 16–18. On the reluctance of some Lakes Indians to return captives, see Alexander McKee to Col. DePeyster, 8 Sept. 1783, in *MPHC,* 11:385.

5. Nugent, *Habits of Empire,* 18–40; David Nichols, *Red Gentlemen and White Savages,* 20–21, 37; Blake Watson, *Buying America from the Indians,* 151; Resolution of 23 April 1784, in *Journals of the Continental Congress,* 26:275–79; Land Ordinance of 20 May 1785, in ibid., 28:375–81; Report of the Committee on Indian Affairs for the Northern Department, 15 Oct. 1783, in ibid., 25:683 (quote).

6. David Nichols, *Red Gentlemen and White Savages,* 58–59; Taylor, "Land and Liberty"; Silver, *Our Savage Neighbors,* 232–60.

7. Larry Nelson, *Man of Distinction,* 150; David Nichols, *Red Gentlemen and White Savages,* 25 (quote), 43, 61, 63; Journal of Richard Butler, 1 and 9 Oct. 1785, in Craig, *Olden Time,* 2:437, 442–43; Kukla, *Wilderness So Immense,* 67–69, 75–84.

8. Alexander McKee to John Johnson, 2 June 1785, in *MPHC,* 11:457–58 (first quote); Denny, *Military Journal,* 75–76, 79, 84–85, 93; David Nichols, *Red Gentlemen and White Savages,* 55, 70; Speech of the United Indian Nations, 28 Nov. and 18 Dec. 1786, in Lowrie and Clarke, *American State Papers, Class II: Indian Affairs* (hereafter ASPIA), 1:8–9 (second quote).

9. Abler, *Chainbreaker,* 167–68; Alan Taylor, *Divided Ground,* 120–23, 125–28; Kelsay, *Joseph Brant,* 370; David Nichols, *Red Gentlemen and White Savages,* 72–73, 220n61.

10. Statement of Indebtedness of John Askin, 20 Dec. 1786, in Quaife, *John Askin Papers,* 1:4–9, 274–75; Askin to Thomas Smith, 5 Jan. 1793, in ibid., 1:457–59; George Ironside to David Gray, 21 March 1785 and 16 Feb. 1787, in Coleman, "Letters from Eighteenth Century Indiana Merchants," 142 and 149; Quaife, *Fort Wayne in 1790,* 336, 338–39; Horsman, *Matthew Elliott,* 97.

11. Richard White, *Middle Ground,* 425–27; Harper, "Powerful Weakness of the Frontier State"; David Nichols, *Red Gentlemen and White Savages,* 65–66, 78–79, 82–83; Calloway, *Shawnees and the War for America,* 83–84.

12. David Nichols, *Red Gentlemen and White Savages,* 66, 68, 87–88, Tanner, *Atlas of Great Lakes Indian History,* 87; Taylor, "Land and Liberty," 89–90 (quote); Calloway, *Shawnees and the War for America,* 88.

13. David Nichols, *Red Gentlemen and White Savages,* 37, 48, 80–87, 106; Denny, *Military Journal,* 22 Oct. 1785, 55, 59–61, 64, 71–73, 101–3; Richard White, *Middle Ground,* 426–27; "Northwest Ordinance; July 13, 1787," *The Avalon Project,* http://avalon.law.yale.edu/18th_century/nworder.asp; Finkelman, *Slavery and the Founders,* 40–50. For white settlers' control of frontier law enforcement, see Ford, *Settler Sovereignty,* 108–20.

14. Treaty of Fort Harmar (9 Jan. 1789), in Kappler, *Indian Affairs*, 2:18–23; David Nichols, *Red Gentlemen and White Savages*, 91, 104.

15. David Nichols, *Red Gentlemen and White Savages*, 91–92, 101, 103–4; Denny, *Military Journal*, 127–30.

16. Account of Depredations Committed in the District of Kentucky, in *ASPIA*, 1:85; Representatives of the Frontier Counties of Virginia to the President, 12 Dec. 1789, in ibid., 1:85–86; David Nichols, *Red Gentlemen and White Savages*, 104–5, 114.

17. Anderson and Cayton, *Dominion of War*, 189–90; Report of the Secretary of War, 15 June 1789, in *ASPIA*, 1:13; David Nichols, *Red Gentlemen and White Savages*, 105–6 (quote).

18. Mr. Gamelin's Journal, 5 April–5 May 1790, in *ASPIA*, 1:93–94 (first quote); David Nichols, *Red Gentlemen and White Savages*, 115–16 (second quote); Tanner, *Atlas of Great Lakes Indian History*, 87–89; Denny, *Military Journal*, 139 (third quote), 141–42.

19. Denny, *Military Journal*, 143, 145–49; Willig, *Restoring the Chain of Friendship*, 32–33; Rufus Putnam to the President, 28 Feb. 1791, in Carter, *Territorial Papers of the United* States (hereafter *TPUS*), 2:338–39; David Nichols, *Red Gentlemen and White Savages*, 115–16; Sugden, *Blue Jacket*, 100–111. On labeling the Battle of Kekionga, see Conlin and Owens, "Bigger Than Little Bighorn."

20. Statement of the Causes of the Indian War, 26 Jan. 1792, in *TPUS*, 2:364–65; David Nichols, *Red Gentlemen and White Savages*, 138–39; Report of General Scott, 8 June 1791, in *ASPIA*, 1:131–32; Lt. Col. Wilkinson's Report, 24 Aug. 1791, in ibid., 1:133–35.

21. Denny, *Military Journal*, 151–69, 171 (first quote 166); Sugden, *Blue Jacket*, 115–27 (second quote 123); Calloway, *Victory with No Name*, 111, 119–20.

22. Dowd, *Spirited Resistance*, 106–7; Calloway, *Shawnees and the War for America*, 94; Calloway, *Victory with No Name*, 125; Harrison, *Philadelphia Merchant*, 99.

23. Cayton, "Meanings of the Wars"; Clarfield, "Protecting the Frontiers"; David Nichols, *Red Gentlemen and White Savages*, 140–43.

24. David Nichols, *Red Gentlemen and White Savages*, 143, 145–46 (quote); Helen Tanner, "The Glaize in 1792"; Calloway, *Shawnees and the War for America*, 96–97, Abler, *Chainbreaker*, 198–99.

25. Buell, *Memoirs of Rufus Putnam*, 342–52, quotes 342, 347; David Nichols, *Red Gentlemen and White Savages*, 143–45; Edmunds, "'Nothing Has Been Effected.'" On Indians' views of treaty councils, see Calloway, *Pen and Ink Witchcraft*, 15–40.

26. Secretary Knox's Instructions to the Commissioners, 26 April 1793, in *ASPIA*, 1:340–42; Proceedings of the Commissioners at Niagara, 5–9 July 1793, in ibid., 1:349–51; Address of the Confederate Council, 27 July 1793, in ibid., 1:352; Speech of the Commissioners to the Deputies of the Confederated Indians, 31 July 1793, in ibid., 1:352–54; Reply of the General Council, in ibid., 1:356–57 (quotes); David Nichols, *Red Gentlemen and White Savages*, 147–50.

27. Sugden, *Blue Jacket*, 150–51; Larry Nelson, *Man of Distinction*, 160–61, 163–67; David Nichols, *Red Gentlemen and White Savages*, 148–49.

28. David Nichols, *Red Gentlemen and White Savages*, 157–58, 160–62, 165–67; Horsman, *Matthew Elliott*, 92–98; David Nichols, *Red Gentlemen and White Savages*, 159–61. In preparation for a 1793 attack on the French West Indies, the British navy had seized 250 American ships, leading Congress to discuss war measures (Henry Knox to Anthony Wayne, 31 March 1794, in Knopf, *Anthony Wayne*, 318–19).

29. Anthony Wayne to Henry Knox, 9 May 1793, 15 Nov. 1793, 8 Jan. 1794 and 3 March 1794, in Knopf, *Anthony Wayne*, 234, 281–83, 298, and 306; Knox to Wayne, 3 Sept. 1793, in ibid., 271 (quote); Benjamin Lincoln et al. to Knox, 10 July 1793, in *ASPIA*, 1:351; David Nichols, *Red Gentlemen and White Savages*, 162–63.

30. Wayne to Knox, 20 June 1793, in Knopf, *Anthony Wayne*, 247; Wayne to Knox, 7 July 1794, in *ASPIA*, 1:487–88; Richard White, *Middle Ground*, 466.

31. Alexander McKee to Joseph Chew, 7 July 1794, in *MPHC*, 20:364; Willig, *Restoring the Chain of Friendship*, 53–54; David Nichols, *Red Gentlemen and White Savages*, 163–64.

32. Richard Wade, *Urban Frontier*, 11–12; Hill, *John Johnston and the Indians*, 150; David Nichols, *Red Gentlemen and White Savages*, 151, 164; Bergmann, *American National State*, 64–72.

33. Wayne to Knox, 28 Aug. 1794, in Knopf, *Anthony Wayne*, 351–55 (quotes 354); Alexander McKee to Joseph Chew, 27 Aug. 1794, in *MPHC*, 20:370–72; David Nichols, *Red Gentlemen and White Savages*, 164–65.

34. Willig, *Restoring the Chain of Friendship*, 56–57. For Jay's Treaty, see "British-American Diplomacy: The Jay Treaty; November 19, 1794," *The Avalon Project*, http://avalon.law.yale.edu/18th_century/jay.asp.

35. Timothy Pickering to Wayne, 8 April 1795, in Knopf, *Anthony Wayne*, 394–96; Cayton, "'Noble Actors,'" 244, 256–62; Treaty of Greenville, 3 Aug. 1795, in Kappler, *Indian Affairs*, 2:41–42; David Nichols, *Red Gentlemen and White Savages*, 172–73.

36. Greenville Treaty Journal, 21–22 July, 24 July, 29–30 July 1795, in *ASPIA*, 1:570–73, 576–78, 580 (quote); Cayton, "'Noble Actors,'" 262–65; Wayne to Knox, 23 Dec. 1794, in Knopf, *Anthony Wayne*, 370.

37. Hurt, *Ohio Frontier*, 197–204, 211–12, 217–21; Calloway, *American Revolution*, 292–301.

38. Dowd, *Spirited Resistance*, 93–113; Jortner, *Gods of Prophetstown*, 56–60.

39. Cayton, *Frontier Indiana*, 98–100. I have extrapolated the expense of Wayne's army from Congressional appropriations for 1793 and 1794, which included $2,580,000 for the pay and equipment of the western army. (Act Making Appropriations for Support of Government, 28 Feb. 1793 and 21 March 1794, both in Peters, *Public Statutes at Large*, 1:328 and 346–47.)

CHAPTER 8: SURVIVAL AND NATION BUILDING ON THE EDGE OF EMPIRE

1. On different "levels" of historic change and the slower pace of material and cultural change, see Braudel, "History and the Social Sciences"; Ladurie, "History That Stands Still"; Tomich, "Order of Historical Time."

2. Kohn, *Eagle and Sword*, 174–93; Prucha, *Sword of the Republic*, 40; Estimate of Posts where Garrisons Will be Expedient, 23 Dec. 1801, in Lowrie and Franklin, *American State Papers, Military Affairs*, 1:156.

3. Hurt, *Ohio Frontier*, 189, 197–204, 217–21, 250–51, 275–77; An Act to Divide the Territory Northwest of the Ohio, 7 May 1800, in *TPUS*, 7:7–10; William Harrison to Henry Dearborn, 15 July 1801, in Esarey, *Governor's Messages*, 1:25–26; David Nichols, *Red Gentlemen and White Savages*, 184–85.

4. Harrison to Dearborn, 15 July 1801, in Esarey, *Governor's Messages*, 1:27; David Nichols, *Red Gentlemen and White Savages*, 185. See also Willig, *Restoring the Chain of Friendship*, 63.

5. In early-modern Europe and North America, "factory" referred to a mercantile establishment with a resident trader or traders, not to an industrial plant.

6. Anthony Wallace, *Jefferson and the Indians*, 207, 220; David Nichols, "'Main Mean of Their Political Management'"; John Mason to Matthew Irwin and Joseph Varnum, 9 Sept. 1808, in *CSHSW*, 19:327 (quote); Partnership for Purchase of the Michigan Peninsula, 27 Sept. 1795, in Quaife, *John Askin Papers*, 1:568–71; J. V. Campbell, "Account of a Plot for Obtaining the Lower Peninsula of Michigan," in *MPHC*, 8:406–10.

7. Magnaghi, "Michigan's Indian Factory at Detroit"; Farmer, *History of Detroit*, 767–68; David Nichols, "Commercial Embassy in the Old Northwest."

8. David Nichols, *Engines of Diplomacy*, 104–7.

9. Frederick Bates to Meriwether Lewis, 7 Nov. 1807, in Marshall, *Life and Papers of Frederick Bates*, 1:230; David Nichols, *Engines of Diplomacy*, 101–2; Nicholas Boilvin to William Eustis, 11 Feb. 1811, in *TPUS*, 14:440.

10. Edmunds, *Shawnee Prophet*, 19–24; Dowd, *Spirited Resistance*, 120.

11. Beck, "Return to Namä'o Uskíwämît," 34, 39–45; George Nelson, *My First Years*, 56, 158n58; Schoolcraft, *Narrative Journal*, 118, 133; Cary Miller, *Ogimaag*, 54–55; Waddell, "Malhiot's Journal," 247–48; Gary Anderson, *Kinsmen of Another Kind*, 3, 6; Faragher, *Sugar Creek*, 16–17.

12. Birk, *John Sayer's Snake River Journal*, 40–43, 46, 49–50, 54; Gary Anderson, *Kinsmen*, 66–67; Waddell, "Malhiot's Journal," 251, 254, 256; George Nelson, *My First Years*, 14–15; Bruce White, "'Give Us a Little Milk,'" 66–67, 70–71; Cary Miller, *Ogimaag*, 61. On "convenient" goods, see Axtell, *Indians' New South*, 62–64.

13. George Nelson, *My First Years*, 14–15, 32, 101 (quote); John Tanner, "White Indian," in Drimmer, *Captured by the Indians*, 142–82, esp. 156, 160–61, 172; Rich, *Montreal and the Fur Trade*, 74–79, 89–92; Haeger, *John Jacob Astor*, 53–54, 73; Morton, "Northwest Company," 14; Davies, "From Competition to Union," 20–24; Mancall, "Men, Women, and Alcohol," 432–35.

14. Willig, *Restoring the Chain of Friendship,* 104, 108, 118.

15. Tanner, *Atlas of Great Lakes Indian History,* 96–103; Denny, *Military Journal,* 145–47 (quote); McConnell, *Country Between,* 211–19; Aron, "Pigs and Hunters," 190–92; Gipson, *Moravian Indian Mission on White River,* 58–60.

16. Spencer, *Indian Captivity,* 82; Faragher, *Sugar Creek,* 11–14, 19–20; Schoolcraft, *Narrative Journal,* 127; Lucy Murphy, "Autonomy and Economic Roles," 76–79, 81–82; Schutt, "Delawares in Eastern Ohio," 117–19, 122.

17. Mancall, "Men, Women, and Alcohol," 428, 434; David Nichols, "Commercial Embassy in the Old Northwest," 9–11 (quote).

18. Robb Mann, "Silenced Miami"; Sugden, *Blue Jacket,* 54, 80, 230–31; Richter, "'Believing That Many Suffer Much,'" 614–16; Oliver Spencer, *Indian Captivity,* 84, 110; Calloway, *Shawnees and the War for America,* 121, 124; Edmunds, *The Potawatomis,* 162–63.

19. Anthony Wayne to William McHenry, 3 Oct. 1796, in Knopf, *Anthony Wayne,* 532; Speech of Little Turtle, 4 Jan. 1802, quoted in Hill, *John Johnston and the Indians,* 16; Dowd, *Spirited Resistance,* 131–35; Willig, *Restoring the Chain of Friendship,* 77; Jefferson to William Harrison, 28 April 1805, in Esarey, *Governor's Messages*, 1:127–28 (first quote); Jefferson to Charles Carroll, 15 April 1791, in Boyd et al., *Papers of Thomas Jefferson,* 20:214–15 (second quote).

20. Owens, *Mr. Jefferson's Hammer,* 78–86; Harrison to Dearborn, 3 March 1803, in Esarey, *Governor's Messages,* 1:76–81; Dearborn to Harrison, 27 June 1804 and 24 May 1805, in ibid., 1:100 and 130; Owens, "Jeffersonian Benevolence on the Ground," 419, 421; Treaties of Fort Wayne (7 June 1803), Vincennes (13 Aug. 1803, 18 Aug. 1804, 27 Aug. 1804), Grouseland (21 Aug. 1805), and Saint Louis (1804), all in Kappler, *Indian Affairs,* 2:64–65, 67–68, 70–72, 72–73, 80–82, and 74–77, respectively; Dearborn to Thomas Jefferson, 11 Jan. 1805, in *TPUS,* 7:256–57; Horsman, *Expansion and American Indian Policy,* 144–49.

21. Horsman, *Expansion and American Indian Policy,* 151, 155; Dearborn to Hull, 22 July 1806, in *TPUS,* 10:63–65; Hull to Dearborn, 18 Nov. 1807, in *MPHC,* 40:219, 221; Treaty of Detroit (17 Nov. 1807), in Kappler, *Indian Affairs,* 2:92–95; Treaty of Brownstown (25 Nov. 1808), in ibid., 2:99–100.

22. Owens, "Jeffersonian Benevolence on the Ground," 423; Harrison to Dearborn, 1804, in Esarey, *Governor's Messages,* 1:114–15; Hull to Henry Dearborn, 18 Nov. 1807, in *MPHC,* 40:219–20 (first quote); Hull to William Eustis, 25 Jan. 1810, in ibid., 40:311; Chitta to Walk-in-the-Water, 6 Aug. 1805, in ibid., 40:76 (second quote); Jacques Laselle to President Jefferson, 12 June 1806, in *TPUS,* 10:59–61; James Wilkinson to Dearborn, 27 July 1805, in *TPUS,* 13:168–69; William Wells to Dearborn, 20 April 1808, in ibid., 7:556–57 (third quote).

23. Jefferson to Harrison, 27 Feb. 1803, in *TPUS,* 7:89–91; Dowd, *Spirited Resistance,* 105–7.

24. Dowd, *Spirited Resistance,* 102–3; Spencer, *Indian Captivity,* 109; Cave, *Prophets of the Great Spirit,* 98; Devens, *Countering Colonization,* 42; Roger Nichols, *Indians in the United States and Canada,* 153–54; Anthony Wallace, *Death and Rebirth of the Seneca,* 239–302. Handsome Lake also urged his

kinsmen to adopt plow agriculture, frame houses, and the English language; his was a hybrid vision of renewal.

25. Edmunds, *Shawnee Prophet*, 28–66; Cave, "Failure of the Shawnee Prophet's Witch Hunt"; Report of Indian Alarms by A.B. Woodward, 14 Aug. 1807, in *MPHC*, 40:175 (quote).

26. Willig, *Restoring the Chain of Friendship*, 233; Speech of Le Maigouis, 4 May 1807, in *MPHC*, 40:128–33 (quotes); Cave, *Prophets of the Great Spirit*, 91–95; Jortner, *Gods of Prophetstown*, 100–102, 106–7.

27. Edmunds, *Shawnee Prophet*, 67–93; Sugden, *Blue Jacket*, 240–42; Witgen, *Restoring the Chain*, 213; Jortner, *Gods of Prophetstown*, 143–48, 153.

28. Willig, *Restoring the Chain of Friendship*, 223–25; Hammond, *Slavery, Freedom, and Expansion*, 110–20; Owens, *Mr. Jefferson's Hammer*, 140–41, 199.

29. Treaties of Fort Wayne, 30 Sept. and 26 Oct. 1809, in Kappler, *Indian Affairs*, 2:101–4; Treaty with the Kickapoos, 9 Dec. 1809, in ibid., 2:104–5; Owens, *Mr. Jefferson's Hammer*, 200–204; John Weaver, *Great Land Rush*, 229.

30. Sugden, *Tecumseh*, 193, 197–200, 212; Tecumseh's Speech to Governor Harrison, 20–21 Aug. 1810, in Esarey, *Governor's Messages*, 1:463–69.

31. Harrison to William Eustis, 15 May 1810 and 13 Aug. 1811, in Esarey, *Governor's Messages*, 1:420–421 and 554–55; Harrison to Tecumseh, 24 June 1811, in ibid., 1:522–24; Sugden, *Tecumseh*, 218–20; Jortner, *Gods of Prophetstown*, 192.

32. Harrison to Eustis, 8 Nov. 1811, in Esarey, *Governor's Messages*, 1:614–15; Jortner, *Gods of Prophetstown*, 191–95.

33. Horsman, *Expansion and American Indian Policy*, 145, 155; Murrin, "Jeffersonian Triumph and American Exceptionalism," 13–14.

CHAPTER 9: RECKONING WITH THE CONQUERORS

1. Aron and Adelman, "From Borderlands to Borders"; Dowd, *Spirited Resistance*, 131–47.

2. Schwartz and Green, "Middle Ground or Native Ground?"

3. Hickey, *War of 1812*, 9–28, 86–90, 139–46, 185–202.

4. Thomas Forsyth to Benjamin Howard, 7 Sept. 1812, in *TPUS*, 16:261–65; Ferguson, *Illinois in the War of 1812*, 55–72; Hickey, *War of 1812*, 80–84; Journal of Thomas Verchères de Boucherville, in Hickey, *War of 1812*, 95–96; Journal of Robert Lucas, in ibid., 113–15 (quote 115); Sugden, *Tecumseh*, 290–305.

5. Daniel Curtis to Jacob Kingsbury, 21 Sept. 1812, in Hickey, *War of 1812*, 145–50; Diary of William Northcutt, in ibid., 181–89, 192; William Russell to William Eustis, 31 Oct. 1812, in *TPUS*, 16:268–69; Ninian Edwards to John Armstrong, 12 April 1813, in ibid., 16:313; Ferguson, *Illinois in the War of 1812*, 81–87; Prucha, *Sword of the Republic*, 111–12; Deposition of Joseph Robert, 4 Feb. 1813, in Lowrie and Franklin, *American State Papers, Military Affairs*, 1:368; Report of Ensign Isaac Baker, 26 Feb. 1813, in ibid., 370; Taylor, *Civil War of 1812*, 211–14.

6. John Richardson, "A Canadian Campaign," in Hickey, *War of 1812*, 220–27; Hickey, *War of 1812*, 135; Sugden, *Tecumseh*, 327–39, 346–49.

7. Dowd, *Spirited Resistance,* 184–85; Skaggs, "Gaining Naval Dominance," 32–43.

8. John Richardson, "War of 1812," in Hickey, *War of 1812,* 326–31; David Nichols, *Red Gentlemen and White Savages,* 198; Sugden, *Tecumseh,* 368–80; Owens, *Red Dreams, White Nightmares,* 217.

9. Hickey, *War of 1812,* 483–85; Davis, *Frontier Illinois,* 148–49; Dunnigan, "'No One Acquired Any Glory.'"

10. Howe, *What Hath God Wrought,* 74–75; David Nichols, *Engines of Diplomacy,* 119; Samuel Watson, *Jackson's Sword,* 216 (quote); Taylor, *Civil War of 1812,* 435–37; Surtees, "Indian Land Cessions in Upper Canada"; Donald Smith, *Sacred Feathers,* 31–32, 37–40. One prominent Mississauga group, the Credit River Band, saw its holdings shrink from eleven thousand acres to two hundred.

11. Willig, *Restoring the Chain of Friendship,* 262–63; Calloway, "End of an Era," 10, 18; George Boyd to John Eaton, 5 March 1831, in *TPUS,* 12:263–64; Boyd to W. P. Slaughter, 28 June 1838, in ibid., 27:1025.

12. Prucha, *American Indian Treaties,* 133; Prucha, *Sword of the Republic,* 120–21; Journal of the Spring Wells Conference, 31 Aug., 4–5 Sept, 1815, in *ASPIA,* 2:20, 23, and 25. The Portage des Sioux treaties are in Kappler, *Indian Affairs,* 2:105–6, 110–17, and 120–22; the Treaty of Spring Wells (8 September 1815) is in ibid., 2:117–19.

13. James Monroe, First Annual Message to Congress (2 Dec. 1817), in Richardson, *Compilation of Messages and Papers,* 2:11–20; Treaty of Ghent, 24 Dec. 1814, in Hickey, *War of 1812,* 629 (quote); Davis, *Frontier Illinois,* 156; Prucha, *American Indian Treaties,* 136–38; Calloway, *Shawnees and the War for America,* 156; Cayton, *Frontier Indiana,* 263–64; Treaty of Maumee Rapids (29 Sept. 1817), in Kappler, *Indian Affairs,* 2:145–55; Treaties of Saint Mary's (2–6 Oct. 1818), in ibid., 2:168–74; Treaty of Edwardsville (30 July 1819), in ibid., 2:182–83; Treaty of Saginaw (24 Sept. 1819), in ibid., 2:185–87. In the Treaty of Vincennes (11 Aug. 1820), the Weas agreed to cede their reservations and move to Illinois (Kappler, *Indian Affairs,* 2:190).

14. Tiro, "View from Piqua Agency," 49–50; Prucha, *American Indian Treaties,* 146–49; Edmunds, *The Potawatomis,* 229; Lewis Cass and Duncan McArthur to the Secretary of War, 30 Sept. 1817, in *ASPIA,* 2:139.

15. Prucha, *American Indian Treaties,* 138–39; Treaties of Chicago (29 Aug. 1821), Washington (4 Aug. 1824), and Saint Louis (7 Nov. 1825), in Kappler, *Indian Affairs,* 2:198–201, 207–8, and 262–64; Treaty of the Wabash (16 Oct. 1826), in ibid., 2:273–77.

16. Kugel, "Planning to Stay," 8–10, 13, 16, 18; Schedule of Grants Referred to in the Treaty of the Wabash, 16 Oct. 1826, in Kappler, *Indian Affairs,* 2:276–77; Lucy Murphy, *Great Lakes Creoles,* 62; Cary Miller, *Ogimaag,* 109; Juliette Kinzie, *Waubun,* Chapter 10; Child, *Holding Our World Together,* 55–56.

17. Lewis Cass to the Secretary of War, 10 July 1815, in *TPUS,* 10:566–67; Bellfy, *Three Fires Unity,* 65, 68–69; Calloway, "End of an Era," 6; Prucha, *Sword of the Republic,* 125–28, 135–37, 147–49.

18. Distribution of Troops, 20 Nov. 1824, in Lowrie and Franklin, *American State Papers, Military Affairs*, 2:706; Prucha, *Sword of the Republic*, 89–90; Prucha, *American Indian Treaties*, 141; Jones, *Citadel in the Wilderness*, 45–51, 76, 84–85.

19. Haeger, *John Jacob Astor*, 184–85; Aron, *American Confluence*, 184–85; Schoolcraft, *Narrative Journal*, 137–38 (first quote); David Nichols, *Engines of Diplomacy*, 141–47 (second quote 146).

20. Haeger, *John Jacob Astor*, 185–86, 199–200, 210–12; Paul Phillips, "Fur Trade in the Maumee-Wabash Country," 105; Dolin, *Fur, Fortune, and Empire*, 221, 268–69, 274–75.

21. Dolin, *Fur, Fortune, and Empire*, 275–78 (quote 278); Susan Wade, "Indigenous Women and Maple Sugar," 68–69, 80–81, 85–87; Nute, "American Fur Company's Fishing Enterprises"; Humins, "Furs, Astor, and Indians," 30. According to Fish Cadle, the AFC annually procured fifteen thousand gallons of whiskey in Mackinac. (Jackson Kemper, "Journal of an Episcopalian Missionary's Tour to Green Bay, 1834," in *CSHSW*, 14:427.)

22. Susan Wade, "Indigenous Women and Maple Sugar," 81; Ingersoll, *To Intermix with Our White Brothers*, 151–55 (quote 153), 161–62; Widder, *Battle for the Soul*, 5–6, 12–13, 113–15; Wyman, *Wisconsin Frontier*, 74; Lucy Murphy, "To Live among Us," 278–79; Berkhofer, *Salvation and the Savage*, 97, 113.

23. Andrew, *Rebuilding the Christian Commonwealth*; Widder, *Battle for the Soul*, 23, 72, 88, 104.

24. Schutt, "Delawares in Eastern Ohio," 126–27; Warren, *Shawnees and Their Neighbors*, 21–22, 49–50, 65; Finley, *Life among the Indians*, 325, 359–60; Berkhofer, *Salvation and the Savage*, 92, 117–18, 143–44; Second Annual Report of Lac Qui Parle Mission School, 16 Aug. 1837, in *TPUS*, 27:881–82; George Schultz, *Indian Canaan*.

25. Berkhofer, *Salvation*, 39; Finley, *Life among the Indians*, 292–94, 319 (quote), 339–42; Warren, *Shawnees and Their Neighbors*, 49, 63.

26. Jackson Kemper, "Journal of an Episcopalian Missionary's Tour," in *CSHSW*, 14:426, 433 (quote); Buss, "Politics of Indian Removal," 175; Finley, *Life among the Indians*, 338–39; Kugel, "Of Missionaries and Their Cattle"; Catherine Spencer to David Greene, 11 Feb. 1830, in Widder, *Battle for the Soul*, 152. On the Wisconsin Oneidas, see chapter 10.

27. Warren, *Shawnees and Their Neighbors*, 47; Davis, *Frontier Illinois*, 155. The contemporary Native American population of the northern Lakes region was about forty thousand. See Henry Schoolcraft to John Calhoun, 6 May 1822, in *TPUS*, 11:238.

28. Susan Wade, "Indigenous Women and Maple Sugar," 48–50, 70–71, 75–76; Schutt, "Delawares in Eastern Ohio," 122; Spring Wells Treaty Journal, 6 Sept. 1815, in *ASPIA*, 2:25; Edmunds, *The Potawatomis*, 215; Schoolcraft, *Narrative Journal*, 104–5; Paul Phillips, "Fur Trade in the Maumee-Wabash Country"; Finley, *Life among the Indians*, 296–97; Brewer and Vankat, "Description of Vegetation," 78, 82–83.

29. James Doty to Henry Schoolcraft, 17 Nov. 1821, in *TPUS*, 11:176; Rosen, *American Indians and State Law*, 21, 114 (quote), 117; David Murphy, *Murder in Their Hearts*.

30. Lucy Murphy, "To Live among Us," 290–95, 296, 299; John Marsh to Lewis Cass, 4 July 1827, in *TPUS*, 11:1096; Cass to James Barbour, 10 July 1827, in ibid., 11:1101–3; Wyman, *Wisconsin Frontier*, 143–45. On the spread of Indian-hating in the early nineteenth century, see Owens, *Red Dreams, White Nightmares*, 183–85.

31. Journal of the Treaty of Wabash, 20 Sept.–16 Oct. 1826, Treaty Number 146 in Documents Relating to the Negotiation of Ratified and Unratified Treaties.

CHAPTER 10: TRAILS OF DEATH AND PATHS OF RENEWAL

1. Ethridge, introduction to Ethridge and Shuck-Hall, *Mapping the Mississippian Shatter Zone*; Calloway, *Pen and Ink Witchcraft*, 36, 106 (quote).

2. On southeastern removal, see Satz, *American Indian Policy in the Jacksonian Era*, 64–110; Howe, *What Hath God Wrought*, 352–57, 414–18; Perdue and Green, *Cherokee Nation and the Trail of Tears*, 91–140.

3. Parkman, *Oregon Trail*, 20 (quote).

4. Anthony Wallace, *Long, Bitter Trail*, 66–101, 105–8.

5. Young, "Exercise of Sovereignty"; Aley, "Bringing about the Dawn"; Cayton, *Frontier Indiana*, 284 (quote).

6. Sheehan, *Seeds of Extinction*, 213–75; Garrison, *Legal Ideology of Removal*, 25–33; Ingersoll, *To Intermix with Our White Brothers*, 194–95, 220.

7. Taylor, "Captain Hendrick Aupaumut"; Tiro, *People of the Standing Stone*, 135–56; Jackson Kemper, "Journal of an Episcopalian Missionary's Tour to Green Bay," in *CSHSW*, 14:418, 423n1.

8. Faragher, "'More Motley than Mackinaw,'" 305–12; Warren, *Shawnees and Their Neighbors*, 74–80; List of Indian Tribes under the Superintendence of the Governor of Missouri, 25 Aug. 1817, in *TPUS*, 15:305.

9. Anthony Wallace, *Jefferson and the Indians*, 224, 254–60, 273–74, 302; Message of President Monroe on Indian Removal, 27 Jan. 1825, in Prucha, *Documents of United States Indian Policy*, 39–40.

10. Anderson and Cayton, *Dominion of War*, 218, 231–34, 237–38, 244–45 (quotes); Howe, *What Hath God Wrought*, 347–52; Satz, *American Indian Policy*, 14–38, 64–85; Indian Removal Act, 28 May 1830, in Prucha, *Documents of United States Indian Policy*, 52–53.

11. Warren, *Shawnees and Their Neighbors*, 67, 81–87, 90–95; Calloway, *Shawnees and the War for America*, 160, 162–63, 166; Edmunds, *Shawnee Prophet*, 165–87; Lakomäki, *Gathering Together*, 162–63, 177–84.

12. Buss, *Winning the West with Words*, 73–75, 91–94; Journal of Concluding Proceedings, 23 Oct. 1834, in Dwight Smith, " Unsuccessful Negotiation for Removal," 326; Robert Lucas to Lewis Cass, 25 March 1835, in ibid., 329; Kappler, *Indian Affairs*, 2:534–37; Bowes, *Land Too Good for Indians*, 143–44; Bowes, *Exiles and Pioneers*, 95.

13. Prucha, *American Indian Treaties,* 193–94, 221; Rinehart, "Miami Resistance and Resilience," 142–43, 148–49; Treaties of Wabash Forks, 6 Nov. 1838 and 28 Nov. 1840, in Kappler, *Indian Affairs,* 2:519–24 (quote) and 531–34.

14. Rinehart, "Miami Resistance and Resilience," 152–53; Stewart Rafert, *Miami Indians of Indiana,* 118, 124; Cayton, *Frontier Indiana,* 263.

15. Calloway, *Pen and Ink Witchcraft,* 118–19; Prucha, *American Indian Treaties,* 187–92, 221; Latrobe, *Rambler in North America,* 2:154–59.

16. Edmunds, *The Potawatomis,* 266, 268–71; Bellfy, *Three Fires Unity,* 99–100; Wyman, *Wisconsin Frontier,* 220–21.

17. Hall, "Red Man's Burden," 128–74; Roger Nichols, *Indians in the United States and Canada,* 185–86, 190–91; Tobias, "Protection, Civilization, Assimilation," 40–41.

18. Edmunds, *The Potawatomis,* 267–68; Cayton, *Frontier Indiana,* 307–10; "Journal of an Emigrating Party of Pottawattomie Indians, 1838," 318, 324–25.

19. Lappas, "'Perfect Apollo,'" 221, 230; Black Hawk, *Life of Black Hawk,* 57, 65.

20. Davis, *Frontier Illinois,* 193–94; Hagan, *Sac and Fox Indians,* 123, 126, 132–34; Black Hawk, *Life of Black Hawk,* 64–72.

21. Lappas, "'Perfect Apollo,'" 232; Hagan, *Sac and Fox Indians,* 134; Jung, *Black Hawk War,* 73–74, 88–91, 94–95; Wyman, *Wisconsin Frontier,* 149–50; Davis, *Frontier Illinois,* 194–98; Black Hawk, *Life of Black Hawk,* 75–77, 80, 83–85.

22. Jung, *Black Hawk War,* 96–97, 108; Wyman, *Wisconsin Frontier,* 150–55; Tanner, *Atlas of Great Lakes Indian History,* 151–53; George Boyd to Gov. G.B. Porter, 12 Aug. 1832, in *CSHSW,* 12:285; Captain Plympton to Captain Clark, 9 Aug. 1832, in ibid., 12:287–88; Black Hawk, *Life of Black Hawk,* 88–93.

23. Prucha, *American Indian Treaties,* 195; Hagan, *Sac and Fox Indians,* 219–24, 228; Memorial to Congress by the Assembly of Wisconsin, 23 Jan. 1837, in *TPUS,* 27:713; Joseph Street to Henry Dodge, 3 Aug. 1836, in ibid., 27:633; Treaty of Fort Armstrong (21 Sept. 1832), in Kappler, *Indian Affairs,* 2:349–51, quote 349; Treaty of Dubuque (28 Sept. 1836), in ibid., 2:474–75; Treaties of Washington (21 Sept. and 21 Oct. 1837), in ibid., 2:495–97; Treaty of Sauk and Fox Agency (11 Oct. 1842), in ibid., 2:546–49; Green, "Sac-Fox Annuity Crisis"; Green, "'We Dance in Opposite Directions,'" 132, 134–35, 137–38. White merchants in Iowa probably supported a Mesquakie reservation in order to tap the nation's annuities.

24. George Brooke to Roger Jones, 16 June 1836, in *TPUS,* 27:59–60; Lewis Cass to Henry Dodge, 7 July 1836, in ibid., 27:612–13; Henry Dodge to the Secretary of War, 12 Aug. 1836, in ibid., 27:638; Alexander Hooe to John Green, 25 March 1836, in ibid., 27:28–30; Talk of Major Green with the Winnebagos, 1 Nov. 1836, in ibid., 27:669–70; Dodge to C.A. Harris, 15 Feb. 1837, in ibid., 27:737.

25. Wallace, *Long Bitter Trail,* 107; Treaty of Washington (1 Nov. 1837), in Kappler, *Indian Affairs,* 2:498–500; Prucha, *American Indian Treaties,* 196; Nicholas Boilvin to Hartley Crawford, 1 July 1839, in *TPUS,* 27:1249–50; Bieder, *Native*

American Communities in Wisconsin, 132; Treaty of Washington (13 Oct. 1846), in Kappler, *Indian Affairs*, 2:565–67; Wingerd, *North Country*, 219–22.

26. Treaty of Washington, 8 Feb, 1831, in Kappler, *Indian Affairs*, 2:319–23 (first quote); Treaty of Cedar Point, 3 Sept. 1836, in ibid., 463–66; Journal of Proceedings of the Treaty with the Menominees, 30 Aug. and 1 Sept. 1836, Treaty Number 209, in Documents Relating to the Negotiation of Ratified and Unratified Treaties; Wyman, *Wisconsin Frontier*, 167, 169 (second quote); Beck, *Siege and Survival*, 124, 146.

27. Treaty of 18 Oct. 1848, in Kappler, *Indian Affairs*, 2:572–4; Treaty of Wolf River Falls (12 May 1854), in ibid., 2:626–27; Beck, *Siege and Survival*, 162–66, 169–71, 174–83 (quotes 171, 177); Saler, *Settlers' Empire*, 223–24, 234.

28. Rosen, *American Indians and State Law*, 129–41, 157–58, 207–8; Mc-Clurken, "Ottawa Adaptive Strategies," 42, 44–48.

29. Treaty of Washington, 28 March 1836, in Kappler, *Indian Affairs*, 2:450–56; McClurken, "Ottawa Adaptive Strategies," 49 (quote); Bellfy, *Three Fires Unity*, 99–100, 104–5, 108, 110; Roger Nichols, *Indians in the United States and Canada*, 190–92; Bowes, *Land Too Good for Indians*, 200; Fletcher, *Eagle Returns*, 24, 27, 33, 38–39, 50; Howe, *What Hath God Wrought*, 517–19, 672–75.

30. Henry Dodge to the Commissioner of Indian Affairs, 7 Aug. 1837, in Documents Relating to the Negotiation of Ratified and Unratified Treaties (Treaty Number 223); Journal of Proceedings of the St. Peters Treaty Conference, 24 and 27 July 1837, in ibid.; Treaty of Saint Peters (29 July 1837), in Kappler, *Indian Affairs*, 2:491–93; Kugel, "Civilizing Missions"; Schenck, *Ojibwe Journals of Edmund Ely*, 215, 299.

31. Child, *Holding Our World Together*, 66–68; Clifton, "Wisconsin Death March."

32. Child, *Holding Our World Together*, 68–78; Wyman, *Wisconsin Frontier*, 223–26; Armstrong, *Early Life among the Indians*, 16–18, 30–31, 34–37; Kvasnicka, "George W. Manypenny."

33. Warren, *Shawnees and Their Neighbors*, 98–99, 127; Green, "'We Dance in Opposite Directions,'" 136; Speech of Pepishkay, 5 Nov. 1838, in "Journal of an Emigrating Party of Pottawattomie Indians," 334 (quote).

34. Savage, *Prairie*, 8, 11–13, 68, 71–72, 79–82; Gitlin, *Bourgeois Frontier*, 106; Warren, *Shawnees and Their Neighbors*, 133, 141; Parkman, *Oregon Trail*, 18, 21–23; Abing, "Holy Battleground," 133–34; Bowes, *Exiles and Pioneers*, 108–9; Wingerd, *North Country*, 220–23.

35. Bowes, *Exiles and Pioneers*, 110, 112; Obermeyer, *Delaware Tribe in a Cherokee Nation*, 45–47; Warren, *Shawnees and Their Neighbors*, 113–14, 128, 131–32; Gary Anderson, *Conquest of Texas*, 91, 134, 138, 160, 200–202, 208–10, 252, 255.

36. Abing, "Holy Battleground," 123–27, 134 (quote); Warren, *Shawnees and Their Neighbors*, 108; Obermeyer, *Delaware Tribe*, 47–48; Foreman, "Journal of a Tour in the Indian Territory," 253–54; Wingerd, *North Country*, 223; McCormick, *Memoir of Miss Eliza McCoy*, 54, 74–76.

37. United States Office of Indian Affairs, *Annual Report of the Commissioner of Indian Affairs for the Year 1862*, 101; Warren, *Shawnees and Their Neighbors*, 103, 142–49; Abing, "Holy Battleground," 125–26; McCormick, *Memoir of Miss Eliza McCoy*, 61; Berkhofer, *Salvation and the Savage*, 85–87; Bowes, *Exiles and Pioneers*, 180–81.

38. Holt, *Fate of Their Country*, 96–98; Etchison, *Bleeding Kansas*, 9–10; Bowes, *Exiles and Pioneers*, 147–48, 183–84; Warren, *Shawnees and Their Neighbors*, 150; Treaties with the Delawares (6 May 1854) (quote), Shawnees (10 May 1854), Kickapoos (18 May 1854), Miamis (5 June 1854), and Wyandots (31 Jan. 1855), all in Kappler, *Indian Affairs*, 2:614–18, 618–26, 634–36, 641–46, and 677–81, respectively.

39. Holt, *Fate of Their Country*, 100–103, 115–17, 144–45; Watts, "How Bloody Was Bleeding Kansas?" 123; Kvasnicka, "George W. Manypenny," 62 (quote); Nichole Etchison, *Bleeding Kansas*, 107–12, 205–6.

40. For fatalities, see Jung, *Black Hawk War*, 172, 179.

41. On the federal government's prioritizing of southern removal, see Wallace, *Long, Bitter Trail*, 6–8, 56, 105.

CONCLUSION: THE LAST IMPERIAL WAR AND THE LAST REMOVALS

1. Horsman, *Race and Manifest Destiny*; Holt, *Fate of Their Country*, 30, 33–34; Hammond, "Slavery, Settlement, and Empire"; Resendez, *Other Slavery*, 277.

2. United States Office of Indian Affairs, *Annual Report of the Commissioner of Indian Affairs for 1861*, 192–93 (quotes); Hauptman, *Between Two Fires*, 131–32.

3. Beck, *Struggle for Self-Determination*, 17, 38; Hauptman, *Between Two Fires*, 133–43; Cassidy, "Assigniack's Canoe and Anishinaabe Bibles."

4. Roger Nichols, *Indians in the United States and Canada*, 199–200; Sally Weaver, "The Iroquois"; Hele, "Anishinaabeg and Metis," 79–80; Riley, *Great Lakes Country*, 146–47.

5. Fletcher, *Eagle Returns*, 54; Beck, *Struggle for Self-Determination*, 25, 27–29; Bogue, *Fishing the Great Lakes*, 77, 80; Riley, *Great Lakes Country*, 120–21, 148; Tiro, "Sorry Tale," 1013–14, 1019; Tiro, *People of the Standing Stone*, 179–86; Sally Weaver, "The Iroquois," 189–97.

6. Warren, *Shawnees and Their Neighbors*, 139, 164–65; Warde, *When the Wolf Came*, 120–21, 230–31.

7. United States Office of Indian Affairs, *Annual Report of the Commissioner of Indian Affairs for 1862*, 99; Warren, *Shawnees and Their Neighbors*, 165; Hauptman, *Between Two Fires*, 28–30, 34.

8. Warren, *Shawnees and Their Neighbors*, 158–59; Rosen, *American Indians and State Law*, 47–48; Obermeyer, *Delaware Tribe in a Cherokee Nation*, 53. One can overstate white Kansans' racism. The state tolerated Indians who submitted to its laws and accepted several thousand black families who migrated from the southeast to Kansas in the late 1870s.

9. Second Annual Report of the Lac Qui Parle Mission School, 16 Aug. 1837, in *TPUS*, 27:882–83; Gary Anderson, *Kinsmen of Another Kind*, 145–202; Keeler, "Mighty Mississippi"; Berg, *38 Nooses*, 24–25, 27–28, 54–55, 123–25.

10. Renville, *Thrilling Narrative*, 13–15, 48; Jerome Big Eagle, "A Sioux Story of the War," in Calloway, *Our Hearts Fell*, 94 (quotes).

11. Howe, *What Hath God Wrought*, 826; Jerome Big Eagle, "A Sioux Story," 92–94; Renville, *Thrilling Narrative*, 58–60, 154 (quote); Gary Anderson, *Kinsmen of Another Kind*, 226–80.

12. Berg, *38 Nooses*, 37–41, 44, 84, 90–91, 129 (quote), 168; Renville, *Thrilling Narrative*, 147.

13. Berg, *38 Nooses*, 163, 172–73, 207–9; Renville, *Thrilling Narrative*, 77–79; Frost, "Roving Savages, Regionalized Americanness," 13–16; Finkelman, "'I Could Not Afford to Hang Men for Votes.'"

14. Wingert, *North Country*, 332–37; United States Office of Indian Affairs, *Annual Report of the Commissioner of Indian Affairs for 1863*, 350; Bieder, *Native American Communities in Wisconsin*, 171–72; Anthony Wallace, *The Long, Bitter Trail*, 107; Kappler, *Indian Affairs*, 1:15–16. Some white Wisconsin settlers helped Ho-Chunk returnees finance their homestead purchases (see Saler, *Settlers' Empire*, 233).

15. Bieder, *Native American Communities in Wisconsin*, 171–72.

Bibliography

PRIMARY SOURCES

Abler, Thomas, ed. *Chainbreaker: The Revolutionary War Memoirs of Governor Blacksnake, as Told to Benjamin Williams*. Lincoln: University of Nebraska Press, 1989.

Armstrong, Benjamin J. *Early Life among the Indians*. Ashland, WI: A. W. Bowron Press, 1892.

Birk, Douglas A., ed. *John Sayer's Snake River Journal, 1804–1805: A Fur Trade Diary from East Central Minnesota*. Minneapolis: Institute for Minnesota Archaeology, 1989.

Black Hawk. *Life of Black Hawk, or Ma-ka-tai-me-she-kia-kiak, Dictated by Himself*. Hollywood, FL: Simon and Brown, 2013.

Blair, Emma Helen, ed. *The Indian Tribes of the Upper Mississippi Valley and Region of the Great Lakes*. 2 vols. Cleveland: Arthur H. Clark, 1911.

Bogaert, Harmer M. van Den, and George O'Connor. *Journey to Mohawk Country*. New York: First Second, 2006.

Bond, Beverly, Jr. "The Captivity of Charles Stuart, 1755–1757." *Mississippi Valley Historical Review* 13 (1926): 58–81.

Boyd, Julian P., et al., eds. *The Papers of Thomas Jefferson*. 43 vols. Princeton: Princeton University Press, 1950– .

Buell, Rowena, ed. *The Memoirs of Rufus Putnam, and Certain Official Papers and Correspondence*. Boston: Houghton, Mifflin, 1903.

Calloway, Colin, ed. *Our Hearts Fell to the Ground: Plains Indian Views of How the West Was Lost*. Boston: Bedford/St. Martin's, 1996.

———, ed. *The World Turned Upside Down: Indian Voices from Early America*. Boston: Bedford/St. Martins, 1994.

Carter, Clarence E., et al., eds. *Territorial Papers of the United States*. 28 vols. Washington, DC: US Government Printing Office, 1934–75.

Coleman, Christopher, ed. "Letters from Eighteenth Century Indiana Merchants." *Indiana Magazine of History* 5 (December 1909): 137–59.

Craig, Neville, ed. *The Olden Time*. 2 vols. Cincinnati: Robert Clarke, 1876.

Davies, K. G., ed. *Documents of the American Revolution, 1770–1783 (Colonial Office Series)*. 21 vols. Shannon: Irish University Press, 1972–1981.

Denny, W. H., ed. *The Military Journal of Major Ebenezer Denny: An Officer in the Revolutionary and Indian Wars.* Philadelphia: J. B. Lippincott, 1859.

Documents Relating to the Negotiation of Ratified and Unratified Treaties with Various Indian Tribes, 1801–1869. Microfilm T-994, Natl. Archives, Washington. Online via http://uwdc.library.wisc.edu/collections/History/IndianTreatiesMicro.

Dumont de Montigny, Jean-François-Benjamin. *The Memoir of Lieutenant Dumont, 1715–1747: A Sojourner in the French Atlantic.* Edited by Gordon Sayre and Carla Zecher. Chapel Hill: University of North Carolina Press, 2012.

Dunn, Caroline, and Eleanor Dunn, trans. *Indiana's First War.* Indianapolis: Indiana Historical Society, 1924.

DuVal, Kathleen, and John DuVal, eds. *Interpreting a Continent: Voices from Colonial America.* Lanham, MD: Rowman and Littlefield, 2009.

Esarey, Logan, ed. *Governor's Messages and Letters.* 2 vols. Indianapolis: Indiana Historical Commission, 1922.

Finley, James B. *Life among the Indians, or, Personal Reminiscences and Historical Incidents Illustrative of Indian Character.* Cincinnati: Methodist Book Concern, 1859.

Foreman, Carolyn, ed. "Journal of a Tour in the Indian Territory." *Chronicles of Oklahoma* 10 (June 1932): 219–56.

Gipson, Lawrence Henry, ed. *The Moravian Indian Mission on White River: Diaries and Letters.* Indianapolis: Indiana Historical Bureau, 1926.

Grumet, Robert, ed. *Journey on the Forbidden Path: Chronicles of a Diplomatic Mission to the Allegheny Country.* Philadelphia: American Philosophical Society, 1999.

Harrison, Eliza Cope, ed. *Philadelphia Merchant: The Diary of Thomas P. Cope, 1800–1851.* South Bend, IN: Gateway Editions, 1978.

Hickey, Donald, ed. *The War of 1812: Writings from America's Second War of Independence.* New York: Library of America, 2013.

James, Alton, ed. *George Rogers Clark Papers.* 3 vols. Springfield: Illinois State Historical Library Collections, 1912.

Jordan, John, ed. "Journal of James Kenny, 1761–1763." *Pennsylvania Magazine of History and Biography* 37 (January and April 1913): 1–47, 152–201.

"Journal of an Emigrating Party of Pottawattomie Indians, 1838." *Indiana Magazine of History* 21 (1925): 315–36.

Journals of the Continental Congress, 1774–1789. 34 vols. Washington, DC: US Government Printing Office, 1907–34.

Kalter, Susan, ed. *Benjamin Franklin, Pennsylvania, and the First Nations: The Treaties of 1736–62.* Urbana: University of Illinois Press, 2006.

Kappler, Charles, ed. *Indian Affairs, Laws, and Treaties.* 7 vols. Washington, DC: US Government Printing Office, 1904–71.

Kellogg, Louise Phelps, ed. *Frontier Advance on the Ohio River, 1778–79.* Madison: Wisconsin Historical Society, 1916.

Kinnaird, Lawrence, ed. *Spain in the Mississippi Valley, 1765–1794*. 3 vols. Washington, DC: US Government Printing Office, 1946–49.

Kinzie, Juliette A. M. *Waubun: The Early Day in the Northwest*. Philadelphia, 1874.

Klinck, Carl F., and James J. Talman, eds. *The Journal of John Norton, 1816*. Toronto: Champlain Society, 1970.

Knopf, Richard, comp. and ed. *Anthony Wayne: A Name in Arms*. Pittsburgh: University of Pittsburgh Press, 1960.

Labaree, Leonard, et al., eds. *The Papers of Benjamin Franklin*. 41 vols. to date. New Haven: Yale University Press, 1959– .

Lambing, A. A., ed. "Céloron's Journal." *Ohio State Archaeological and Historical Quarterly* 29 (1920): 335–96.

Latrobe, Charles Joseph. *The Rambler in North America, 1832–33*. 2 vols. New York: Harper and Brothers, 1835.

Lowrie, Walter, and Matthew St. Clair Clarke, eds. *American State Papers, Class II: Indian Affairs*. 2 vols. Washington, DC: Gales and Seaton, 1832.

Lowrie, Walter, and Walter Franklin, eds. *American State Papers, Class V: Military Affairs*. 7 vols. Washington, DC: Gales and Seaton, 1832–61.

Marshall, Thomas Maitland, ed. *The Life and Papers of Frederick Bates*. 2 vols. St. Louis: Missouri Historical Society, 1926.

McCormick, Calvin, ed. *The Memoir of Miss Eliza McCoy*. Dallas: printed by author, 1892.

McDonald, Forrest, ed. *Empire and Nation: Letters from a Farmer in Pennsylvania and Letters from the Federal Farmer*. 2nd ed. Indianapolis: Liberty Fund, 1999.

Michigan Pioneer and Historical Society. *Michigan Pioneer and Historical Collections*. 40 vols. Lansing: Michigan Pioneer and Historical Society and Michigan Historical Commission, 1876–1929.

Morris, Thomas. *Journal of Captain Thomas Morris*. Ann Arbor, MI: University Microfilms, 1966.

Mulkearn, Lois, comp. and ed. *The George Mercer Papers Relating to the Ohio Company of Virginia*. Pittsburgh: University of Pittsburgh Press, 1954.

Nelson, George. *My First Years in the Fur Trade: The Journals of 1802–1804*. Edited by Laura Peers and Theresa Schenk. St. Paul: Minnesota Historical Society Press, 2002.

Parkman, Francis. *The Oregon Trail*. Lincoln: University of Nebraska Press, 1994 (1849).

Pennsylvania Archives, Selected and Arranged from Original Documents in the Office of the Secretary of the Commonwealth, 1st ser. 12 vols. Philadelphia: Joseph Severns, 1852–56.

Peters, Richard, ed. *The Public Statutes at Large of the United States of America*. 8 vols. Boston: Little, Brown, 1845–67.

Prucha, Francis Paul, ed. *Documents of United States Indian Policy*. 3rd ed. Lincoln: University of Nebraska Press, 2000.

Quaife, Milo M., ed. *Alexander Henry's Travels and Adventures in the Years 1760–1776*. Chicago: Lakeside Press, 1921.

———, ed. *Fort Wayne in 1790*. Indiana Historical Society Publications No. 7. Greenfield: William Mitchell, 1921.

———, ed. *The John Askin Papers*. 2 vols. Detroit: Detroit Library Commission, 1928.

Radin, Paul, ed. *Crashing Thunder: The Autobiography of an American Indian*. Lincoln: University of Nebraska Press, 1983.

Renville, Mary Butler. *A Thrilling Narrative of Indian Captivity: Dispatches from the Dakota War*. Edited by Carrie Reber Zeman and Kathryn Zabelle Derounian-Stodola. Lincoln: University of Nebraska Press, 2012.

Richardson, James, ed. *A Compilation of the Messages and Papers of the Presidents, 1789–1897*. 11 vols. Washington, DC: US Government Printing Office, 1896–1904.

Rowland, Dunbar, Patricia Galloway, et al., eds. *Mississippi Provincial Archives: French Dominion*. 5 vols. Jackson and Baton Rouge: Mississippi Department of Archives and History and Louisiana State University Press, 1927–34, 1984.

Schenck, Theresa M., ed. *The Ojibwe Journals of Edmund F. Ely, 1833–1849*. Lincoln: University of Nebraska Press, 2012.

Schoolcraft, Henry Rowe. *Narrative Journal of Travels through the Northwestern Regions of the United States*. Albany: E. and E. Hosford, 1821.

Seaver, James. *A Narrative of the Life of Mrs. Mary Jemison*. Edited by June Namias. Norman: University of Oklahoma Press, 1995.

Shannon, Timothy J., ed. *The Seven Years' War in North America: A Brief History with Documents*. Boston: Bedford/St. Martin's, 2014.

Smith, Dwight L., ed. "An Unsuccessful Negotiation for Removal of the Wyandot Indians from Ohio, 1834." *Ohio Archaeological and Historical Quarterly* 58 (1949): 305–31.

Smith, James. "Prisoner of the Caughnawagas." In *Captured by the Indians: 15 Firsthand Accounts*, edited by Frederick Drimmer, 25–60. New York: Dover, 1985.

Smith, Peter et al., eds. *Letters of Delegates to Congress, 1774–1789*. 26 vols. Washington, DC: Library of Congress, 1976–2000.

Spencer, Oliver M. *Indian Captivity: A True Narrative of the Capture of Rev. O. M. Spencer*. New York: Carlton and Porter, 1834.

State Historical Society of Wisconsin. *Collections of the State Historical Society of Wisconsin*. 40 vols. Madison: State Historical Society of Wisconsin, 1888–1931.

Stearns, Raymond. "Joseph Kellogg's Observations on Senex's Map of North America (1710)." *Mississippi Valley Historical Review* 23 (December 1936): 345–54.

Sullivan, James, et al., eds. *The Papers of Sir William Johnson*. 19 vols. Albany: University of the State of New York, 1921–65.

Tanner, John. "White Indian." In *Captured by the Indians: 15 Firsthand Accounts*, edited by Frederisk Drimmer, 142–82. New York: Dover, 1985.

Secondary Sources 239

Thwaites, Reuben Gold, ed. *Early Western Travels, 1748–1816*. 42 vols. Cleveland: A. H. Clark, 1904.

———, ed. *The Jesuit Relations and Allied Documents: Travels and Explorations of the Jesuit Missionaries in North America*. 73 vols. Cleveland: Burrows Brothers, 1896–1901.

Thwaites, Reuben Gold, and Louise Phelps Kellogg, eds. *Documentary History of Dunmore's War*. Madison: Wisconsin Historical Society, 1905.

———, eds. *Frontier Defense on the Upper Ohio, 1777–1778*. Madison: Wisconsin Historical Society, 1912.

———, eds. *The Revolution on the Upper Ohio, 1775–1777*. Madison: Wisconsin Historical Society, 1908.

United States Office of Indian Affairs. *Annual Report of the Commissioner of Indian Affairs for the Year 1861*. Washington, DC: US Government Printing Office, 1861.

———. *Annual Report of the Commissioner of Indian Affairs for the Year 1862*. Washington, DC: US Government Printing Office, 1862.

———. *Annual Report of the Commissioner of Indian Affairs for the Year 1863*. Washington, DC: US Government Printing Office, 1863.

Wallace, Paul, ed. *The Travels of John Heckewelder in Frontier America*. Pittsburgh: University of Pittsburgh Press, 1985.

Webster, J. Clarence, ed. *The Journal of Jeffery Amherst*. Toronto: Ryerson Press, 1931.

SECONDARY SOURCES

Abing, Kevin. "A Holy Battleground: Methodist, Baptist, & Quaker Missionaries among Shawnee Indians, 1830–1844." *Kansas History* 21 (Summer 1998): 118–37.

Abrams, Marc D., and Gregory J. Nowacki. "Native Americans as Active and Passive Promoters of Mast and Fruit Trees in the Eastern USA." *Holocene* 18 (2008): 1123–37.

Aley, Ginette. "Bringing about the Dawn: Agriculture, Internal Improvements, Indian Policy, and Euro-American Hegemony in the Old Northwest, 1800–1846." In *The Boundaries between Us: Natives and Newcomers along the Frontier of the Old Northwest Territory, 1750–1850*, edited by Daniel Barr, 196–218. Kent, OH: Kent State University Press, 2006.

Anderson, Fred. *Crucible of War: The Seven Years' War and the Fate of Empire in British North America, 1754–1766*. New York: Knopf, 2000.

———. *The War That Made America: A Short History of the French and Indian War*. New York: Penguin Books, 2006.

Anderson, Fred, and Andrew Cayton. *The Dominion of War: Empire and Liberty in North America, 1500–2000*. New York: Viking Penguin, 2005.

Anderson, Gary Clayton. *The Conquest of Texas: Ethnic Cleansing in the Promised Land, 1820–1875*. Norman: University of Oklahoma Press, 2005.

———. *Kinsmen of Another Kind: Dakota-White Relations in the Upper Mississippi Valley, 1650–1862*. Saint Paul: Minnesota Historical Society, 1997 (1984).

Andrew, John. *Rebuilding the Christian Commonwealth: New England Congregationalists and Foreign Missions, 1800–1830*. Lexington: University Press of Kentucky, 1976.

Andrews, Charles. *The Colonial Background of the American Revolution: Four Essays in American Colonial History*. Rev. ed. New Haven, CT: Yale University Press, 1961.

Aron, Stephen. *American Confluence: The Missouri Frontier from Borderland to Border State*. Bloomington: Indiana University Press, 2006.

———. *How the West Was Lost: The Transformation of Kentucky from Daniel Boone to Henry Clay*. Baltimore: Johns Hopkins University Press, 1996.

———. "Pigs and Hunters: 'Rights in the Woods' on the Trans-Appalachian Frontier." In *Contact Points: American Frontiers from the Mohawk Valley to the Mississippi, 1750–1830*, edited by Andrew Cayton and Fredrika Teute, 175–204. Chapel Hill: University of North Carolina Press, 1998.

Aron, Stephen, and Jeremy Adelman. "From Borderlands to Borders: Empires, Nation-States, and the Peoples in between in North American History." *American Historical Review* 104 (October 1999): 814–41.

Atkinson, James. *Splendid Land, Splendid People: The Chickasaw Indians to Removal*. Tuscaloosa: University of Alabama Press, 2004.

Axtell, James. "Ethnohistory: An Historian's Viewpoint." *Ethnohistory* 26 (Winter 1979): 1–13.

———. *The Indians' New South: Cultural Change in the Colonial Southeast*. Baton Rouge: Louisiana State University Press, 1997.

———. *The Invasion Within: The Contest of Cultures in Colonial America*. New York: Oxford University Press, 1985.

Barr, Daniel P. *A Colony Sprung from Hell: Pittsburgh and the Struggle for Authority on the Western Pennsylvania Frontier, 1744–1794*. Kent, OH: Kent State University Press, 2014.

Beck, David R. M. "Return to Namä'o Uskíwämît: The Importance of Sturgeon in Menominee Indian History." *Wisconsin Magazine of History* 79 (Autumn 1995): 32–48.

———. *Siege and Survival: History of the Menominee Indians, 1634–1856*. Lincoln: University of Nebraska Press, 2002.

———. *The Struggle for Self-Determination: History of the Menominee Indians since 1854*. Lincoln: University of Nebraska Press, 2005.

Bellfy, Paul. *Three Fires Unity: The Anishinaabeg of the Lake Huron Borderlands*. Lincoln: University of Nebraska Press, 2011.

Belue, Ted. *The Long Hunt: Death of the Buffalo East of the Mississippi*. Mechanicsburg, PA.: Stackpole Books, 1996.

Benn, David. "Woodland People and the Roots of the Oneota." In *Oneota Archaeology: Past, Present, and Future*, edited by William Green, 91–139. Iowa City: University of Iowa, 1995.

Benson, Larry, Timothy Pauketat, and Edward Cook. "Cahokia's Boom and Bust in the Context of Climate Change." *American Antiquity* 74 (July 2009): 467–83.

Berg, Scott W. *38 Nooses: Lincoln, Little Crow, and the Beginning of the Frontier's End.* New York: Pantheon Books, 2012.

Bergmann, William H. *The American National State and the Early West.* Cambridge: Cambridge University Press, 2012.

Berkhofer, Robert, Jr. *Salvation and the Savage: An Analysis of Protestant Missions and American Indian Response, 1787–1862.* Lexington: University of Kentucky Press, 1965.

Bieder, Robert E. *Native American Communities in Wisconsin, 1600–1960: A Study of Tradition.* Madison: University of Wisconsin Press, 1995.

Birmingham, Robert, and Leslie Eisenberg. *Indian Mounds of Wisconsin.* Madison: University of Wisconsin Press, 2000.

Birzer, Bradley. "French Imperial Remnants on the Middle Ground: The Strange Case of Auguste de la Balme and Charles Beaubien." *Journal of the Illinois Historical Society* 94 (Summer 2000): 135–54.

Black, B. A., C. M. Ruffner, and M. D. Abrams. "Native American Influences on the Forest Composition of the Allegheny Plateau." *Canadian Journal of Forest Research* (May 2006): 1266–75.

Bogue, Margaret Beattie. *Fishing the Great Lakes: An Environmental History.* Madison: University of Wisconsin Press, 2000.

Bohaker, Heidi. "*Nindoodemag:* The Significance of Algonquian Kinship Networks in the Eastern Great Lakes Region, 1600–1701." *William and Mary Quarterly,* 3rd ser., 58 (January 2006): 23–52.

Bowes, John P. *Exiles and Pioneers: Eastern Indians in the Trans-Mississippi West.* Cambridge: Cambridge University Press, 2007.

———. *Land Too Good for Indians: Northern Indian Removal.* Norman: University of Oklahoma Press, 2016.

Bradburn, Douglas. "The Visible Fist: The Chesapeake Tobacco Trade in War and the Purpose of Empire, 1690–1715." *William and Mary Quarterly,* 3rd ser., 68 (July 2011): 361–86.

Brandão, José António. *"Your Fyre Shall Burn No More": Iroquois Policy toward New France and Its Native Allies to 1701.* Lincoln: University of Nebraska Press, 1997.

Braudel, Fernand. "History and the Social Sciences." *Annales: Économies, Sociétés, Civilisations* 4 (October–December 1958): 725–33.

———. *The Structures of Everyday Life.* Vol. 1 of *Civilization and Capitalism, 15th–18th Century.* Berkeley: University of California Press, 1992.

Breen, T. H. *American Insurgents, American Patriots: The Revolution of the People.* New York: Hill and Wang, 2010.

Brewer, Lawrence G., and John L. Vankat. "Description of Vegetation of the Oak Openings of Northwestern Ohio at the Time of Euro-American Settlement." *Ohio Journal of Science* 104 (September 2004): 76–85.

Buikstra, Jane, Lyle Konigsburg, and Jill Bullington. "Fertility and the Development of Agriculture in the Prehistoric Midwest." *American Antiquity* 51 (July 1986): 528–46.

Buss, James Joseph. "The Politics of Indian Removal on the Wyandot Reserve, 1817–1843." In *Contested Territories: Native Americans and Non-Natives in the Lower Great Lakes, 1700–1850,* edited by Charles Beatty-Medina and Melissa Rinehart, 167–93. East Lansing: Michigan State University Press, 2012.

———. *Winning the West with Words: Language and Conquest in the Lower Great Lakes.* Norman: University of Oklahoma Press, 2011.

Byers, A. Martin. "The 'Heartland' Woodland Settlement System: Cultural Traditions and Resolving Key Puzzles." In *Hopewell Settlement Patterns, Subsistence, and Symbolic Landscapes,* edited by A. Martin Byers and DeeAnne Wymer, 276–96. Gainesville: University Press of Florida, 2010.

Calloway, Colin. *The American Revolution in Indian Country: Crisis and Diversity in Native American Communities.* Cambridge: Cambridge University Press, 1995.

———. "The End of an Era: British-Indian Relations in the Great Lakes Region after the War of 1812." *Michigan Historical Review* 12 (Fall 1986): 1–20.

———. *New Worlds for All: Indians, Europeans, and the Remaking of Early America.* 2nd ed. Baltimore: Johns Hopkins University Press, 2013.

———. *Pen and Ink Witchcraft: Treaties and Treaty-Making in American Indian History.* New York: Oxford University Press, 2013.

———. *The Scratch of a Pen: 1763 and the Transformation of North America.* Oxford: Oxford University Press, 2006.

———. *The Shawnees and the War for America.* New York: Viking Penguin, 2007.

———. *The Victory with No Name: The Native American Defeat of the First American Army.* Oxford: Oxford University Press, 2015.

Cassidy, Michelle. "Assigniack's Canoe and Anishinaabe Bibles: Anishinaabe Men and Their Journeys on the Great Lakes from the War of 1812 through the Civil War." Paper presented at the Annual Meeting of the American Society for Ethnohistory, New Orleans, September 13, 2013.

Cave, Alfred. "The Failure of the Shawnee Prophet's Witch Hunt." *Ethnohistory* 42 (Summer 1995): 445–75.

———. *Prophets of the Great Spirit: Native American Revitalization Movements in Eastern North America.* Lincoln: University of Nebraska Press, 2006.

Cayton, Andrew. *Frontier Indiana.* Bloomington: Indiana University Press, 1996.

———. "The Meanings of the Wars for the Great Lakes." In *The Sixty Years' War for the Great Lakes, 1754–1814,* edited by David Skaggs and Larry Nelson, 373–90. East Lansing: Michigan State University Press, 2001.

———. "'Noble Actors' upon the 'Theatre of Honour': Power and Civility at the Treaty of Greenville." In *Contact Points: American Frontiers from the Mohawk Valley to the Mississippi, 1750–1830,* edited by Andrew Cayton and Fredrika Teute, 235–69. Chapel Hill: University of North Carolina Press, 1998.

Child, Brenda J. *Holding Our World Together: Ojibwe Women and the Survival of Community.* New York: Penguin, 2012.

Clarfield, Gerard. "Protecting the Frontiers: Defense Policy and the Tariff Question in the First Washington Administration." *William and Mary Quarterly,* 3rd ser., 32 (July 1975): 443–464.

Clark, Jerry. *The Shawnee.* Lexington: University Press of Kentucky, 2007 (1993).

Cleary, Patricia. *The World, the Flesh, and the Devil: A History of Colonial Saint Louis.* Columbia: University of Missouri Press, 2011.

Clifton, James A. *The Prairie People: Continuity and Change in Potawatomi Indian Culture, 1665–1965.* Lawrence: Regents Press of Kansas, 1977.

———. "Wisconsin Death March: Explaining the Extremes in Old Northwest Indian Removal." *Proceedings of the Wisconsin Academy of Sciences, Arts, and Letters* 75 (1987): 1–39.

Colley, Linda. *Captives: Britain, Empire, and the World, 1600–1850.* New York: Anchor Books, 2004.

Conlin, Michael F., and Robert M. Owens. "Bigger Than Little Bighorn: Improving the Name of the Greatest Amerindian Victory over the United States." *Ohio Valley History* 12 (Summer 2012): 3–23.

Conn, Steven. *History's Shadow: Native American and Historical Consciousness in the Nineteenth Century.* Chicago: University of Chicago Press, 2004.

Coon, Matthew. "Variation in Ohio Hopewell Political Economies." *American Antiquity* 74 (January 2009): 49–76.

Cordell, Linda, and Bruce Smith. "Indigenous Farmers." In *The Cambridge History of the Native Peoples of the Americas.* Vol. 1, *North America,* edited by Bruce Trigger and Wilcomb Washburn, 201–66. Cambridge: Cambridge University Press, 1996.

Crosby, Alfred. *The Columbian Exchange: Biological and Cultural Consequences of 1492.* Westport, CT: Greenwood Press, 1972.

———. "Virgin Soil Epidemics as a Factor in the Aboriginal Depopulation in America." *William and Mary Quarterly,* 3rd ser., 33 (April 1976): 289–99.

Curry, Andrew. "Ancient Migration: Coming to America." *Nature,* May 2, 2012.

Darwin, John. *After Tamerlane: The Rise and Fall of Global Empires, 1400–2000.* New York: Bloomsbury, 2007.

David, James Corbett. *Dunmore's New World: The Extraordinary Life of a Royal Governor in Revolutionary America.* Charlottesville: University of Virginia Press, 2013.

Davies, K. G. "From Competition to Union." In *Aspects of the Fur Trade: Selected Papers of the 1965 North American Fur Trade Conference,* edited by Dale Morgan, 18–29. St. Paul: Minnesota Historical Society, 1967.

Davis, James. *Frontier Illinois.* Bloomington: Indiana University Press, 1998.

Deloria, Vine, Jr. *Red Earth, White Lies: Native Americans and the Myth of Scientific Fact.* Golden, CO: Fulcrum, 1997 (1995).

Dennis, Jerry. *The Living Great Lakes: Searching for the Heart of the Inland Seas.* New York: Thomas Dunne Books, 2003.

Devens, Carol. *Countering Colonization: Native American Women and Great Lakes Missions, 1630–1900.* Berkeley: University of California Press, 1992.

Diamond, Jared. *Guns, Germs, and Steel: The Fates of Human Societies.* New York: W. W. Norton, 1997.

Dolin, Eric Jay. *Fur, Fortune, and Empire: The Epic History of the Fur Trade in America.* New York: W. W. Norton, 2010.

Dowd, Gregory Evans. "The French King Wakes Up in Detroit: 'Pontiac's War' in Rumor and History." *Ethnohistory* 37 (Summer 1990): 254–78.

———. "Indigenous Catholicism and St. Joseph Potawatomi Resistance in 'Pontiac's War,' 1763–1766." *Ethnohistory* 63 (January 2016): 143–66.

———. *A Spirited Resistance: The North American Indian Struggle for Unity, 1745–1815.* Baltimore: Johns Hopkins University Press, 1992.

———. *War under Heaven: Pontiac, the Indian Nations, and the British Empire.* Baltimore: Johns Hopkins University Press, 2002.

Downes, Randolph. *Council Fires on the Upper Ohio: A Narrative of Indian Affairs in the Upper Ohio Valley until 1795.* Pittsburgh: University of Pittsburgh Press, 1968.

Dunnigan, Brian Leigh. "'No One Acquired Any Military Glory in This Affair': The American Attempt to Retake Mackinac, 1814." In *The Battle of Lake Erie and Its Aftermath: A Reassessment,* edited by David Skaggs, 81–97. Kent, OH: Kent State University Press, 2013.

DuVal, Kathleen. "Interconnectedness and Diversity in 'French Louisiana.'" In *Powhatan's Mantle: Indians in the Colonial Southeast,* edited by Gregory Waselkov, Peter Wood, and Tom Hatley, 133–62. Rev. ed. Lincoln: University of Nebraska Press, 2006.

———. *The Native Ground: Indians and Colonists in the Heart of the Continent.* Philadelphia: University of Pennsylvania Press, 2006.

Eccles, W. J. *The Canadian Frontier, 1534–1760.* Albuquerque: University of New Mexico Press, 1984.

———. "The Fur Trade and Eighteenth-Century Imperialism." *William and Mary Quarterly,* 3rd ser., 40 (July 1983): 341–62.

Edling, Max. *A Revolution in Favor of Government: Origins of the U.S. Constitution and the Making of the American State.* New York: Oxford University Press, 2003.

Edmunds, R. David. "'Nothing Has Been Effected': The Vincennes Treaty of 1792." *Indiana Magazine of History* 74 (March 1978): 23–35.

———. *The Potawatomis: Keepers of the Fire.* Norman: University of Oklahoma Press, 1978.

———. *The Shawnee Prophet.* Lincoln: University of Nebraska Press, 1983.

Edmunds, R. David, and Joseph Peyser. *The Fox Wars: The Mesquakie Challenge to New France.* Norman: University of Oklahoma Press, 1993.

Elliott, J. H. *Empires of the Atlantic World: Britain and Spain in America, 1492–1830.* New Haven: Yale University Press, 2006.

Emrick, Isaac. "The Monyton Diaspora: A History of the Middle Ohio River Valley, 1640–1700." Master's thesis, West Virginia University, 2005.

Etchison, Nicole. *Bleeding Kansas: Contested Liberty in the Civil War Era.* Lawrence: University Press of Kansas, 2004.

Ethridge, Robbie. Introduction to *Mapping the Mississippian Shatter Zone,* edited by Robbie Ethridge and Sheri M. Shuck-Hall, 1–62. Lincoln: University of Nebraska Press, 2009.

Fagan, Brian. *The Great Warming: Climate Change and the Rise and Fall of Civilizations.* New York: Bloomsbury Press, 2008.

———. *People of the Earth: An Introduction to World Prehistory.* 7th ed. New York: HarperCollins, 1992.

Faragher, John Mack. "'More Motley than Mackinaw': From Ethnic Mixing to Ethnic Cleansing on the Frontier of the Lower Missouri, 1783–1833." In *Contact Points: American Frontiers from the Mohawk Valley to the Mississippi, 1750–1830,* edited by Andrew Cayton and Fredrika Teute, 304–26. Chapel Hill: University of North Carolina Press, 1998.

———. *Sugar Creek: Life on the Illinois Prairie.* New Haven: Yale University Press, 1986.

Farmer, Silas. *History of Detroit and Wayne County and Early Michigan.* New York: Munsell, 1890.

Fenn, Elizabeth. "Biological Warfare in Eighteenth-Century America: Beyond Jeffrey Amherst." *Journal of American History* 86 (March 2000): 1552–80.

Fenton, William. *The Great Law and the Longhouse: A Political History of the Iroquois Confederacy.* Norman: University of Oklahoma Press, 1998.

Ferguson, Gillum. *Illinois in the War of 1812.* Urbana: University of Illinois Press, 2012.

Finkelman, Paul. "'I Could Not Afford to Hang Men for Votes': Lincoln the Lawyer, Humanitarian Concerns, and the Dakota Pardons." *William Mitchell Law Review* 39 (2013): 405–49.

———. *Slavery and the Founders: Race and Liberty in the Age of Jefferson.* Armonk, NY: M. E. Sharpe, 1994.

Fischer, David Hackett. *Champlain's Dream: The European Founding of North America.* New York: Simon and Schuster, 2008.

Fischer, Joseph R. *A Well-Executed Failure: The Sullivan Campaign against the Iroquois, July–September 1779.* Columbia: University of South Carolina Press, 1997.

Fitting, James, Jerry De Visscher, and Edward Wahla. *The Paleo-Indian Occupation of Holcombe Beach.* Ann Arbor: University of Michigan Press, 1966.

Flannery, Tim. *The Eternal Frontier: An Ecological History of North America and Its Peoples.* New York: Grove Press, 2002.

Fletcher, Matthew. *The Eagle Returns: The Legal History of the Grand Traverse Band of Ottawa and Chippewa Indians.* East Lansing: Michigan State University Press, 2012.

Ford, Lisa. *Settler Sovereignty: Jurisdiction and Indigenous People in America and Australia, 1788–1836.* Cambridge, MA: Harvard University Press, 2009.

Fowler, William, Jr. *Empires at War: The French and Indian War and the Struggle for North America, 1754–1763.* New York: Walker, 2005.

Frazier, Patrick. *The Mohicans of Stockbridge.* Lincoln: University of Nebraska Press, 1992.

Friend, Craig. *Kentucke's Frontiers*. Bloomington: Indiana University Press, 2010.

Frost, Linda. "Roving Savages, Regionalized Americanness, and the 1862 Dakota War." In *Never One Nation: Freaks, Savages, and Whiteness in U.S. Popular Culture*, 1–29. Minneapolis: University of Minnesota Press, 2005.

Fur, Gunlög. *A Nation of Women: Gender and Colonial Encounters among the Delaware Indians*. Philadelphia: University of Pennsylvania Press, 2009.

Gallay, Allan. *The Indian Slave Trade: The Rise of the English Empire in the American South, 1670–1717*. New Haven: Yale University Press, 2002.

Galloway, Patricia. "'The Chief Who Is Your Father': Choctaw and French Views of the Diplomatic Relation." In *Powhatan's Mantle: Indians in the Colonial Southeast*, edited by Peter H. Wood, Gregory A. Waselkov, and M. Thomas Hatley, 254–78. Lincoln: University of Nebraska Press, 1989.

———. "Choctaws at the Border of the Shatter Zone: Spheres of Exchange and Spheres of Social Value." In *Mapping the Mississippian Shatter Zone*, edited by Robbie Ethridge and Sheri Shuck-Hall, 333–64. Lincoln: University of Nebraska Press, 2009.

———. *Practicing Ethnohistory: Mining Archives, Hearing Testimony, Constructing Narrative*. Lincoln: University of Nebraska Press, 2006.

Garrad, Charles. "Champlain and the Odawa." *Midcontinental Journal of Archaeology* 24 (Spring 1999): 57–77.

Garrison, Tim Alan. *The Legal Ideology of Removal: The Southern Judiciary and the Sovereignty of Native American Nations*. Athens: University of Georgia Press, 2002.

Gitlin, Jay. *The Bourgeois Frontier: French Towns, French Traders and American Expansion*. New Haven: Yale University Press, 2010.

Goldsworthy, Adrian. *How Rome Fell*. New Haven: Yale University Press, 2009.

Graymont, Barbara. *The Iroquois in the American Revolution*. Syracuse: Syracuse University Press, 1972.

Green, Michael D. "The Sac-Fox Annuity Crisis of 1840." *Arizona and the West* 16 (Summer 1974): 141–50.

———. "'We Dance in Opposite Directions': Mesquakie (Fox) Separatism from the Sac and Fox Tribe." *Ethnohistory* 30 (Summer 1983): 129–40.

Greene, Evarts B., and Virginia D. Harrington. *American Population before the Federal Census of 1790*. 1932; repr., New York: Columbia University Press, 1992.

Greer, Allan. *Mohawk Saint: Catherine Tekakwitha and the Jesuits*. Oxford: Oxford University Press, 2005.

Greer, Allan, and Kenneth Mills. "A Catholic Atlantic." In *The Atlantic in Global History, 1500–2000*, edited by Jorge Ca izares-Esguerra and Erik Seeman, 3–20. Upper Saddle River, NJ: Prentice-Hall, 2007.

Griffin, Patrick. "Destroying and Reforming Canaan: Making America British." In *Between Sovereignty and Anarchy: The Politics of Violence in the American Revolutionary Era*, edited by Patrick Griffin, Robert Ingram, Peter Onuf, and Brian Schoen, 40–59. Charlottesville: University of Virginia Press, 2015.

Haeger, John D. *John Jacob Astor: Business and Finance in the Early Republic.* Detroit: Wayne State University Press, 1991.

Hagan, William. *The Sac and Fox Indians.* Norman: University of Oklahoma Press, 1980.

Hall, Anthony. "The Red Man's Burden: Land, Law, and the Lord in the Indian Affairs of Upper Canada, 1791–1858." PhD dissertation, University of Toronto, 1984.

Hammon, Neal O., and Richard Taylor. *Virginia's Western War, 1775–1786.* Mechanicsburg, PA: Stackpole Books, 2002.

Hammond, John Craig. *Slavery, Freedom, and Expansion in the Early American West.* Charlottesville: University of Virginia Press, 2007.

———. "Slavery, Settlement, and Empire: The Expansion and Growth of Slavery in the Interior of the North American Continent, 1770–1820." *Journal of the Early Republic* 32 (Summer 2012): 175–206.

Harper, Rob. "The Powerful Weakness of the Frontier State: Manipulative Mobilization and the 1786 Clark-Logan Expedition." Paper presented at the Annual Meeting of the Society for Historians of the Early American Republic, Rochester, NY, July 2010.

Hatch, Robert McConnell. *Thrust for Canada: The American Attempt on Quebec in 1775–1776.* Boston: Houghton-Mifflin, 1979.

Hauptman, Laurence. *Between Two Fires: American Indians in the Civil War.* New York: Free Press, 1995.

Havard, Gilles. "'Protection' and 'Unequal Alliance': The French Conception of Sovereignty over Indians in New France." In *French and Indians in the Heart of North America, 1630–1815,* edited by Robert Englebert and Guillaume Teasdale, 113–37. East Lansing: Michigan State University Press, 2013.

Heidenreich, Conrad. "Huron." In *Handbook of North American Indians.* Vol. 15, *Northeast,* edited by Bruce Trigger and William Sturtevant, 368–88. Washington, DC: Smithsonian Institution, 1978.

———. *Huronia: A History and Geography of the Huron Indians, 1600–1650.* Toronto: McClelland and Stewart, 1971.

Hele, Karl S. "The Anishinaabeg and Metis in the Sault Sainte Marie Borderlands: Confronting a Line Drawn upon the Water." In *Lines Drawn upon the Water: First Nations and the Great Lakes Borders and Borderlands,* edited by Karl Hele, 65–84. Waterloo, ON: Wilfred Laurier University Press, 2008.

Hickerson, Harold. *The Chippewa and Their Neighbors: A Study in Ethnohistory.* New York: Holt, Rinehart, and Winston, 1970.

Hickey, Donald R. *Don't Give Up the Ship! Myths of the War of 1812.* Urbana: University of Illinois Press, 2006.

———. *The War of 1812: A Forgotten Conflict.* Urbana: University of Illinois Press, 1989.

Hill, Leonard U. *John Johnston and the Indians in the Land of the Three Miamis.* Columbus, OH: Stoneman Press, 1957.

Hinderaker, Eric. *Elusive Empires: Constructing Colonialism in the Ohio Valley, 1673–1800*. Cambridge: Cambridge University Press, 1997.

Hofstra, Warren. "The Extension of His Majesties Dominions: The Virginia Backcountry and the Reconfiguration of Imperial Frontiers." *Journal of American History* 84 (1998): 1281–1312.

Holt, Michael. *The Fate of Their Country: Politicians, Slavery Extension, and the Coming of the Civil War*. New York: Hill and Wang, 2004.

Holton, Woody. *Forced Founders: Indians, Debtors, Slaves, and the Making of the American Revolution in Virginia*. Chapel Hill: University of North Carolina Press, 1999.

Horsman, Reginald. *Expansion and American Indian Policy, 1783–1812*. Norman: University of Oklahoma Press, 1992 (1967).

———. *Matthew Elliott, British Indian Agent*. Detroit: Wayne State University Press, 1964.

———. *Race and Manifest Destiny: The Origins of American Racial Anglo-Saxonism*. Cambridge, MA: Harvard University Press, 1981.

Howard, James H. *Shawnee! The Ceremonialism of a Native American Tribe and Its Cultural Background*. Athens: Ohio University Press, 1981.

Howe, Daniel Walker. *What Hath God Wrought: The Transformation of America, 1815–1848*. New York: Oxford University Press, 2007.

Humins, John. "Furs, Astor, and Indians: The American Fur Company in the Old Northwest Territory." *Michigan History* 69 (March/April 1985): 24–31.

Huppert, George. *After the Black Death: A Social History of Early Modern Europe*. Bloomington: Indiana University Press, 1986.

Hurt, R. Douglas. *The Ohio Frontier: Crucible of the Old Northwest, 1720–1830*. Bloomington: Indiana University Press, 1996.

Ingersoll, Thomas N. *To Intermix with Our White Brothers: Indians in the United States from the Earliest Times to the Indian Removals*. Albuquerque: University of New Mexico Press, 2005.

Ingram, James. *Indians and British Outposts in Eighteenth-Century America*. Gainesville: University Press of Florida, 2012.

Jennings, Francis. *The Ambiguous Iroquois Empire: The Covenant Chain Confederation of Indian Tribes with English Colonies*. New York: Norton, 1984.

———. *Benjamin Franklin, Politician*. New York: Norton, 1996.

———. *The Creation of America: Through Revolution to Empire*. Cambridge: Cambridge University Press, 2000.

———. *Empire of Fortune: Crowns, Colonies, and Tribes in the Seven Years War in America*. New York: Norton, 1988.

Jennings, Matthew. *New Worlds of Violence: Cultures and Conquests in the Early American Southeast*. Knoxville: University of Tennessee Press, 2011.

Jones, Evan. *Citadel in the Wilderness: The Story of Fort Snelling and the Northwest Frontier*. New York: Coward-McCann, 1966.

Jortner, Adam. *The Gods of Prophetstown: The Battle of Tippecanoe and the Holy War for the American Frontier*. Oxford: Oxford University Press, 2012.

Jung, Patrick. *The Black Hawk War of 1832*. Norman: University of Oklahoma Press, 2007.

Keeler, Kasey. "The Mighty Mississippi: Power and Politics on the Upper Mississippi River Valley." Paper presented at the Annual Meeting of the American Society for Ethnohistory, New Orleans, September 13, 2013.

Kelsay, Isabel Thompson. *Joseph Brant: Man of Two Worlds, 1743–1807*. Syracuse: Syracuse University Press, 1986.

Kerr, Ronald Dale. "'Why Should You Be So Furious?' The Violence of the Pequot War." *Journal of American History* 85 (December 1998): 876–909.

Knouff, Gregory. "Soldiers and Violence on the Pennsylvania Frontier." In *Beyond Philadelphia: The American Revolution in the Pennsylvania Hinterland*, edited by John Frantz and William Pencak, 171–93. University Park: Penn State University Press, 1998.

Kohn, Richard. *Eagle and Sword: The Federalists and the Creation of the Military Establishment in America, 1783–1802*. New York: Free Press, 1975.

Kugel, Rebecca. "Civilizing Missions." *Thamyris* 25 (2012), 169–85.

———. "Of Missionaries and Their Cattle: Ojibwa Perceptions of a Missionary as Evil Shaman." *Ethnohistory* 41 (Spring 1994): 227–44.

———. "Planning to Stay: Native Strategies to Remain in the Great Lakes, Post-War of 1812." *Middle West Review* 2 (Spring 2016): 1–26.

———. *To Be the Main Leaders of Our People: A History of Minnesota Ojibwe Politics, 1825–1898*. East Lansing: Michigan State University Press, 1998.

Kukla, Jon. *A Wilderness So Immense: The Louisiana Purchase and the Destiny of America*. New York: Knopf, 2003.

Kupperman, Karen Ordahl. *The Atlantic in World History*. New York: Oxford University Press, 2012.

Kurlansky, Mark. *Cod: A Biography of the Fish That Changed the World*. New York: Penguin, 1997.

Kvasnicka, Robert M. "George W. Manypenny, 1853–57." In *The Commissioners of Indian Affairs, 1824–1977*, edited by Robert Kvasnicka and Herman J. Viola, 57–67. Lincoln: University of Nebraska Press, 1979.

Labelle, Kathryn Magee. "'Faire la Chaudière': The Wendat Feast of Souls, 1636." In *French and Indians in the Heart of North America, 1630–1815*, edited by Robert Englebert and Guillaume Teasdale, 1–20. East Lansing: Michigan State University Press, 2013.

Ladurie, E. Le Roy. "History That Stands Still." In *The Mind and Method of the Historian*, translated by Sian Reynolds and Ben Reynolds, 1–27. Chicago: University of Chicago Press, 1978.

Lakomäki, Sami. *Gathering Together: The Shawnee People through Diaspora and Nationhood, 1600–1700*. New Haven: Yale University Press, 2014.

Landsman, Ned. *Crossroads of Empire: The Middle Colonies in British North America*. Baltimore: Johns Hopkins University Press, 2010.

Lappas, Thomas J. "'A Perfect Apollo': Keokuk and Sac Leadership during the Removal Era." In *The Boundaries between Us: Natives and Newcomers along* the Frontier of the Old Northwest Territory, 1750–1850, edited by Daniel Barr, 219–35. Kent, OH: Kent State University Press, 2006.

Lee, Jacob. "'At War with All Nations': Chickasaw Indians and the Greater Illinois Country in the Eighteenth Century." Paper presented at the 78th Annual Meeting of the Southern Historical Association, Mobile, AL, November 3, 2012.

Leeming, David, ed. Creation Myths of the World: An Encyclopedia. 2 vols. Santa Barbara, CA: ABC-Clio, 2010.

Lepper, Bradley. "The Ceremonial Landscape of the Newark Earthworks and the Raccoon Creek Valley." In Hopewell Settlement Patterns, Subsistence, and Symbolic Landscapes, edited by A. Martin Byers and DeeAnne Wymer, 97–127. Gainesville: University Press of Florida, 2010.

MacLeod, D. Peter. "Microbes and Muskets: Smallpox and the Participation of the Amerindian Allies of New France in the Seven Years' War." Ethnohistory 39 (Winter 1992): 42–64.

Magnaghi, Russell. "Michigan's Indian Factory at Detroit, 1802–1805." Inland Seas 38 (Fall 1982): 172–78.

Maier, Pauline. American Scripture: Making the Declaration of Independence. New York: Vintage, 1997.

Mancall, Peter C. Deadly Medicine: Indians and Alcohol in Early America. Ithaca: Cornell University Press, 1995.

———. "Men, Women, and Alcohol in Indian Villages in the Great Lakes Region in the Early Republic." Journal of the Early Republic 15 (Fall 1995): 425–48.

Mann, Charles C. 1493: Uncovering the New World Columbus Created. New York: Knopf, 2011.

Mann, Robb. "The Silenced Miami." Ethnohistory 46 (Summer 1999): 399–427.

Mapp, Paul. The Elusive West and the Contest for Empire, 1713–1763. Chapel Hill: University of North Carolina Press, 2011.

McBride, Genevieve, ed. Women's Wisconsin: From Native Matriarchs to the New Millennium. Madison: Wisconsin Historical Society Press, 2014.

McClurken, James M. "Ottawa Adaptive Strategies to Indian Removal." Michigan Historical Review 12 (Spring 1986): 29–55.

McConnell, Michael. A Country Between: The Upper Ohio Valley and Its Peoples, 1724–1774. Lincoln: University of Nebraska Press, 1992.

McDonnell, Michael. Masters of Empire: Great Lakes Indians and the Making of America. New York: Hill and Wang, 2015.

Merrell, James. The Indians' New World: Catawbas and Their Neighbors from European Contact through the Era of Removal. Chapel Hill: University of North Carolina Press, 1989.

Merritt, Jane T. "Metaphor, Meaning, and Misunderstanding: Language and Power on the Pennsylvania Frontier." In Contact Points: American Frontiers from the Mohawk Valley to the Mississippi, 1750–1830, edited by Andrew Cayton and Fredrika Teute, 60–87. Chapel Hill: University of North Carolina Press, 1998.

Miller, Cary. *Ogimaag: Anishinaabeg Leadership, 1760–1845*. Lincoln: University of Nebraska Press, 2010.

Miller, Jay. "Old Religion among the Delawares: The Gamwing (Big House Rite)." *Ethnohistory* 44 (Winter 1997): 113–34.

Morgan, Kenneth O., ed. *The Oxford History of Britain*. Oxford: Oxford University Press, 2010.

Morris, Christopher. *The Big Muddy: An Environmental History of the Mississippi River and Its Peoples*. New York: Oxford University Press, 2012.

Morrissey, Robert Michael. "The Power of the Ecotone: Bison, Slavery, and the Rise and Fall of the Grand Village of the Kaskaskia." *Journal of American History* 102 (December 2015): 667–92.

———. "The Terms of Encounter: Language and Contested Visions of French Colonization in the Illinois Country, 1673–1702." In *French and Indians in the Heart of North America, 1630–1815*, edited by Robert Englebert and Guillaume Teasdale, 43–75. East Lansing: Michigan State University Press, 2013.

Morton, W. L. "The Northwest Company: Pedlars Extraordinary." In *Aspects of the Fur Trade: Selected Papers of the 1965 North American Fur Trade Conference*, edited by Dale Morgan, 9–17. St. Paul: Minnesota Historical Society, 1967.

Murphy, David Thomas. *Murder in Their Hearts: The Fall Creek Massacre*. Indianapolis: Indiana Historical Society Press, 2010.

Murphy, Lucy Eldersveld. "Autonomy and the Economic Roles of Indian Women of the Fox-Wisconsin River Region, 1763–1822." In *Negotiators of Change: Historical Perspectives on Native American Women*, edited by Nancy Shoemaker, 72–89. New York: Routledge, 1995.

———. *Great Lakes Creoles: A French-Indian Community on the Northern Borderlands, Prairie du Chien, 1750–1860*. Cambridge: Cambridge University Press, 2014.

———. "To Live among Us: Accommodation, Gender, and Conflict in the Western Great Lakes Region, 1760–1832." In *Contact Points: American Frontiers from the Mohawk Valley to the Mississippi, 1750–1830*, edited by Andrew Cayton and Fredrika Teute, 270–303. Chapel Hill: University of North Carolina Press, 1998.

Murrin, John. "The Jeffersonian Triumph and American Exceptionalism." *Journal of the Early Republic* 20 (Spring 2000): 1–25.

Nassaney, Michael, William Cremin, and Lisamarie Malischke. "Native American-French Interactions in Eighteenth-Century Southwest Michigan: The View from Saint Joseph." In *Contested Territories: Native Americans and Non-Natives in the Lower Great Lakes, 1700–1850*, edited by Charles Beatty-Medina and Melissa Rinehart, 55–79. East Lansing: Michigan State University Press, 2012.

Nelson, Larry. *A Man of Distinction among Them: Alexander McKee and the Ohio Country Frontier, 1754–1799*. Kent, OH: Kent State University Press, 1999.

Nester, William R. *"Haughty Conquerors": Amherst and the Great Indian Uprising of 1763*. Westport, CT: Greenwood Publishing, 2000.

Nichols, David Andrew. "A Commercial Embassy in the Old Northwest: The United States' Indian Factory at Fort Wayne, 1803–1812." *Ohio Valley History* 8, no. 4 (Winter 2008): 1–16.

———. *Engines of Diplomacy: Indian Trading Factories and the Negotiation of American Empire*. Chapel Hill: University of North Carolina Press, 2016.

———. "'The Main Mean of Their Political Management': George Washington and the Practice of Indian Trade in the Early Republic." In *George Washington in and as Culture,* edited by Kevin Cope, 143–61. New York: AMS Studies in the Eighteenth Century, 2001.

———. *Red Gentlemen and White Savages: Indians, Federalists, and the Search for Order on the American Frontier.* Charlottesville: University of Virginia Press, 2008.

Nichols, Roger. *Indians in the United States and Canada: A Comparative History.* Lincoln: University of Nebraska Press, 1998.

Nugent, Walter. *Habits of Empire: A History of American Expansion.* New York: Knopf, 2008.

Nute, Grace Lee. "The American Fur Company's Fishing Enterprises on Lake Superior." *Mississippi Valley Historical Review* 12 (March 1926): 483–503.

Obermeyer, Brice. *Delaware Tribe in a Cherokee Nation.* Lincoln: University of Nebraska Press, 2009.

Owens, Robert M. "Jeffersonian Benevolence on the Ground: The Indian Land Cession Treaties of William Henry Harrison." *Journal of the Early Republic* 22 (Fall 2002): 405–35.

———. *Mr. Jefferson's Hammer: William Henry Harrison and the Origins of American Indian Policy.* Norman: University of Oklahoma Press, 2007.

———. *Red Dreams, White Nightmares: Pan-Indian Alliances in the Anglo-American Mind, 1763–1815.* Norman: University of Oklahoma Press, 2015.

Pacheco, Paul. "Why Move? Ohio Hopewell Sedentism Revisited." In *Hopewell Settlement Patterns, Subsistence, and Symbolic Landscapes,* edited by A. Martin Byers and DeeAnne Wymer, 37–55. Gainesville: University Press of Florida, 2010.

Pagden, Anthony. *Lords of All the World: Ideologies of Empire in Spain, Britain, and France, c. 1500—c. 1800.* New Haven: Yale University Press, 1995.

Parkman, Francis. *The Jesuits in North America in the Seventeenth Century.* Boston: Little, Brown, 1910.

Parmenter, Jon. "Pontiac's War: Forging New Links in the Anglo-Iroquois Covenant Chain." *Ethnohistory* 44 (Fall 1997): 617–54.

Parsons, Christopher M. "Natives, Newcomers, and Nicotiana: Tobacco in the History of the Great Lakes Region." In *French and Indians in the Heart of North America, 1630–1815,* edited by Robert Englebert and Guillaume Teasdale, 21–41. East Lansing: Michigan State University Press, 2013.

Patterson, Orlando. "Slavery: The Underside of Freedom." *Slavery and Abolition* 5 (1984): 87–104.

Pauketat, Timothy. *Cahokia: Ancient America's Great City on the Mississippi.* New York: Viking, 2009.

———. "Resettled Farmers and the Making of a Mississippian Polity." *American Antiquity* 68 (January 2003): 39–66.

Perdue, Theda, and Michael D. Green. *The Cherokee Nation and the Trail of Tears.* New York: Viking Penguin, 2007.

Phillips, Kevin. *1775: A Good Year for Revolution.* New York: Viking, 2012.

Phillips, Paul Chrisler. "The Fur Trade in the Maumee-Wabash Country." In *Studies in American History Dedicated to James Albert Woodburn*, 89–118. Bloomington: Indiana University Studies, 1925.

Pleger, Thomas, and James Stoltman. "The Archaic Tradition in Wisconsin." In *Archaic Societies: Diversity and Complexity across the Midcontinent*, edited by Thomas Ermerson, Dale McElrath, and Andrew Fortier, 697–723. Albany: State University of New York Press, 2009.

Pollack, David. *Caborn-Welborn: Constructing a New Society after the Angel Chiefdom Collapse.* Tuscaloosa: University of Alabama Press, 2004.

Prucha, Francis Paul. *American Indian Treaties: The History of a Political Anomaly.* Berkeley: University of California Press, 1994.

———. *The Sword of the Republic: The United States Army on the Frontier, 1783–1846.* New York: Macmillan, 1969.

Pulsipher, Jenny Hale. *Subjects unto the Same King: Indians, English, and the Contest for Authority in Colonial New England.* Philadelphia: University of Pennsylvania Press, 2005.

Quaife, Milo M. "When Detroit Invaded Kentucky." *Filson History Quarterly* 1 (January 1927): 53–67.

Rafert, Stewart. *The Miami Indians of Indiana: A Persistent People, 1654–1994.* Indianapolis: Indiana Historical Society Press, 1996.

Ramsey, J. G. M. *The Annals of Tennessee to the End of the Eighteenth Century.* Charleston: John Russell, 1853.

Resendez, Andres. *The Other Slavery: The Uncovered Story of Indian Enslavement in America.* Boston: Houghton Mifflin Harcourt, 2016.

Rich, Edwin Ernest. *Montreal and the Fur Trade.* Montreal: McGill University Press, 1966.

Richter, Daniel. *Before the Revolution: America's Ancient Pasts.* Cambridge, MA: Harvard University Press, 2011.

———. "'Believing That Many of the Red People Suffer Much for the Want of Food': Hunters, Agriculture, and a Quaker Construction of Indianness in the Early Republic." *Journal of the Early Republic* 19 (Winter 1999): 601–29.

———. *Facing East from Indian Country: A Native History of Early America.* Cambridge, MA: Harvard University Press, 2001.

———. "Onas, the Long Knife." In *Trade, Land, Power: The Struggle for Eastern North America*, 202–26. Philadelphia: University of Pennsylvania Press, 2013.

————. *The Ordeal of the Longhouse: The Peoples of the Iroquois League in the Era of European Colonization.* Chapel Hill: University of North Carolina Press, 1992.

————. "The Plan of 1764: Native Americans and a British Empire that Never Was." In *Trade, Land, Power: The Struggle for Eastern North America,* 177–201. Philadelphia: University of Pennsylvania Press, 2013.

Riley, John L. *The Once and Future Great Lakes Country: An Ecological History.* Montreal: McGill-Queens University Press, 2013.

Rinehart, Melissa. "Miami Resistance and Resilience during the Removal Era." In *Contested Territories: Native Americans and Non-Natives in the Lower Great Lakes, 1700–1850,* edited by Charles Beatty-Medina and Melissa Rinehart, 137–65. East Lansing: Michigan State University Press, 2012.

Rosen, Deborah. *American Indians and State Law: Sovereignty, Race, and Citizenship, 1790–1880.* Lincoln: University of Nebraska Press, 2007.

Rushforth, Brett. *Bonds of Alliance: Indigenous and Atlantic Slaveries in New France.* Chapel Hill: University of North Carolina Press, 2012.

————. "Slavery, the Fox Wars, and the Limits of Alliance." *William and Mary Quarterly,* 3rd ser., 63 (January 2006): 53–80.

Sadosky, Leonard. "Rethinking the Gnadenhutten Massacre: The Contest for Power in the Public World of the Revolutionary Pennsylvania Frontier." In *The Sixty Years' War for the Great Lakes, 1754–1814,* edited by David Skaggs and Larry Nelson, 187–213. East Lansing: Michigan State University Press, 2001.

Saler, Bethel. *The Settlers' Empire: Colonialism and State Formation in America's Old Northwest.* Philadelphia: University of Pennsylvania Press, 2015.

Satz, Ronald N. *American Indian Policy in the Jacksonian Era.* Lincoln: University of Nebraska Press, 1975.

Savage, Candace. *Prairie: A Natural History.* Vancouver: Greystone Books, 2011.

Schmalz, Peter. *The Ojibwa of Southern Ontario.* Toronto: University of Toronto Press, 1991.

Schultz, George A. *An Indian Canaan: Isaac McCoy and the Vision of an Indian State.* Norman: University of Oklahoma Press, 1971.

Schultz, Gwen. *Wisconsin's Foundations: A Review of the State's Geology and Its Influence on Geography and Human Activity.* Madison: University of Wisconsin Press, 1986.

Schutt, Amy. "Delawares in Eastern Ohio after the Treaty of Greenville: The Goshen Mission in Context." In *Contested Territories: Native Americans and Non-Natives in the Lower Great Lakes, 1700–1850,* edited by Charles Beatty-Medina and Melissa Rinehart, 111–36. East Lansing: Michigan State University Press, 2012.

Schwartz, Saul, and William Green. "Middle Ground or Native Ground? Material Culture at Iowaville." *Ethnohistory* 60 (Fall 2013): 537–65.

Shackelford, Alan G. "The Illinois Indians in the Confluence Region: Adaptation in a Changing World." In *Enduring Nations: Native Americans in the*

Midwest, edited by R. David Edmunds, 15–35. Urbana: University of Illinois Press, 2008.

Shannon, Timothy. *Indians and Colonists at the Crossroads of Empire: The Albany Congress of 1754.* Ithaca, NY: Cornell University Press, 2000.

———. *Iroquois Diplomacy on the Early American Frontier.* New York: Penguin, 2008.

Sheehan, Bernard. *Seeds of Extinction: Jeffersonian Philanthropy and the American Indian.* Chapel Hill: University of North Carolina Press, 1973.

Shoemaker, Nancy. *A Strange Likeness: Becoming Red and White in Eighteenth-Century North America.* Oxford: Oxford University Press, 2004.

———. "Kateri Tekakwitha's Tortuous Path to Sainthood." In *Negotiators of Change: Historical Perspectives on Native American Women,* edited by Nancy Shoemaker, 49–71. New York: Routledge, 1995.

Shy, John. *A People Numerous and Armed: Reflections on the Military Struggle for American Independence.* Rev. ed. Ann Arbor: University of Michigan Press, 1990.

———. *Toward Lexington: The Role of the British Army in the Coming of the American Revolution.* Princeton: Princeton University Press, 1965.

Silver, Peter. *Our Savage Neighbors: How Indian War Transformed Early America.* New York: Norton, 2008.

Silverberg, Robert. *The Mound Builders.* Athens: Ohio University Press, 1986.

Skaggs, David. "Gaining Naval Dominance on Lake Erie." In *The Battle of Lake Erie and Its Aftermath: A Reassessment,* edited by David Skaggs, 32–43. Kent, OH: Kent State University Press, 2013.

Skinner, Claiborne. *The Upper Country: French Enterprise in the Colonial Great Lakes.* Baltimore: Johns Hopkins University Press, 2008.

Sleeper-Smith, Susan. *Indian Women and French Men: Rethinking Cultural Encounter in the Western Great Lakes.* Amherst: University of Massachusetts Press, 2001.

———. "Women, Kin, and Catholicism: New Perspectives on the Fur Trade." *Ethnohistory* 47 (Spring 2000): 423–52.

Sleeper-Smith, Susan, Richard White, Philip Deloria, Heidi Bohaker, Brett Rushforth, and Catherine Desbarats. "Forum: The Middle Ground Revisited." *William and Mary Quarterly,* 3rd ser., 63 (January 2006): 3–96.

Smith, Bruce. "Agricultural Chiefdoms of the American Woodlands." In *The Cambridge History of the Native Peoples of the Americas, Volume 1, North America,* edited by Bruce Trigger and Wilcomb Washburn, 267–303. Cambridge: Cambridge University Press, 1996.

Smith, David Lee. *Folklore of the Winnebago Tribe.* Norman: University of Oklahoma Press, 1997.

Smith, Donald B. *Sacred Feathers: The Reverend Peter Jones (Kahkewaquonaby) and the Mississauga Indians.* Toronto: University of Toronto Press, 1987.

Smith, Timothy. "Wampum as Primitive Valuables." *Research in Economic Anthropology* 5 (1983): 225–46.

Snow, Dean. "Disease and Population Decline in the Northeast." In *Disease and Demography in the Americas,* edited by John Verano and Douglas Ubelaker, 177–86. Washington, DC: Smithsonian Institution Press, 1992.

———. "The First Americans and the Differentiation of Hunter-Gatherer Cultures." In *The Cambridge History of the Native Peoples of the Americas.* Vol. 1, *North America,* edited by Bruce Trigger and Wilcomb Washburn, 125–99. Cambridge: Cambridge University Press, 1996.

———. "Migrations in Prehistory: The Northern Iroquoian Case." *American Antiquity* 60 (January 1995): 57–79.

Snyder, Christina. *Slavery in Indian Country.* Cambridge, MA: Harvard University Press, 2010.

Sosin, Jack. *The Revolutionary Frontier, 1763–1783.* Albuquerque: University of New Mexico Press, 1974.

———. *Whitehall and the Wilderness: The Middle West in British Imperial Policy, 1760–1775.* Lincoln: University of Nebraska Press, 1961.

Spero, Patrick. *Frontier Country: The Politics of War in Early Pennsylvania.* Philadelphia: University of Pennsylvania Press, 2016.

Standage, Tom. *An Edible History of Humanity.* New York: Walker, 2009.

Sturtevant, Andrew. "'Inseparable Companions' and Irreconcilable Enemies: The Hurons and Odawas of French Detroit, 1701–38." *Ethnohistory* 60 (Spring 2013): 219–43.

Styles, Bonnie and R. Bruce McMillan. "Archaic Faunal Exploitation in the Prairie Peninsula and Surrounding Regions of the Midcontinent." In *Archaic Societies: Diversity and Complexity across the Midcontinent,* edited by Thomas Ermerson, Dale McElrath, and Andrew Fortier, 39–80. Albany: State University of New York Press, 2009.

Sugden, John. *Blue Jacket: Warrior of the Shawnees.* Lincoln: University of Nebraska Press, 1999.

———. *Tecumseh: A Life.* New York: Henry Holt, 1997.

Sunderman, Jack A. "Fort Wayne, Indiana: Paleozoic and Quaternary Geology." In *North-Central Section of the Geological Society of American (Centennial Field Guide),* 325–32. Boulder, CO: Geological Society of America, 1987.

Surtees, Robert J. "Indian Land Cessions in Upper Canada, 1815–1830." In *As Long as the Sun Shines and Water Flows: A Reader in Canadian Native Studies,* edited by Ian A. L. Getty and Antoine S. Lussier, 65–81. Vancouver: University of British Columbia Press, 1983.

Tanner, Helen Hornbeck. *The Atlas of Great Lakes Indian History.* Norman: University of Oklahoma Press, 1986.

———. "The Glaize in 1792: A Composite Indian Community." *Ethnohistory* 25 (Winter 1978): 15–34.

Taylor, Alan. "Captain Hendrick Aupaumut: The Dilemmas of an Intercultural Broker." *Ethnohistory* 43 (Summer 1996): 431–57.

———. *The Civil War of 1812: American Citizens, British Subjects, and Indian Allies.* New York: Knopf, 2010.

———. *Colonial America: A Very Short Introduction.* New York: Oxford University Press, 2012.

———. *The Divided Ground: Indians, Settlers, and the Northern Borderland of the American Revolution.* New York: Knopf, 2006.

———. "Land and Liberty on the Post-Revolutionary Frontier." In *Devising Liberty: Preserving and Creating Freedom in the New American Republic,* edited by David Konig, 178–216. Stanford: Stanford University Press, 1995.

Thornton, Russell. *American Indian Holocaust and Survival: A Population History since 1492.* Norman: University of Oklahoma Press, 1987.

Tiro, Karim. *The People of the Standing Stone: The Oneida Nation from the Revolution through the Era of Removal.* Amherst: University of Massachusetts Press, 2011.

———. "A Sorry Tale: Natives, Settlers, and the Salmon of Lake Ontario, 1780–1900." *Historical Journal* 59 (December 2016): 1001–25.

———. "The View from Piqua Agency: The White River Delawares, the War of 1812, and the Origins of Indian Removal." *Journal of the Early Republic* 35 (Spring 2015): 25–54.

Titus, James. *The Old Dominion at War: Society, Politics, and Warfare in Late Colonial Virginia.* Columbia: University of South Carolina Press, 1991.

Tobias, John. "Protection, Civilization, Assimilation: An Outline History of Canada's Indian Policy." In *As Long as the Sun Shines and Water Flows: A Reader in Canadian Native Studies,* edited by Ian A. L. Getty and Antoine S. Lussie, 39–55. Vancouver: University of British Columbia Press, 2011.

Tomich, Dale. "The Order of Historical Time: The *Longue Durée* and Micro-History." In *The Longue Durée and World-Systems Analysis,* edited by Richard E. Lee, 9–33. Albany: State University of New York Press, 2012.

Tooker, Elizabeth. "Wyandot." In *Handbook of North American Indians.* Vol. 15, *Northeast,* edited by Bruce Trigger and William Sturtevant, 398–406. Washington, DC: Smithsonian Institution, 1978.

Trigger, Bruce. *The Children of Aataentsic: A History of the Huron People to 1660.* 2 vols. Montreal: McGill-Queens University Press, 1976.

———. "Ethnohistory: Problems and Prospects." *Ethnohistory* 29 (Winter 1982): 1–19.

Trubitt, Mary Beth. "Mound Building and Prestige Goods Exchange: Changing Strategies in the Cahokia Chiefdom." *American Antiquity* 65 (October 2000): 669–90.

Turgeon, Laurier. "French Fishers, Fur Traders, and Amerindians during the Sixteenth Century: History and Archaeology." *William and Mary Quarterly,* 3rd ser., 55 (October 1998): 585–610.

Vinovetsky, Ilya. *Russian America: An Overseas Colony of a Continental Empire, 1805–1867.* New York: Oxford University Press, 2011.

Vennum, Thomas, Jr. *American Indian Lacrosse: Little Brother of War.* Washington, DC: Smithsonian Institution Press, 1994.

Veracini, Lorenzo. *Settler Colonialism: A Theoretical Overview*. New York: Palgrave Macmillan, 2010.

Vizenor, Gerald. *Native Liberty: Natural Reason and Cultural Survivance*. Lincoln: University of Nebraska Press, 2009.

Wade, Richard. *The Urban Frontier: The Rise of Western Cities, 1790–1830*. Cambridge, MA: Harvard University Press, 1959.

Wade, Susan Deborah. "Indigenous Women and Maple Sugar in the Upper Midwest, 1760 to 1848." Master's thesis, University of Wisconsin-Milwaukee, 2011.

Waddell, Jack. "Malhiot's Journal: An Ethnohistoric Account of Chippewa Alcohol Behavior in the Nineteenth Century." *Ethnohistory* 32 (Summer 1985): 246–68.

Wallace, Anthony F. C. *The Death and Rebirth of the Seneca*. New York: Vintage, 1972.

———. *Jefferson and the Indians: The Tragic Fate of the First Americans*. Cambridge, MA: Harvard University Press, 1999.

———. *The Long, Bitter Trail: Andrew Jackson and the Indians*. New York: Hill and Wang, 1993.

Ward, Matthew. *Breaking the Backcountry: The Seven Years' War in Virginia and Pennsylvania, 1754–1765*. Pittsburgh: University of Pittsburgh Press, 2003.

———. "'The Indians Our Real Friends': The British Army and the Ohio Indians, 1758–1772." In *The Boundaries between Us: Natives and Newcomers along the Frontier of the Old Northwest Territory, 1750–1850*, edited by Daniel Barr, 66–86. Kent, OH: Kent State University Press, 2006.

Warde, Mary Jane. *When the Wolf Came: The Civil War and Indian Territory*. Fayetteville: University of Arkansas Press, 2013.

Warren, Stephen. *The Shawnees and Their Neighbors, 1795–1870*. Urbana: University of Illinois Press, 2005.

———. *The Worlds the Shawnees Made: Migration and Violence in Early America*. Chapel Hill: University of North Carolina Press, 2014.

Watson, Blake A. *Buying America from the Indians: Johnson v. McIntosh and the History of Native Land Rights*. Norman: University of Oklahoma Press, 2012.

Watson, Samuel. *Jackson's Sword: The Army Officer Corps on the American Frontier*. Lawrence: University Press of Kansas, 2012.

Watts, Dale E. "How Bloody Was Bleeding Kansas? Political Killings in Kansas Territory, 1854–1861." *Kansas History* 18 (Summer 1995): 116–29.

Weaver, John. *The Great Land Rush and the Making of the Modern World, 1650–1900*. Montreal: McGill-Queens University Press, 2003.

Weaver, Sally M. "The Iroquois: The Consolidation of the Grand River Reserve in the Mid-Nineteenth Century, 1847–1875." In *Aboriginal Ontario: Historical Perspectives on the First Nations*, edited by Edward S. Rogers and Donald B. Smith, 182–212. Toronto: Dundurn Press, 1994.

Weyhing, Richard. "'Gascon Exaggerations': The Rise of Antoine Laumet dit de Lamothe, Sieur de Cadillac, and the Origins of the Fox Wars." In *French and Indians in the Heart of North America, 1630–1815,* edited by Robert Englebert and Guillaume Teasdale, 77–112. East Lansing: Michigan State University Press, 2013.

White, Bruce. "'Give Us a Little Milk': The Social and Cultural Meanings of Gift-Giving in the Lake Superior Fur Trade." *Minnesota History* 48 (Summer 1982): 60–71.

White, Richard. *The Middle Ground: Indians, Empires, and Republics in the Great Lakes Region, 1650–1815.* Cambridge: Cambridge University Press, 1991.

White, Sophie. *Wild Frenchmen and Frenchified Indians: Material Culture and Race in Colonial Louisiana.* Philadelphia: University of Pennsylvania Press, 2012.

Wiant, Michael, Kenneth Farnsworth, and Edwin Hajic. "The Archaic Period in the Lower Illinois River Basin." In *Archaic Societies: Diversity and Complexity across the Midcontinent,* edited by Thomas Ermerson, Dale McElrath, and Andrew Fortier, 229–85. Albany: State University of New York Press, 2009.

Widder, Keith R. *Battle for the Soul: Métis Children Encounter Evangelical Protestants at Mackinaw Mission, 1823–1837.* East Lansing: Michigan State University Press, 1999.

Willig, Timothy D. *Restoring the Chain of Friendship: British Policy and the Indians of the Great Lakes, 1783–1815.* Lincoln: University of Nebraska Press, 2008.

Wingerd, Mary Lethert. *North Country: The Making of Minnesota.* Minneapolis: University of Minnesota Press, 2010.

Witgen, Michael. *An Infinity of Nations: How the Native New World Shaped Early America.* Philadelphia: University of Pennsylvania Press, 2012.

Wyman, Mark. *The Wisconsin Frontier.* Bloomington: Indiana University Press, 1998.

Young, Mary. "The Exercise of Sovereignty in Cherokee Georgia." *Journal of the Early Republic* 10 (Spring 1990): 43–63.

Index

Where multiple translations or versions of a Native American personal name appear in the text, they have been indexed under the first version of that name to appear in the book.

References to illustrations are denoted by the letter "i" following the page number.